Fifty Contemporary Poets

McKAY ENGLISH AND HUMANITIES SERIES

ADVISORY EDITOR: Lee A. Jacobus
University of Connecticut, Storrs

Fifty Contemporary Poets:

THE CREATIVE PROCESS

Edited by ALBERTA T. TURNER
The Cleveland State University

DAVID McKAY COMPANY, INC.
NEW YORK

FIFTY CONTEMPORARY POETS

THE CREATIVE PROCESS

MANUFACTURED IN THE UNITED STATES OF AMERICA

Developmental Editor: Gordon T. R. Anderson
Editorial and Design Supervisor: Nicole Benevento
Design: Bob Antler
Manufacturing and Production Supervisor: Donald W. Strauss
Composition: Maryland Linotype Composition Company
Printing and Binding: The Maple Press

Library of Congress Cataloging in Publication Data

Main entry under title:
Fifty Contemporary Poets

(McKay English and humanities series)
1. American poetry—20th century—History and criticism—Addresses, essays, lectures. 2. Poets, American—20th century—Biography—Addresses, essays, lectures. I. Turner, Alberta T.
PS325.F5 811'.5'09 76-56750
ISBN 0-697-30318-9
ISBN 0-697-30317-0 pbk.

To Lou Milic and Gordon Anderson without whom—

ACKNOWLEDGMENTS

Ray Amorosi, "Nothing Inside and Nothing Out," was first published in *Ironwood* 3, no. 2 (Fall 1975): 40. Copyright © 1975 by Ironwood Press. Reprinted by permission of the publisher.

Jon Anderson, "Lives of the Saints," was first published under the title "Lives of the Saints, Part I" in *The Iowa Review* 7, no. 1 (Winter 1976). Copyright © 1976 by *The Iowa Review*. Reprinted by permission of the author.

Marvin Bell, "Gemwood," was first published in *Field* 15 (Fall 1976). Copyright © 1976 by Marvin Bell. Reprinted by permission of the publisher and the author.

Michael Benedikt, "The Meat Epitaph," was first published in *Field* 12 (Spring 1975). Copyright © 1975 by Michael Benedikt. Reprinted from *Night Cries* by permission of Wesleyan University Press. Analysis of "The Meat Epitaph," copyright © 1977 by Michael Benedikt. Reprinted by permission of the author.

Philip Booth, "Dreamscape." From *Available Light* by Philip Booth. Copyright © 1973 by Philip Booth. Reprinted by permission of The Viking Press, Inc.

Hayden Carruth, "Loneliness: An Outburst of Hexasyllables," was first published in *New Letters* 41, no. 4 (Summer 1975). Copyright © 1975 by Hayden Carruth. Reprinted by permission of the author and publisher.

Laura Chester, "Pavane for the Passing of a Child." From *Primagravida* by Laura Chester. Copyright © 1975 by Laura Chester. Reprinted by permission of the author and Christopher's Books.

Norman Dubie, "Monologue of Two Moons, Nudes With Crests. 1938." Reprinted from *In the Dead of the Night* by Norman Dubie by permission of the University of Pittsburgh Press. Copyright © 1975 by the University of Pittsburgh Press.

Richard Eberhart, "A Snowfall," was first published in the *Atlantic Monthly*, February 1976. Copyright © 1976, by The Atlantic Monthly company, Boston, Mass. Reprinted by permission of the author and publisher.

Russell Edson, "Counting Sheep," in *The Intuitive Journey and Other Works* by Russell Edson. Copyright © 1976 by Russell Edson. Reprinted by permission of Harper & Row, Publishers, Inc., the author, and Georges Borchardt, Inc.

Peter Everwine, "Routes," was first published in *Field* 11 (Fall 1974): 42. Copyright © 1974 by *Field* Magazine. Reprinted by permission of the publisher.

Robert Francis, "Silent Poem." Reprinted by permission of Robert Francis and The University of Massachusetts Press from *Like Ghosts of Eagles*, © Copyright 1970 by Robert Francis.

Stuart Friebert, "The Apron." Copyright © 1977 by Stuart Friebert. Reprinted by permission of the author. "The Aquarium" was first published in *The Midwest Quarterly* 7, no. 4 (Summer 1966). Copyright © 1966 by *The Midwest Quarterly*. Reprinted by permission of the publisher.

Gary Gildner, "Then." Copyright © 1977 by Gary Gildner. Reprinted by permission of the author.

Louise Glück, "The Garden," was first published in *Antaeus* 18 (Summer 1975). Copyright © 1975 by *Antaeus*. Reprinted by permission of the publisher.

John Haines, "At White River," was first published in *Poetry* NOW II, no. 6, issue 12 (1975). Copyright © 1975 by E. V. Griffith. Reprinted by permission of the publisher.

Donald Hall, "The Town of Hill," was first published in the *American Poetry Review*, February 1975. Copyright © 1975 by Donald Hall. Reprinted by permission of the author.

James Baker Hall, "The Song of the Mean Mary Jean Machine." From *Getting It On Up To The Brag* by James Baker Hall, published by the Larkspur Press. Copyright © 1975 by James Baker Hall. Reprinted by permission of the author.

Michael S. Harper, "Grandfather." From *Nightmare Begins Responsibility* by Michael S. Harper, published by the University of Illinois Press. Copyright © 1975 by Michael S. Harper. Reprinted by permission of the publisher and author.

Phil Hey, "Old Men Working Concrete," was first published in *Oakwood* I (January 1975). Copyright © 1974 by Phil Hey. Reprinted by permission of the publisher and author.

Donald Justice, "First Death," was first published in the *Ohio Review* XVI, no. 4 (1975). Copyright © 1975 by Donald Justice. Reprinted by permission of the author and publisher. Worksheets for "First Death," Copyright © 1977 by Donald Justice. Reprinted by permission of the author.

Shirley Kaufman, "Dinosaur Tracks in Beit Zayit." Copyright © 1977 by Shirley Kaufman. Reprinted by permission of the author.

X. J. Kennedy, "Consumer's Report." From *Breaking and Entering* by X. J. Kennedy, published by Oxford University Press, Oxford. Copyright © 1971 by X. J. Kennedy. Reprinted by permission of the publisher and author.

Peter Klappert, "O'Connor the Bad Traveler." Copyright © 1977 by Peter Klappert. Reprinted by permission of the author.

Maxine Kumin, "How It Goes On," was first published in *New Letters* 42, no. 4 (Summer 1976). Copyright © 1976 by the Curators of the University of Missouri. Reprinted by permission of the publisher.

Denise Levertov, "The 90th Year," first appeared in the *Boston University Journal* XXIII, no. 3 (1975). Copyright © 1975 by Denise Levertov. Reprinted by permission of the publisher and author. Analysis of "The 90th Year," Copyright © 1977 by Denise Levertov. Reprinted by permission of the author.

Lou Lipsitz, "Conjugation of the verb, 'to hope.'" Copyright © 1977 by Lou Lipsitz. Reprinted by permission of the author.

Cynthia Macdonald, "The Stained Glass Man." George Braziller, Inc.—from *Transplants* by Cynthia Macdonald; reprinted with the permission of the publisher and author. Copyright © 1976 by Cynthia Macdonald. Analysis of "The Stained Glass Man," Copyright © 1977 by Cynthia Macdonald. Reprinted by permission of the author.

Sandra McPherson, "A Coconut for Katerina," was first published in *Field* 13 (Fall 1975): 48–49. Copyright © 1975 by *Field* Magazine. Reprinted by permission of the publisher.

William Matthews, "Nurse Sharks," was first published by the Slow Loris Press in *Rapport* 3, no. 3 (1976). Copyright © 1976 by William Matthews. Reprinted by permission of the publisher and author.

Jerome Mazzaro, "At Torrey Pines State Park." Copyright © 1977 by Jerome Mazzaro. Reprinted by permission of the author.

Vassar Miller, "Accepting," was first published in *Fiction and Poetry by Texas Women*, edited by Janice L. White, published by Texas Center for Writers Press. Copyright © 1975 by Texas Center for Writers Press. Reprinted by permission of the publisher and author.

Judith Minty, "The End of Summer." From *Heartland II: Poets of the Midwest*, edited by Lucien Stryk. Copyright © 1975 by Northern Illinois University Press, DeKalb. Reprinted by permission of the publisher.

Linda Pastan, "Old Woman," was first published in *The Ohio Review* XVII, no. 1 (Fall 1975). Copyright © 1975 by the Editors of *The Ohio Review*. Reprinted by permission of the publisher. "Whom Do You Visualize As Your Reader?" Copyright © 1976 by The Atlantic Monthly company, Boston, Mass. Reprinted by permission of the publisher and author.

Charles Wright, "Death," was first published in the *Chicago Review* 27, no. 1 (Summer 1975). Copyright © 1975 by the *Chicago Review*. Reprinted by permission of the publisher and author.

David Young, "Occupational Hazards," was first published in *Poetry* NOW III, no. 2 (Summer 1976). Copyright © 1976 by E. V. Griffith. Reprinted by permission of the publisher.

PREFACE

I asked over a hundred poets a question, a rude question, yet one that had to be asked. A poet is more concerned *that* a poem happen than *how* it happens. In fact, in the poet's role as maker this is all that matters. To be concerned with how a poem began, how it changed, why it took the form it did, how it compares with other poems he has written, he has to exchange the role of maker for that of teacher. Poets play this role easily with the poetry of other poets but are often reluctant to play it with their own.

Still, it will be played. Any poem successful enough to be noticed will be analyzed, categorized, and explained—by those who had nothing to do with its making. In their struggle to take it and have it, they may ennoble or deform it. (Imagine the foaming rage of Milton as he elbows his way up to the table in a contemporary graduate seminar when the students are trying to decide whether he felt real sorrow at the death of Lycidas or whether the "two-handed engine at the door" was the keys of Saint Peter or the houses of Parliament.) Granted, the poet may not know everything about his own poem, but he knows more about it than anyone else does, and a direct question to the poet will reveal more about some aspects of a poem than the most ingenious or educated guess by another—to say nothing of how much misdirected effort and outright misinterpretation it will save. So it was as a teacher that I asked representative contemporary American poets whether they would be willing to select one of their poems that they considered typical of their best current work and explain how it started, what changes it went through, what principles of technique they consciously used, whom they visualized as their readers, whether they perceived in the poem a paraphrasable meaning, and how it compared to their earlier work. The hundred poets who responded to my initial query had one of three reactions:

1. About one-fourth did not wish to, or did not feel they could, assume the role of teacher and declined to participate in the project.
2. Another fourth knew well the time and labor necessary to teach any poem and did not have the time and energy to spare.
3. About half agreed to assume the teaching role and answered the questionnaire.

Analyses of fifty poems are not enough to make any definitive generalizations about contemporary American poetics. What they can do is to show a reader used mostly to reading exposition and argument a number of ways of reading specific poems. These poets' answers are like the fingers that close over a small boy's hand when he first writes his name or ties his shoelace. They enable the reader to get the feel of the poem as the author felt it. Both directly and indirectly he perceives what the poet was trying to do, and so comes as close as it is possible to come to actually writing the poem. This is not going to make it unnecessary to read the poem, nor will it invalidate other analyses; but it is a firsthand source for that poem, it will provide ways of approaching other poems by the same poet, and it will suggest ways of approaching the poems of other contemporary poets. A child may be rude but not really impertinent when he picks up your shoe and asks, "Whose is it? What did you buy it for? Why is it brown? Where are the laces? Did you put the hole in the bottom? May I try it on?" The reader, like the child, *needs* to know, and the poet needs readers to feel that need.

The poets who answered the questionnaire range in age from the twenties to the seventies; in geographical location from the east coast to the west. Most are college graduates, many with advanced degrees either in literature or creative writing. Many are college or university teachers, some exclusively in creative writing programs. Few have or have had no teaching responsibilities. Nearly all have published one or more volumes of poetry.

Many have published literary criticism. Several are editors of literary magazines.

Together, these poets represent a cross section of "established" American poets in 1976—no more. But no less either. The book does not claim to represent all facets of American poetry, such as Third World poetry or oral poetry or antipoetry, but it does represent a considerable range of the attitudes toward the function of the poet and methods of writing poetry that, by means of writing programs and literary magazines, are influencing both the style and the taste of the young men and women who are just now beginning to read poetry seriously and to write it.

The poems are widely different. They range in length from 2 to 231 lines; in form from single-word units to prose paragraphs; in method from simple concrete description to surrealism; in structure from dream fragments to logical arguments. Each has in common with the others only its author's conviction that it represents his or her current work, working habits, and critical standards.

The questionnaire that provoked these responses was designed to produce a book more thorough and more factual than the many interviews with poets on their general poetic theory and habits now available, and to furnish analyses more parallel and so more easily and accurately comparable than the essays by single poets on single poems now scattered in magazines and anthologies.

To emphasize the individual differences among the poets and to avoid the danger of making the project a series of dialogues with the editor, I kept the questions pedestrian, colorless, as objective as a graduate examination. They were designed to reveal the poet's attitudes as much by his omissions and rejections as by his compliances. The intention worked. Some answers came under protest; some questions were passed over. Two forms of answer were possible: short phrases answering specific questions about process and technique, and brief essays incorporating the same material but allowing for fuller explanation and the introduction of relevant material not directly asked for in the questions. The poets used both forms. As a result, the reader can compare direct statements about lineation or metaphor or eye appeal and can also infer a number of things that perhaps even the poets did not know they were revealing, such as their fear/reverence for the unseen sources of poems, their tendency to paraphrase while expressing a profound reluctance to paraphrase, their pet peeves. Whichever form they used, they spoke throughout in their poets' language—the touch of humor, the vivid metaphor, the effective rhythm. The answers are as much more than the sum of their parts as the poems are. So much would have been lost had I extracted only statistics from them that I decided to reproduce the answers entire. The book thus became, not the documented research about poetic theory and method that I had originally intended, but first a collection of primary sources and only second an interpretation of these. My summarizing introduction may be read first or last or not at all—depending on whether the reader is interested in one poem or poet alone, whether he wants to make his own comparisons, or whether he wants to react to mine. Standing in austere isolation at the head of the collection is the questionnaire—the red rag that provoked these poets to snort, paw, lower their heads, and charge.

CONTENTS

Fifty Contemporary Poets

Part I

INTRODUCTION

That about half the poets who were asked agreed to answer the questionnaire and that about half of those refusing alleged other commitments or lack of time is not surprising. Lack of time is a faceless *no*, which neither explains nor offends. What did seem surprising was the emotional intensity of many of the refusals and the reluctance even in some of the acceptances.

Some were frankly hostile, explaining that they did not believe in analyzing poetry in so academic a manner:

> This is disgusting. Truly. Don't you see that you will just reduce everyone to their lowest common denominator—thus most boring answers? The language you use is out of *1984* or the CIA.

> As a poet my primary concern is not with the facilitation of understanding. Therefore I am not inclined to answer your questions.

> I am opposed to what in the end must be a mechanistic approach to writing poetry and I am doubtful of the good it does.

> Accounting for things is lengthy, tedious, and finally incomplete. . . . I'm afraid it's the intrusion of mystery in what we do that makes poems interesting.

Some said nothing against critical analysis in general, but were unwilling to apply it to one of their own poems:

> I guess I agree with Randall Jarrell's remark that writing a poem is a way of making yourself forget how you wrote it.

> I DON'T enjoy talking about such things as my poetics, my influences, etc. . . . It's not fun, and it's sometimes stultifying, for me to be that conscious of my inside processes.

Several claimed that they didn't do that sort of criticism well enough to undertake an analysis:

> I'm not much good at talking about poetry, and worse than that at talking about my own.

Underlying these rejections and even some of the acceptances of the questionnaire is an attitude of distrust toward the traditional academic approach to poetry. Will anything so different from the poem, they seem to say, and so inferior to the poem as an analysis of it harm the poem by being substituted for it? Isn't anything one can rationally say about a poem really a lie? John Haines expresses most fully for all the participants both the value of the project and its limitations:

> I find surveys like this interesting, and the questions occasionally force me to think about details of poems I might not otherwise confront. At the same time, I am bothered by the tone of many of the items on the checklist. They have too studied or contrived a meaning. It is difficult for me to imagine any worthwhile poem coming from (conscious) attention to all these things. Granted that any poet will in some way be paying attention to many of these things in actual composition, too much thinking about what he is going to do in a poem may rob the poem of mystery and surprise. In fact, I think that too much of this kind of thing might end by drying up some of the sources of poetry itself. There *is* a way of talking about poems that adds to and deepens them, that explores the world of thought and experience from which the poems emerge, and without attempting to reveal too much. In discussing my own poems, I try to do this, aware that the poems may be saying things I never thought of when I wrote them. I need to concede a considerable area to what I don't know and can't know, and perhaps don't wish to know. Only to understand in a way I do not quite understand.

HOW DOES A POEM START?

At one extreme the poet has no idea; at the other he can give you everything he saw, heard, or read that in any way affected the poem. More often he can give you a date, place, bit of experience that started him putting pencil to paper. Wilbur's poem was started by a visit to Saint Thomas, Gildner's by a rainy-day regret that he had not bet on a filly named Mocha Bear, Tate's by staring into a closet full of old clothes, Haines' by a roadside stop in the Yukon, Hey's by helping a retired friend pour a cement floor. But these are only the circumstances accompanying the poem's surfacing into consciousness. Behind these lie preoccupations, often lifelong, which the poet only recognizes later, if at all, as the source of the poem. Wilbur: "It is hard to say when the poem started, because I have been thinking about the various senses, and the justice of their perceptions for many years." Woods: "I wrote the Camus passage in a journal several years ago, feeling that there was something about its gravity that would be a source. . . . Then I realized that most of the poems I had written that I cared for had already taken some resonance from the passage." Bell: "One has the literal fact . . . and the sense that there is more to say, connections to be allowed to surface—not simply to be planned or designed." Levertov: The poem "is a distillation of long and complex experience."

All the evidence suggests that whether the poet is aware of it or not, *emotion* (mood) determines what ideas and bits of experience are to become poems. The *intellect* can only recognize these, and the *will* can only apply the choices of the intellect after the emotion has determined the poem's direction and tone.

Realizing emotion as the source, most poets prefer a poem to happen (be given) rather than to be made. The poet respects it enough to finish it only if it has surprised—and continues to surprise—him or her. As Simpson put it, "I don't consider that I have a poem unless it begins to excite me by telling me something that I haven't consciously known." Poets use words like *happen, come, arrive, occur, appear, burst.* "Strongly impelled and yet loosely defined, that's an emerging poem—like a burst of buckshot" (Kennedy). "The poem started with a phrase: 'I am Chopin, I enclose a little time,' I had no idea what it meant" (Anderson). "I still can't tell you how the lines happened, at least until the last part" (Woods). "Came to me suddenly and unexpectedly" (Benedikt). "Out of nowhere" (Lipsitz). In cases where the poet consciously begins with a theme and a focus, he may be frustrated until he lets his subconscious mind show him that the poem is really about something else. "It was to be a poem of lambs, of going off to slaughter, and I had intended to make a parallel with the suicide of a close friend. I couldn't do it. It didn't work" (Kumin). "Every time I tried to write directly from the [epigraph's] demands, the poem failed" (Woods). "There is a sheet of paper on which at some time or other I tried to begin a poem with the line 'Others are bodies,' but got no farther than that" (Wilbur). "That shy totem . . . insisted upon itself . . . in a moment when I thought I was thinking about something else" (Bell). If the poems do not come to them in this fashion, the poets may consider them inferior poems: James Baker Hall says that he chose to analyze *The Song of the Mean Mary Jean Machine* because he *could* give an account of its growth, but he adds, "the origins and execution of most of my poems, at least the ones I like best, are characteristically far too complex and obscure to account for. . . . This poem . . . was more pieced together out of existing stuff than created. . . . I would guess that that has something to do with the poem being no better than it is."

Aware of the ways that poems take them by surprise, the poets record every surprise that comes in the form of either their own words or another's and that might later become a poem. The commonest method is to keep a notebook of ideas, quotations, and given yet undeveloped fragments. They hope these scraps may fuse or generate or trigger the preconscious workings of felt ideas and present themselves in the form of poems later. Further conscious stimulation or at least facilitation of the preconscious given is provided by Stafford, who deliberately free-associated with no specific expectation; by McPherson, who initiated her poem by means of a class exercise in sensory perception; by Francis, who made a list; by Reiss, who played the first movement of Mahler's Ninth Symphony "over and over again. Loud"; by Chester, who played Ravel's *Pavane pour une infante défunte*, which was "a perfect complement to my melancholy," and by Klappert, who, intrigued by the character of Dr. O'Connor in Djuna Barnes' *Nightwood*, retired to the MacDowell Colony and then to Yaddo to read relevant historical and psychological material, a process he calls reading reactively—that is, reading with "a pad at hand for anything that might trigger O'Connor's voice."

As might be expected, these efforts meet with erratic success. Stafford throws away a large part of what occurs; and at one point Klappert "experienced an almost neurasthenic blocking of the faculties: whether reading or writing I could not comprehend units longer than one sentence."

HOW DOES A POEM CHANGE?

Though there is always a given and some kind of conscious editorial development of it, the form in which the given occurs and the length of time, number of drafts, and kinds of change it goes through differ widely. For some poets, and only rarely even for them, a poem is given whole and trusted and let alone. Eberhart's *A Snowfall* "came whole" and was "written in a mood of calmness and control." He "changed no word" and sent it to the *Atlantic Monthly* at once, but he admits that this presentation of a finished poem to the consciousness is relatively rare, even for him. Pastan's *Old Woman* "almost wrote itself." But she adds: "Usually my poems expand and contract endlessly during the month or so it takes to write them, and usually they go through nearly a hundred pages of revision." Stafford says of *Ask Me*, "The first writing of the poem was much more clear and *set* than most; . . . And I believe the poem was essentially complete within three days." And Kennedy says, "Unlike most things that I write, that are rewritten of greater length than they are written, this one emerged in very nearly the same way it now remains."

At the other extreme, Donald Hall's *The Town of Hill* went through fifty or sixty drafts and took three years. Wilbur waited a year and a half before beginning to write *The Eye* after the poem had surfaced on Saint Thomas, and took several months to complete it. Simpson took thirteen years from notebook entries to finished poem: "I had no idea how it would work out; I had some images and clusters of lines that I would push around. Sometimes I would think I had a poem in view, then it would disintegrate. I would be ashamed to have people see just how hard it is for me to finish what I consider a real poem."

Between these extremes the poets more usually report multiple drafts over days, weeks, or months: Young, about twenty drafts in six months; Amorosi, seven or eight drafts in two months; Willard, six or seven drafts in one evening and two changes a month later; Ray, "at least four, with intervals of a few days." Stanford revised his poem orally over a period of a year: "Everyday in the woods at work I would say it. . . . It became what they call a floater. That's a work song, a chant. Once I thought it sounded right, and undramatic, I wrote it down without changing a word."

The extent of these differences in time and number of revisions indicates very different temperaments and ways of working: decisive vs. indecisive; intellectual control vs. further invitation of the given; minor changes in punctuation or phrasing vs. major changes in structure and even theme or tone. Eberhart, McPherson, Pastan, Stafford, and Bell strongly trust the poem-as-given: Eberhart's revisions consisted of one substitution of *and* for *but* and the addition of one pair of parentheses at the suggestion of his editor. As he explains, "I always believe in the sacredness or special quality of the creative time or onset and have not been addicted to changing lines because of my strong belief in the power of the imagination when the creative drive and mood is on. Why is there not a fifty-fifty chance of making a poem worse by tinkering with it in cold intellect?" For McPherson revision consisted chiefly in "cutting words which did not add to the poetry." For Stafford, "the changes were a teasing out of opportunities perceived in the first draft." For Pastan, "it was a matter of polishing rather than true revision." And for Bell, "sometimes my method of revision may be more of a method for acceptance (and then completion) than for making major alterations. I want to be able to accept as much as possible of the poem-in-process: to understand the underlying terms of the poem, the givens, and to make the connections thereby required."

At the opposite extreme are the poets who work to bring the poem in line with certain principles that they feel should control all their poems: Young was "trying to bring all the elements of the poem up to the quality I felt was in the best lines, a certain kind of resonance inhering mainly in the imagery but supported by sound and movement, and of course 'voice.' A little like thickening and seasoning a sauce." Wallace says, "The process seems to have mainly involved replacing vague, generalizing epithets with additional images." Simic: "My additions and revisions had one aim: economy." Justice: "Most of the revisions seem to have been made for the sake of coherence—narrative, stylistic, and especially tonal." And Kaufman seeks to counter specific recurrent tendencies in her work: for example, the tendency to "find a felicitous phrase and get carried away with it . . . I have to force myself later to ask how honest it is."

Several poets never quite trusted their revisions, either given or imposed, and still consider their poems possibly incomplete: Donald Hall's poem became shorter, then longer; parts exchanged places. He is still not sure that it is finished or whether it is really good ("This one is far too new for that kind of knowledge"). Also he is "not *sure* what it is secretly about, not yet." Haines, too, having been given much of the fifth stanza and the last half dozen lines in 1973, after putting the poem through six or seven drafts trying to decide "how much else I wanted to say, and to find a satisfying way to begin the poem," and after exposing it in a public reading and a college workshop in 1975, was "still not quite satisfied with a few things, especially the first three or four lines," and made further revisions while this book was in process. The same hesitation or fluctuation or change of mind occurred in Simpson's *The Hour of Feeling*: "At times it expanded—then, rapidly, it would shrink," and Benedikt's *The Meat Epitaph*: "After a first attempt at beginning, . . . I struck the typescript entirely . . . and started anew, retaining only a phrase or two. . . . The second typescript, the one completed, was begun with a determination to face the necessity of an inventiveness more adequate to the subject." This determination or relaxing or opening allowed him to be surprised by the concrete and absurd example of Blackie, the labeled lamb, which permitted draft three to be a penciled-over but recognizable version of draft two, and allowed draft four to be virtually the final poem. But, he adds, "Usually the struggle is more complicated."

BY WHAT PRINCIPLES OF TECHNIQUE DOES A POEM CHANGE?

Since analysis of rhetoric and prosody is a strictly academic process, the poets more often wince at than welcome questions about specific techniques. They tend to insist that the lineation, diction, assonance, metaphor, etc., were unconscious or that they became aware of them only part way through the poem: "A poet in the process of writing," says Booth, "need be no more or less aware of 'techniques' than a skijumper approaching the lip of a jump. On hills where darkness has closed down early, he has already learned by example, and practiced every possible technique. Readied, he is full of experience and feeling, set to inhabit blank air. What may once have felt mechanical becomes, in process, organic: his form is an event; an act of intensely concentrated motion both grounded in common sense and defying it. First courage, then skill, then luck. The luck that courage and skill help make." Nevertheless, most of these poets, even those who disclaim prior awareness of technique, show considerable awareness of it in hindsight, and they tend to agree in the kinds of technique they emphasize and the kinds they avoid (though, of course, within these categories there is a considerable range of individual difference).

Most are strongly aware of structure. For some that structure was part of the given. Francis, after making a list of random compound nouns, discovered a picture, which contained both spatial and cultural sequence: "A picture of old-time New England, a picture moving from wildwood to dwelling, outdoors and in, then out and up to pasture and down to millstream." Levertov's poem assumed "a psychological order." McPherson let "sensuous effects" structure her poem: "The poem sort of fans out. I wanted to do justice to Katerina and to the coconut. When justice was done, I stopped." Simic waited and hoped that his ending would surprise him: "I had a premonition that it would come as a surprise and my revisions were really a way of preparing the ground for the inevitable to happen."

For some others the structure was the first intellectual operation performed on the raw material of the given. Young, after having been given the four woodcutter lines and one line about a baker, recognized that he was wryly comparing and contrasting coordinates, and chose the series or list. Carruth early recognized that his unifying factor was an emotion of total isolation and deliberately tried to create a cyclical movement. Haines recognized the central emotion of his poem as a moment's awareness of place and time, a transcendent lengthening of prospect out of the ordinary and a lapse into the ordinary again, and so edited out contradictory or irrelevant details of the actual experience and structured a narrative of climax and anticlimax. Harper explains, "I have always been a poet who had a pattern for a poem at conception, a means of balancing form and content in formal rather than traditional lines; the original pattern was the ballad form, because it is economical and dramatic and does not require too much right-sounding rhyme."

But for some the poem's structure came only after one or more false starts. Woods had originally thought that he was shaping a philosophical comment, an expository answer to a question, but eventually chose structures of counting, of reverse narrative, and of regression into the preconscious state of both the individual and the race. These decisions came hard, almost against his will. Dubie had to abandon his poem until he discovered its structure as dramatic monologue, a speaker writing narrative flashbacks in a diary during the last few moments before suicide. Amorosi, whose source was dream, had to re-create the structure of dream: "The poem wouldn't begin until I realized I had to write the dream back into a fully conscious world, in other words I had to have a dream awake." Wilbur's poem lay for years in the form of philosophical statements in a notebook and became a poem only when the ideas became embodied in a dramatic incident.

But once they had recognized the kind of structure the poem was insisting upon, the poets became decisive about such matters as order, length, proportion, and kind of ending. Some, for example, created deliberately firm endings. Hey: "Everything conspires to end. Anticlimax in ideas. Short sentences of flat sounds. Full pauses." Justice: "I wanted a big ending, quietly done." Kumin: "My pet peeve is the poem that leaves me turning the page in search of its ending—only to discover it *has* ended." Others just as carefully avoided firm endings. Stafford: "I was using the tug of narrative, a thing I like to do. And I was avoiding anything high at the end." Kaufman: "I would prefer to write my poems with more open-ended conclusions, and I struggle to avoid tying things up in a neat package."

Only a few poets are concerned with appeals to the eye, the appearance of the poem on the page, and except where space is important to movement and meaning, they do not make it a primary consideration: Levertov says, "The appearance of the poem is a purely secondary effect, as accidental as the visual effect of a musical score." Young admits that the finished *Occupational Hazards* has "a certain tidy attractiveness, but my sense of that was and is rather vague." Donald Hall: "The poem began to make this spacey, skinny thing, and I liked that. But I did not look forward to it." Wilbur: "The poem is not arranged on the page to appeal to the reader's eye: I think such effects may amuse, but that they usually do not *move* the reader, and may interfere with emotional response." Evidently the theories and emphases of the concrete poets have not infused the main body of contemporary American poetics very deeply.

The poets are more concerned with poetry as sound, though none, I think, would call themselves oral poets. Most expect that their poems will be read both silently and aloud and indicate no preference. Wilbur specifies that his should be "read silently or heard twice." None expresses need for musical accompaniment, but several specify that they would *prefer* their poems to be read aloud. Donald Hall adds "by me." Even Charles Wright, who wishes his poem to "be read silently, by one reader at a time," says, "My ear likes lots of sound. Sound and repetition. I like 'music' in poems."

The prosody of these poems ranges from prose poem and free verse through loose meter to stricter meter and syllabics. As might be expected, fewer use meter or syllabics than free verse, and those who use meter take conscious pains to avoid too much regularity. None of the poems included here is in a fixed form, such as sonnet or villanelle or sestina, though a number of these poets have written elsewhere in these forms. The rhythm of the poem may be chosen in advance (Francis' four words to a line); may be determined by the form of the first line or two (Carruth's hexasyllables, Wilbur's couplets); or may change, becoming more regular or less regular as the poem advances (Wallace's "rough two-beat lines," "intuitive" in the first draft and "formalized" in the second).

For the majority, who choose free verse, the chief technical problem is determining where the line shall end to best indicate the individual poem's unique cadence. The cadences are determined by idea (which controls grammatical units) and by emotion (which controls bodily rhythm), usually by an indivisible combination of the two. Most often the rhythm of the poem is determined preconsciously, reflecting, when they think about it later, the poets' rhythms of breathing and speaking. They mention "cadence of emotion and bodily rhythm" (Young), "conversational tone of voice" (Kumin), "the cadence of my own thinking and speaking voice" (Haines). With some poets it is enough to trust the subconscious hearing of that personal bodily and emotional rhythm. Everwine suggests that it may be out of reach of consciousness: "Probably every poet has a characteristic energy to his voice, modified by the demands of any given poem. The way one 'hears' rhythm being adjusted over the spectrum of the poem—its speed, timing, recurrence—may not reside in pure choice, and may be a personal characteristic that is discoverable in areas other than writing." And Hey: "There is a coherence in the way sounds occur in my writing, a subdued but constant repetition and near-repetition; but no more planned or preordained than the phrases of a good jazzman." With other poets, the personal rhythm has to be *listened for* by means of many trial substitutions—especially of line endings. Pastan says, "I use little conscious technique myself. I do, however, seem to spend hours over line breaks." And Kaufman: "When I arrive at the final breaks in line . . . they seem to me inevitable. In the process I experiment with many alternative breaks, but when I get it the way I want it no alternative seems possible. I can't explain this logically."

When the poets become conscious of using principles of lineation, they articulate some fairly specific ones. Stafford: "My lines are generally just about equal; where a line breaks, though, means something to me, and some of the juggling was meant to preserve how definite the slash line is in such change-over sequences as me/mistakes, have/done, and/some, etc. I was aware of current *is there . . . there are*, things like that—willingnesses to repeat, coasting the sounds." Schmitz: "The line breaks should make the sense of the poem clearer by showing the delivery the poet intended. . . . I slow or speed up the lines so that the ear may help the eye." Young uses onomatopoeia as one of his rhythmic principles: "a two-stress line (chop, chop?) for the wood cutter, pretty regular. Two-stress for the butcher (another chopper?)." Miller, considering her poem "fairly conventional," wants each line to end with a strong word, not a *the* or *and.* Dubie breaks his line according to the "principles of ordinary speech. . . . The stanzas are built like paragraphs and the basic instinct is toward the sentence rather than the line." Shelton says, "I tried to break the lines into natural syntactical units. I tried, above all, for clarity, so that no line could possibly be misread." And Minty says that her line breaks depend on "how the piece sounds orally," but adds that they are also determined by imagery: "To compound image on image within the same line produces far more energy than if the mind pictures were to remain separated."

But most pervasive in determining line breaks is the cadence of emotional speech. Even when the poet is relying on his idea to determine the line ends syntactically, he is hearing that idea as speech: "the cadence of my own thinking and speaking voice" (Haines); "the cadence of the thinking-feeling process" (Levertov); "wherever the body or speech seemed stronger it took preference over any ideational pattern" (Amorosi). "Asymmetrical lines, indentation, line and stanza break are ways for me to indicate the flow of my voice—to cancel or elaborate emphasis. I am encouraged to continue a poem only when I like my own singing in it" (Schmitz).

For a beginning poet, who has not yet learned to hear his own voice, learning about the lineation practices of these professionals is not much help. What the novice hears may be a self-conscious attempt to sound like "a poet." It takes years of reading and living and listening to develop a voice that sounds like a self, and more years to sound like an interesting self. But this evidence does show, I think conclusively, that there is no other way.

In keeping with this reverence for the hidden and distrust of the academic and the obvious, the poets tend to be shy of easy or conspicuously familiar rhetorical effects, of esoterica. Everwine goes so far as to say, "Sometimes I think technique is mostly a matter of avoiding whatever commits the poem to behaving in a predictable way." They tend to disclaim conscious use of metaphor and/or say that concrete details or bits of action or free-associated surrealistic images came to have metaphorical overtones *after* they had used them.

Only a few even mention literary or historical allusion. Kumin says, "I am leery of literary allusions unless they are pretty readily accessible—Biblical, say, or mythic—as I dislike esoterica in poetry. I would especially want to stay away from private allusive stuff directed at fellow poets." Ray prefers contemporary reference and allusion recognizable by the public at large. Donald Hall disclaims using any allusion at all. And Kaufman says she has "no hesitation to use obscure references or allusions in a poem if they work in the poem," but clearly implies that their "working" effectively prevents their being really obscure.

Esoterica also includes any strained or overobvious or self-indulgent use of sound repetition. While disclaiming any fixed principles by which they select sound effects, they agree in wanting to make these seem inevitable. Haines says that attention "to syllables, to vowels and consonants, seems to me intensely important," that rhymes and near rhymes occur in his poems and "I let these things happen," but "without letting the rhyme become too obvious." Young says that "assonance and consonance show up most consistently in my work and I have a tendency to remove effects that seem too obvious, e.g., excessive alliteration. . . . Too rich a sound texture, as in Thomas and early Lowell, makes it impossible for words to retain their lovely singularity." Kumin: "I try to stay away from heavy alliteration and other pyrotechnics because I think they detract from the sense of the poem and blur the imagery." Wallace: "An early temptation to rhyme . . . disappeared as the first draft gathered momentum, though occasional and slant rhymes still occur frequently." Even Justice, who uses a conventionally strict form such as the couplet, is careful to keep it from sounding mechanical: "Wishing to keep the tone casual and unsophisticated, in tension with the apparent severity of the couplet, I was happy to find a handful of inexact rhymes." And Joan Swift makes the same point: "The couplets were deliberately unconventional, the rhymes all slant with the exception of two."

From this examination of fifty contemporary poems emerge several basic agreements common enough to all the poets to be called principles of contemporary poetics: The poem should seem to be spontaneous, effortless, inevitable. It cannot usually be so; it requires much editorial effort. But patience as much as ingenuity controls the effort, and a large part of the ingenuity consists in positioning and isolating and enhancing the qualities in the poem that are indeed spontaneous. In this process of editing the poets make the choices that will most nearly give the appearance of unself-conscious immersion in the poem's original experience: choice of their everyday diction; concrete rather than abstract diction; a persona more often the poet's own *I*; a bodily rhythm, chiefly of their own emotional speech; metaphor implied from literal detail; avoidance of obvious rhetorical emphases of eye, ear, or logic; an occasional courting of open-ended structures; even a flirting with cliché for the sake of seeming not to strain after originality or to avoid making the poem unnecessarily obscure.

The individual differences among the poets in their methods of attaining these objectives seem less determined by poetic theory than by temperament. One can attribute to temperament the force of the initial emotional, preconscious verbal thrust, the extent to which it delights and surprises the poet, and the resulting confidence that he has in it. One may also attribute to temperament the extent to which the poet wants and needs to revise and the amount of literary background he is aware of in making those revisions. The ends of the range may be represented by Eberhart and Klappert. Eberhart received his poem whole, in a single emotional thrust, felt comfortable and controlled throughout the time of writing, made no revisions himself, sent out the poem at once, and can make almost no analytical comments about it. Klappert received the initial impulse of his poem from a novel, kept bits and pieces for years in notebooks, researched the subject extensively, discarded many drafts, and was able to write 18 pages of detailed explanation of the process. More like Eberhart's are the methods of Stafford, Donald Hall, McPherson, Hey; more like Klappert's are the methods of Wilbur, Dubie, Mazzaro, Simpson.

FOR WHOM DO THE POETS WRITE?

The reader these poets imagine is most often, explicitly or implicitly, the poet's self. This is not surprising. Everyone who has ever proofread one of his or her own letters is standing over the shoulder of that letter's recipient approving or qualifying that recipient's reactions. Similarly, it is both the perceiving and critical selves that the poet addresses: "I wrote it to catch and clarify for myself a mysterious sort of experience . . . to objectify, and so to verify . . . a part of my feelings" (Wallace). "The poem began to be its own audience, speaking to me and back to itself" (Amorosi). "I visualize as my reader a me who somehow wasn't present when I wrote the poem, and can thus read it as if it were written by somebody else" (Matthews). "I was not aiming toward any reader: my entry into the process was through inward satisfactions I felt as the language led me onward" (Stafford). "Usually, I think I write for myself. I try to work my way through an emotional complex or series of impressions and arrive at a conclusion I was not previously aware of" (Shelton).

When the poets visualize a reader outside of themselves, they tend to select "ideal" readers with the same critical standards and same range of perception as themselves. They may choose specific people: "My workshop" (Glück). "A few close friends. . . . Three are poets, one is a painter, one a political scientist, one a doctor, one a folksinger" (McDonald). "Robert Bly, Galway Kinnell, Jane Kenyon, Gregory Orr, Louis Simpson, and Thom Gunn" (D. Hall). When they speak more generally, they still tend to visualize friends and other poets: "A few old and close friends to whom I show my poems, and I trust their critical intelligence almost as much as I do their enduring sympathy" (Everwine). "Friends of mine who read poetry, who write any/or who have high standards for what they read" (Young). To the extent that the poets write to an unknown, it is still likely to be a selected unknown—an extension of that part of themselves they admire and hope is universal: "Not only professors" (Eberhart). A concerned person "capable of feeling" (Ray); the "willingly innocent," a reader "open to the possibility that old men working concrete are beautiful, that unspectacular style can be most appropriate and good. And that many poems now written are a kind of vitiated, obscure mush" (Hey). Or they may visualize those whom, like themselves, poetry may liberate or help in their own self-discovery:

"The woman who is too busy folding the laundry to read poetry and who reads it anyhow" (Willard). "One person and one person and one person . . . reading late by simple light" (Booth). And finally,

> the humanities 5 section man
> who has been sharpening
> his red pencil
> these twenty years
>
> my mother
> who suspected me
> of such thoughts
> all along
>
> the running back
> who after the last touchdown
> reads my poems by his locker
> instead of the sports page
>   *"whom do you visualize*
>   *as your reader?"*
>   Linda Pastan

This emphasis on the soul's selecting her own society is hardly new. Even Milton had to console himself with "fit audience though few" for *Paradise Lost,* but it does indicate that in the 1970s a significant number of the poets currently writing have withdrawn from the podium. The upsurge of poetry addressed to the national conscience that marked the late 1960s seems for the moment to have subsided.

HOW WOULD THE POETS HELP A NOVICE READ THEIR POEMS?

The poets queried for this project are generally more hesitant to answer the question on paraphrase than any other. They agree that no paraphrase can equal a poem and fear that the novice might take the paraphrase as a substitute for the poem (as of course novices will, as every teacher who has introduced a Shakespeare sonnet to English 102 well knows). Several decline to paraphrase by saying that anyone can do it or that the poem is so obvious that no paraphrase could possibly be necessary. Others say that the poem cannot be paraphrased or they suppose it can be but wouldn't know how, or they suppose it could but hope it won't be. Some accompany their *no* with the explanation that the paraphrase could only violate the poem: "A real blizzard is better than 'it snows'" (McPherson). "If I could paraphrase a poem, I wouldn't write the poem" (Kaufman). "The poem is the only possible way in which whatever needed to be said was said" (Simic). "A paraphrase usually involves the translation of the irrational into the rational . . . therefore, the mystery which exists in the plot would not be translated . . . the sound would be lost, the images manhandled" (D. Hall). Paraphrase "probably provides a comfortable feeling of clarity or purpose, especially for rather direct poems. But mostly it simply abandons the poem and steps out into the one-dimensional world of clichés and ad men and reducing salons" (Everwine). "For me, the best paraphrase is an analogue and ends in being a new work of art" (Mazzaro). "Sure we can paraphrase. But who would it help? The matter seems to me like a man who is out floating on a huge lake desperately searching for water" (Amorosi). Those who undertake a paraphrase usually feel it necessary to warn that they cannot make it the equivalent of the poem: "I think my poem can be paraphrased—and that any poem can be paraphrased. But every pass through the material, using other words, would have to be achieved at certain costs, either in momentum or nuance, or dangerously explicit (and therefore misleading in tone) adjustments" (Stafford). Most of the poets, I would say, express or imply a feeling of guilt. Linda Pastan speaks for the majority of them, I believe, when she says, "Unless I take to teaching, 'paraphrasing' is something I would never knowingly commit."

"Unless I take to teaching." But some do take to teaching. With or without reservations about its validity, Stafford, Young, Wilbur, Eberhart, Dubie, Haines, Miller, Levertov, and Shelton talk about what their poems are *doing* or are *about* or are *concerned with*. Others do it even after denying that the poem can or should be paraphrased. Still others give bits of paraphrase while answering other questions, such as those on origin or theme.

When asked how they would help a novice unfamiliar with contemporary poetry to read their poems, only a few answered, and their answers suggest that a better method than paraphrase would be to soak the learner in the elements of the experience that made the poem possible so that he will finally be able to apprehend the poem directly, without the need for paraphrase or other help: Of *A Coconut for Katerina*, McPherson says, "If forced to help him, I'd give him a coconut." Of *Dinosaur Tracks*, Kaufman says, I would explain "how it grew out of my sensory awareness while standing in the footprints of the dinosaur. And how our feelings are irrational and unconnected, and only the poem as a whole can begin to make the connections." Of *The Town of Hill*, Donald Hall explains, "I wouldn't attempt to help him read this poem. I would try to help him read poetry. I would tell him, for instance, that he should not ask for a poem to do any particular thing. I would ask him to relax and listen and float. I would ask him to allow himself to associate. I would ask him—as I would ask anyone about any poems—not to translate but to listen. Most people read poems as if they were reading French badly, translating it into English as they went. To read the poem, you must *stop* paraphrasing, stop 'thinking' in the conventional way, and do some receiving instead." Says Levertov: "If a reader were baffled, one could of course explain; but really what would be indicated would be a longer process of re-education so that the associative, figurative imagination would be stimulated." In other words, these poets seem to agree that if a reader's nose is rubbed often enough and deeply enough into the experience, both as fact and as poem, the poem will become experience for the reader too; if not, no amount of teaching on anyone's part will enable him to grasp the experience that is the poem.

HOW DO THE POETS COMPARE THE POEM WITH THEIR EARLIER POETRY?

The poets presumably picked these poems because they considered them among their successful ones—because each saw this poem as a culmination or extension or reassertion of some combination of theme, tone, and technique that had excited or satisfied him or her before. I wondered to what extent the poets were aware of the inevitable progression that separates the artisan from the artist, the need for each work to succeed rather than just to equal its predecessors. As with the other questions, some poets were hesitant to admit that they had exercised or could exercise so detached and analytic a critical faculty on their own work. Hey sees his poem as similar to but "perhaps slightly better" than previous poems, but adds, "How should I know that? . . . Judgments like these are always retrospective, somehow not lived." Young: "I can't really perceive the differences well, if they exist." Booth: "I rarely look back at my earlier books; when I do, I find myself mostly amazed. I am always more interested in what I am writing than what I have written."

But more often the poets *are* able to explain how the chosen poem realized or departed from long-recognized preoccupations of theme, tone, and technique. Willard, Wright, Shelton, Pastan, Stafford, Donald Hall, Carruth, Hey—all say that they are pursuing persistent or recurrent themes. Wright, Carruth, Francis, and Kumin deny any new departures in technique. Donald Hall finds himself returning to an earlier technique and perhaps for that reason distrusting the poem.

Most interesting are those who see their poem as a break with old self-restrictions of various kinds, and value it for this reason. Benedikt detects a change of tone from lighter to darker, a shift "from a lyrical framing of tensions to a bearing down harder on what I believe are the essences of the issues that face us. At this point in my life, not to mention the life of the period, I can trust no other way to go." McPherson: "It has longer lines than any poem I've written before. It has more energy than any I've written in years. It has more of an unconscious rhetoric than I've used before." Everwine: "I've written poems that are clearer than *Routes*, poems that stay closer to their occasions. I'm less and less interested in certain ways of narrating and informing. One desires to break away from personal limits and formulas that proved adequate." Kaufman: "I think I am moving in a more open direction, less organized, letting my incoherence spill over." Amorosi: "Insofar as the poem goes toward an unknown victory, it's a new force in my writing." Shelton: "My more recent work is less surrealistic, less imagistic, and less complex linguistically. I now seem to be using fewer images and more statements in an attempt to be more direct and clear. This shift has not been a conscious shift." A greater freedom from conscious control seems to be what these poets rejoice in—a greater surge of emotion at first and an increasingly later takeover of craftsmanship.

But there is also rejoicing when change moves in the direction of greater conscious control. Friebert is glad that his poem illustrates a conscious effort "to work against an earlier tendency to use more and more effects, go wall to wall with blazing colors. By keeping them low key, with a kind of flatness. I want to see how quiet I can be without your drifting off; but I also want to see how fast I can be without your just skimming." Mazzaro says that his greatest change is in the "area of workmanship." After warning that such change is not "necessarily an advance," he devotes a page of detailed analysis to his new poem's conscious craft. And Simpson is pleased that "the material is presented in a new way and with greater understanding on my part. It is my understanding that gives the disparate elements their coherence. This is an important poem for me, one of the most important I have written."

These fifty answers to the questionnaire may formulate no new principles, but they do accumulate evidence to support the recurrent suspicions that poets cannot *create* poems, they can only edit them, that the precise moment when the emotional reaction to experience is going to fuse experience into an artifact of words cannot be planned or predicted but only invited, induced; that too much intellectual manipulation may stop the process of creation; that the greatest part of craftsmanship is recognizing what has happened *after* it has happened; that poets as poets distrust and look down upon poets as critics and that even in telling what they *think* they know about their poems, they are uneasy and emotionally sure they must be telling lies about them. "It would be foolish of me," says Russell Edson, "to claim to be an expert on Edson's work. Writing it does not make the work any more open to me, perhaps less so than anyone else. I approach my work as a *reader*, rather than as a writer writing it."

In a sense, any readers who ask poets these questions about their poems are asking other readers. But they are asking readers who have read the poems more closely and earlier in their development and with greater funds of information about the authors' biographies, critical theories, and work habits than any other readers can have. This book has been written on the assumption that if one is to *have* a poem, one must know it in as many ways and with the help of as many kinds of readers as one can.

Part II

QUESTIONNAIRE

Select one of your recent poems which you feel is representative of your best current work and answer the following questions about it.

1. How did the poem start?
2. What changes did it go through from start to finish?
3. What principles of technique did you consciously use?
4. Whom do you visualize as your reader?
5. Can the poem be paraphrased? How?
6. How does this poem differ from earlier poems of yours in (a) quality (b) theme (c) technique?

Please add any other remarks about the poem which you consider pertinent.

CHECKLIST*

1. Was this poem initiated by free-association, by means of an epigraph, by answering the needs of an occasion, by deciding on a theme and seeking to embody it, by reaction to a strong emotion, by other means?

* For use of poet in forming answers to above six questions.

Did this poem (or a part of it) first occur to you as a picture, a rhythm, a cluster of sounds, a statement, a comparison, other?

When you were writing the poem, did you imagine any particular person or persons listening to it or arguing with it? If so, who?

2. How many drafts did the poem go through?

What intervals of time elapsed between the drafts?

Did the poem shrink or expand?

Did the structure change? How?

The theme? How?

The tone? How?

Which lines remained unchanged? Why?

Of those lines which changed, did the changes fall more in the area of rhythm, sound, imagery, denotation, connotation, other? Why?

3. On what principle or principles did you lineate the poem? Are alternative lineations possible?

On what principle or principles did you provide stanza or paragraph breaks? Are alternative breaks possible?

What rhythmical principle did you use? Iambic, accentual, syllabic, speech cadence, the cadence of idea groups, the cadence of a particular emotion, the cadence of a bodily rhythm, other?

On what principle or principles did you use sound repetition (end or internal): exact rhyme, assonance, alliteration, consonance, onomatopoeia, phonetic intensives, other?

Would you prefer this poem to be read silently, aloud, to musical accompaniment?

On what principles did you use the metaphorical process (conventional metaphor, simile, symbol, etc.; surrealism; or literal statement of details implying metaphor)? Or did you consciously avoid metaphor? Or did you unconsciously achieve metaphor by using literal details in such a way that they implied metaphor?

Did you consciously avoid or seek abstract language, esoteric language, "poetic" diction, or any other specific kind or mannerism of diction?

Did you consciously avoid or seek any pattern or mannerism of sentence structure, such as questions, imperatives, direct address, series, parenthetical expressions, fragments, other?

On what principles did you use reference and allusion: conventional historical and literary reference and allusion, personal reference and allusion recognizable by only a small group of friends or fellow poets, contemporary reference and allusion recognizable by the public at large, other?

By what principles did you structure the poem? A familiar prose structure such as cause and effect, thesis-amplification, question-answer, or a psychological order as in dreams or free-association? Other?

Did you consciously avoid or seek an open-ended conclusion, a firmly conclusive ending, a climactic or anti-climatic ending, other?

Is the persona in the poem yourself, a part of yourself, other? Why did you use this persona?

How did you use cliché in writing this poem? Avoid it altogether, incorporate recognizable cliché phrases with a new twist, exaggerate and so satirize clichés, other?

By what principles did you appeal to the reader's eye in arranging the poem on the page? Or did you make no conscious attempt to appeal to his eye?

How would you describe the tone of this poem? Nostalgic, satiric, reflective, ambivalent, other? What factors most conspicuously create this tone? Did you create it deliberately?

4. Students, fellow poets, the general newspaper-reading public?

5. If it cannot be paraphrased by a prose statement, why not?

If it can, give that paraphrase and explain what aspects of the poem are necessarily omitted in the paraphrase.

If a person who had had no experience with poetry written since World War II were confused by this poem, what steps would you take to help him read it?

With gratitude to the FDR library for placing this on display. Lois Gordon.

Part III

THE POETS, THE POEMS, THE ANALYSES

Ray Amorosi

NOTHING INSIDE AND NOTHING OUT

Not believing that igneous dream
that below her skin was a leaf thin sheaf of stone
she unhooked herself and was the woman
who became her own effect, in fact, beautiful
smoothed by neglect, an oracular pebble
in the hand of the now tolerable dread whose hair
binds whatever we touch or sing.

There is another light inside any dead star which we see for a thousand years after it crumbles through its hole. That light soothes the land, masks the water, so that if a man look long enough, disguising his love as a crime, he will know how light starts from inside his own earth, a fugitive wing falling through and up until a clear survival floats out. In this way he feels the body as a vase containing nothing and when it breaks it's all the same—nothing inside and nothing out. In this way I ask for a woman to brush against my life again. My term succinct like the light's tin hand spreading water. Barcelona. Las Ramblas. A woman who is a constant and level threat, now a horned goddess charging in the haphazard joy of mutilation.

But what if a man who always snapped
what he adored built a cage
threw himself in and didn't realize
he was his own love, a cove of light
would he pace his one wing
through that inward air, bracing its curl
along his ribs for some half-flight?
Or confess, say only; she lowered
her human pelt and charged
consumed the lord dread as if
the drop of skin alone were enough.

What type of dream makes your own room so strange? It's like those fourteenth century prisoners kept in one position for years and then suddenly forced up. I ran back to make sure my body was gone, our preordained fear, that I was still in it, awake, and I found her luminous skin so I stretched through knowing I would believe in death, rubbing her dust over my hair my hands pushing out through the nails as a joyful light squirmed in my neck, anxious for another night, singing.

DRAFT

NOTHING INSIDE AND NOTHING OUT

Not believing that igneous dream
that below her skin was a leaf thin sheaf of stone
she unhooked herself and was the woman
who became her own effect, in fact, beautiful
smoothed by neglect, an oracular pebble
in the hand of the now tolerable dread whose hair
binds whatever we touch or sing.

There is another light inside any dead star which
we see for a thousand years after it crumbles
through its hole. That light soothes the land,

masks the water so that if a man look long enough, disguising his love as a crime, he will know how light starts from inside his own earth, a fugitive wing already falling inside him until a clear survival floats out, which is death. In this way he feels the body as a vase containing nothing and when it breaks it's all the same nothing as outside. He asked it to contain nothing. Nothing inside and nothing out. In this way I ask for a woman to brush against my life again. My term succinct like the light's tin hand spreading across the water. She must agree. She must. Barcelona. Las Ramblas, a woman who is a constant and beautiful threat, now a horned goddess charging in the haphazard joy of mutilation. We are inside a dreams memory and I'm singing.

But what if a man who always snapped
what he adored built a cage
threw himself in and didn't realize
he was his own love, a cove of light
would he pace his one wing
through that inward air, bracing its curl
along his ribs for some half-flight?
Or confess, say only; she lowered
her human pelt and charged
consumed the Lord Dread as if
the drop of skin alone were enough.

What type of dream makes your own room so strange, like those prisoners in the fourteenth century kept in one position for years and then suddenly forced

up. I ran back to make sure my body was gone, that
I was still in it awake, and I found her luminous
skin that shouldn't come through this level so
I stretched myself through knowing I would believe
in death, rubbing her dust over my hair my hands
pushing out through the nails as a joyful light
squirmed in my neck anxious for another night.

This poem matured from an increasingly vivid distortion of reality. For a month I was regularly awakened by a dream, which the poem tries to embody, but the startling aspect was the nature, at once distant almost hostile, of familiar objects immediately upon awakening. In order to begin I had to have daylight, complete consciousness as an attempt to conjure the dream's sequence. The poem wouldn't begin until I realized I had to write the dream back into a fully conscious world; in other words, I had to have a dream awake. This is different from daydreaming which is controlled by the "I" insofar as this is begun by an "I" and then lost to it. To write this poem would both free me from the dream and ego's game of control, the self's realization.

While I was writing I had no compulsive idea of an audience outside of myself, and when this indifference was strongest the poem began to be its own audience, speaking to me and back to itself. In effect answering my insistence and choosing another of its own, a willing deference on my part!

It went through seven or eight drafts covering a period of eight weeks. At first it was all verse and then something began to shout inside it which I ignored. But then it began to grow hands, feet, and would run away if I didn't let the second and fourth passages become prose-poem. The tension of opposites was so severe I think a natural break could only have happened as a break into prose. Breathlessness, almost frenzy, a relapsing into the haziness of a twilight world necessitated the break, the release into prose. The poem decided this, and during this time the dream stopped. It had convinced itself up into consciousness, its own theme.

My rhythmical principle was the chant I had to discover to create the right situation, the perfect focus for the dream's new life. It became basically a combination of body rhythm, speech cadence, and idea grouping. Wherever the body or speech seemed stronger it took preference over any ideational pattern.

The poem should be read to someone who is sleeping, or at least wandering. I tried to avoid being abstract because Lord Dread's power is very literal, his own physical appearance. In one aspect I felt as a reporter for the sublime in all of us, the hunger our dreams have to be born beside us, to gift us with knowledge to survive the light.

Persona works if I were a detail relating the whole experience. But since the poem becomes the dream again, it enacted itself for me as a play, showing me its conflicts and offering a resolution which said roughly, "Listen, you are the dream's poem and any mythic element, persona, will be the daily self, personality in touch with a collection of 'I's." This broke the egoistic wall and the poem flowed from there, somewhere in the beginning of the second passage.

It would be false to say I didn't have the idea that fellow poets would read it, perhaps even enjoy it. But where the poem flies and is strongest is where my notions of it and its readability dissolved and it became its own experience, the dream come back, for itself, willed into being with words and living again in them.

No paraphrase is going to equal any poem. A good paraphrase may be another poem in itself but rather a shoddy experiment since the original is still around. What I mean is that I can't understand the need for paraphrasing since it's a return to the old straight-line thinking. This is what the poem is indirectly in contrast to; its reality is that there's no desire for this reshaping since the original was so beautiful. It's like loving the reflection of a beautiful woman while she's standing right there! Sure we can paraphrase. But who would it help? The matter seems to me like a man who is out floating on a huge lake desperately searching for water.

Anyone who stopped reading poetry before World War II shouldn't really have that much of a problem since the experiential data is probably a collective intuition. Lineation might be a problem but easily resolved by reading William Carlos Williams or slowing the mental/physical world to a realization of objective sanctity in everything we deal with. So a break in a line may come with breath, idea, vision, or a combination of all three. It's an intuitional technique refined in the last fifty years to a grace, like when Wallace Stevens ends *The Man on the Dump* with "the The." Hard process to catch up. Better to meditate around that process. There's really no such thing as catching up. We're all where we've always been. No?

Insofar as the poem goes toward an unknown victory, it's a new force in my writing. By this I mean that the Lord Dread is dissolved by absorption. The monster is recognized as a projection of mind and therefore loved. This love dissolves it. It wasn't planned this way. It happened in the poem and I understood the dream's direction, what it was trying to say about my own life. An affirmation about underlying health is becoming more of a force in my poetry. This poem is its manifestation and beginning. That I did have a dream of a monster called Dread whose hair bound the world, fought with a bull-woman, and in that process of love Lord Dread disappeared leaving me singing; that I channeled that dream through the body and let it speak to me, is a fundamental aspect of letting go, flying inside; I want to say toward my ecstasy, forever.

Ray Amorosi was born in 1946 in Boston. He grew up in Barcelona where he worked as a racing consultant for Ferrari. He graduated from the University of Massachusetts in 1970 with a Master of Fine Arts degree. He has published two books of poetry, *A Generous Wall* and *The Congo Itself*, and his poems have been printed in a number of journals. At present he is teaching at the Mission School in Boston.

Jon Anderson

LIVES OF THE SAINTS

I.

This is the rain on Mozart's grave,
Sheering to glissandi.
Where do you little lie, exhausted, whole,
& wholly done?
Sweet Amadeus,
When I sip my bourbon,
Weaving myself toward pure abstraction—
The recollection
Of emotion without the tired events,
I'd trade my part in this to bear your song:
Even the most,
Last, broken, Wolfgang, human moan.
You are so friendly, & your pillow was a stone.

This is Mozart:
A curtain of rain,
The turning heads of certain women,
The sweetness of bourbon,
Sweetness of music,
The poor politeness of oblivion.

*

"Dear Sir
I am in a Madhouse & quite
Forget your Name or who you are
You must excuse me
For I have nothing to communicate
Or tell & why
I am shut up I don't know
I have nothing to say so must conclude
Yours respectfully
John Clare"

Was this his letter into the earth?
Was it wholly composed
Of solitude?
It was wholly composed.
Did he bear extravagant pain,
Whose poems, of such light fragrance
As to be
(Dear Sir, forgive us) small?
You are minor, Sir, & would not offend.
I am, respectfully,
Yours.

*

Under the gathering, luminous clouds
He walked his grounds, thought:
Another reigns;
I must not, Tolstoy, be myself!
& fled from home.
We have the early flickering films.
The mourning strangers, waving.
All day
He lay at Astapovo Station,
Over & over: "I do not understand
What it is I have to do!"

"Yes, one good deed,
A cup of water, given . . ."
Prevailed: his gentleness, his pride,
Who would not bow
(The light: a small tin lamp w/o a shade)
To read himself:
"I have no passport,
I am a servant of God."

*

The age demanded acquiescence.
Stalin's cock, a stone.
The heart
Of Mandelstam, in exile, pumps & dries.
The bells of Petrograd,
The bells of Leningrad,
Limed with ice,
Are hollow;
Silence stalks the frozen snow.

We threw our matches
Three times in our Yankee vodka,
Hoping for a conflagration—
Anger!
For Mandelstam, for Mayakovsky,
Anna Akhmatova!
For timid Mandelstam, three times a fool,
Accused & blessed:
Poet!   Russian!   Jew!

*

I am Chopin,
I enclose a little time,
I bow & play:
The sea, the chandelier, this room, the sky,
The cliffs at Sourash,
Even the whole of Europe,
Blown black, spin—
The music speeds . . . retreats . . .
& I am Robert Schumann,
Mad & done,
Yet must, a little time, go on.

Now
At the hour we lately lie awake,
Give us that surety
On which our fragile art depends.
I am Robert Schumann,
Bewildered, woken
By a strange sonata in a foreign bed.
Give me a little time,
Eternity,
& I will mend.

Lives . . . is a section of a longer project, much of it quite different, though each section is meant to be almost fulfilling in itself.

The poem started with a phrase: "I am Chopin, I enclose a little time." I had no idea what it meant (something, I think, to do with that inscrutable flurry that concludes the B-flat "Funeral March" sonata), but it seemed obsessively important, something to be worked out, discovered, in a poem. Only a poor, manufactured beginning came of it, so I gave it up.

The actual poem came simply and directly. I had consciously sat down to write with (as usual) nothing consciously in mind. I was listening to a

Mozart sonata. A windswept rain began outside the window. I thought, sentimentally, of Mozart, who had offered so much of himself, his vulnerability, buried in a pauper's grave. "This is the rain on Mozart's grave," and then the second line, stolen from my earlier, failed Chopin poem: "Sheering to glissandi." From there, as always, the poem seemed to invent itself. I only had to be attentive to *how* I wrote.

When I read it (the Mozart section) the next day, I liked it but knew it wasn't complete, though it was all I wanted of Mozart—the tone and experience, but only a hint of the contemplation. From this came the possibility of writing small, connecting "vignettes," each composed of an outer and inner voice, a "call & response," which would when placed in series accumulate a central vision. The section of the book of which these "lives" are a part will have the epigraph: "Life overcomes life./The sound fades out./Something is always missing./There's no time to remember it." from Osip Mandelstam.

Much of the syntax of the poem probably came from John Berryman, whose work, for personal reasons, became an obsession for a while. I'd usually rather write a more open, approachable kind of poetry. The centering of each line is more difficult to explain, though I'm sure of its correctness. One guess is that it somehow inhibits the sentimentality; another, that it gives each part of the line equal weight. Also, it allows, for me, more energetic rhythm and internal rhyme. I *do* know that my first conscious choice in writing a poem is usually its form: its language, syntax, rhythm, line, tone, voice—how the poem will talk—and from this choice comes the poem's emotional contexts and, ultimately, its content.

I should pause here to say that, before this, I had intentionally stopped writing for a year. For some time I'd felt I had to put my safety at stake in every poem, to use poetry as an approach to those fatal elements of character I most feared in myself. The motive made possible better poems, but it accented my attention toward those fears. I decided to watch television.

When I began again, I needed the protection of turning poetry toward lives other than my own, though their particular poignance or meaning was subjective. (I love only a few of John Clare's poems, I generally dislike Schumann's music, but the particular poignance of their madness and its disassociation with their "simple" art deeply moves me. I know very little of Mozart's life, but his music has consoled and sometimes changed my own.) Nevertheless, I feel a more than subjective obligation to them, and, in letting them take me up—in spending some time with their work before writing about them—I feel the value of apprenticeship to lives which are more than my own. I'd like the *Lives* . . . sections of the book to serve as a minor homage and requiem.

Jon Anderson was born July 4, 1940; grew up in Lexington, Massachusetts; studied at Northeastern University (Boston) and the University of Iowa. He is currently a visiting lecturer at the University of Iowa. He has published three books, *Looking for Jonathan* (1968), *Death & Friends* (1970), and *In Sepia* (1974). *Death & Friends* was a 1972 National Book Award nominee. Mr. Anderson received a grant from the John Simon Guggenheim Foundation in 1976.

Marvin Bell

GEMWOOD

to Nathan and Jason, our sons

In the *shoppes*
they're showing "gemwood":
the buffed-up flakes of dye-fed pines—
bright concentrics or bull's-eyes,
wide-eyed on the rack of
this newest "joint effort
of man and nature." But then

those life-lines circling
each target chip of "gemwood"
look less like eyes, yours or mine,
when we have watched a while.
They are more like the whorls
at the tips of our fingers,
which no one can copy. Even on

the photocopy Jason made of
his upraised hands, palms down
to the machine, they do not appear.
His hands at five-years-old—
why did we want to copy them, and
why does the grey yet clear print
make me sad? That summer,

the Mad River followed us
through Vermont—a lusher state than
our own. A thunderous matinee
of late snows, and then the peak
at Camel's Hump was bleached.
As a yellow pear is to the sky—
that was our feeling. We had with us
a rat from the lab—no, a pet
we'd named, a pure friend who changed
our minds. When it rained near
the whole of the summer, in that
cabin Nathan made her a social creature.
She was all our diversion, and brave.
That's why, when she died

in the heat of our car
one accidental day we didn't intend,
it hurt her master first and most,
being his first loss like that,
and the rest of our family felt badly
even to tears, for a heart that small.
We buried her by the road

in the Adirondack Mountains,
and kept our way to Iowa.
Now it seems to me the heart
must enlarge to hold the losses
we have ahead of us. I hold to
a certain sadness the way others
search for joy, though I like joy.

Home, sunlight cleared the air
and all the green's of consequence. Still
when it ends, we won't remember
that it ended. If parents must receive
the sobbing, that is nothing
when put next to the last crucial fact
of who is doing the crying.

HOW WE THINK BACK

In answering your questions about the origin and evolution of a poem, I have chosen for example a poem which is itself an attempt to follow the mind and emotions backwards, then forwards beyond the present.

The circumstance was this. I keep in a workroom out back—one room under a wild cherry tree—a xerox of my youngest son's hands. Four years earlier, showing him the operations of a Xerox copier, I had had him place his hands—he was five—on the machine. It was just a way of demonstrating the workings of the copier, but I could not throw away the print that resulted. It would always make me sad to look at it.

At five, a child's hands are still fatty with innocence. The xerox showed the innocence, and nothing of experience or the particular: not the fingerprints, for example. I knew this was the obvious reason the print could sadden me.

Still, that shy totem would not have shown up in a poem had not it insisted upon itself, four years later, in a moment when I thought I was thinking about something else.

I had passed through O'Hare Airport in Chicago for the umpteenth time. O'Hare, I'm told, is the world's busiest airport. It is also the one which provides the least to do between planes. Because I live in Iowa City, and must fly to Cedar Rapids to reach home, I often face a long layover in Chicago. Therefore, I have developed a routine with which to pass the time.

Following my routine, I had seen a new item in the gift shop: "gemwood." I disliked the idea at once: "gemwood" is produced by force-feeding pine trees with dyes, as if the wood of a tree were not enough in itself. The result is a batch of wooden eyes, hung row upon row. "Gemwood" seemed to me an example of one unfortunate meaning of "art" in our time: violation of the natural.

Well, I began with "gemwood." Something of a catty description of "gemwood" was all I intended. That would suffice to refuse it. But the print of Jason's hands looked up at me once more.

What sadness! There was much behind it. That print of a child's hands had been made the summer we had gone to Vermont so that I could teach for Goddard College—the summer my older son's unlikely first pet, a rat, had died unnecessarily.

Now you reading this will probably think a rat a ludicrous pet, and you will almost surely—if your defenses are up—think it silly to feel deeply the death of a rodent. Well, what *did* make us terribly sad, even weepy? Was it the death of the rat, the pain of our son's sudden loss, or both? Does it matter that we know?

I think not. Rather, it matters that we feel. And acknowledge that we do. Writing in my little study, it was enough to acknowledge one's own backyard.

But of course there were other thoughts and impulses that surfaced. I wondered at the cause of my sadness, but also at the way we think from one matter to another. For a year, the poem was titled *How We Think Back.* Furthermore, the "joint effort of man and nature" (the phrase used to advertise gemwood) signalled to me also the inevitable *difference* between man and nature. So too, the past and present came together, as did sadness and joy.

Thus, the poem began, as do so many, because there was present a strong emotion (sadness), tempered and shaped by my attention to occasions and objects. And surely there were general concerns at the time which encouraged the particular combination. For example, I had wanted to write sensible poems to my sons. I was aware that the parent learns too late. I had tried to be a good parent, and I was trying to get better.

One has the literal fact ("gemwood") and the sense that there is more to say, connections to be allowed to surface—not simply to be planned or designed. That is why the poem wanders about, gives and takes back. Its movement is a kind of "hesitation forward."

You ask next about revisions. I remember carrying a draft of the poem—at first, yellow sheets; later, ironically, a xerox of a draft—on trips, finally all the way to Europe. I let it lie, awaiting a clearer perspective. I didn't want to make the poem too shapely. Partly, this was because I had come to desire another sort of movement than my previous poems had shown; but it was also because I wanted the poem to speak as the objects and occasions had spoken to me: haltingly, correctingly, without a posed moment to make famous.

The poem was not to be called "finished" until a year after it had begun. I know now that my practice has been to let drafts sit quite some time, even years, and to publish finished poems long after they are written. Sometimes, my method of revision may be more of a method for acceptance (and then completion) than for making major alterations. I want to be able to accept as much as possible of the poem-in-process: to understand the underlying terms of the poem, the givens, and to make the connections thereby required. In the case of *Gemwood*, the poem did not change size significantly from what I had been able to manage during those first days when I had written most of it. I removed one line and added two. Beyond that, I made changes in the service of rhythm, sequencing, emphasis and small clarities. I may have made a change or two in what I took to be dull language.

You inquire, too, about conscious principles of technique. That is, perhaps, the most difficult question you have asked, because almost any answer must remain partial and misleading. I could say that my technique in this poem—and in the poems which were to follow, in some sense, from it—has been to be as much of myself as possible, but without any insistence. This may be a question of tone, which subsumes all technical matters. I wished, as I have already said, to allow the poem to wander with the mind—not without direction, but without preemptive designing. I wished to be colloquial, and to avoid specially "poetic" diction but not abstract words. I wished to write the poem so that it could be read without reference to another text. I trusted my ear, and tried to phrase the sentences, and line the poem, so that it would be graceful, clear and engaging—but not so smooth that it might become a static record of the mind more than it would be an embodiment of process to be participated in anew with each rereading.

Could another writer line the poem differently? Perhaps. Not, however (I hope), without changing it, if subtly. It seems to me that the first few lines of a poem create a relationship between line and syntax, and that the phrasing and lineation which follow necessarily derive from those first lines.

Notice the little transitions between stanzas. The subject matter of the poem changes slightly with each new stanza; with each new stanza, the poem takes a step forward. Yet I was reluctant to permit neat breaks in what was a flow of association, memory and thought. One theme of the poem may be that very flow.

The ending I hope for is the inevitable, earned one. The ending here is not too surprising, but it is also not a simple repetition of all that has gone before. Hopefully, it is the next step, containing all the rest but requiring nothing more.

I prefer the poem to be read silently or aloud, but not with musical accompaniment, though perhaps someone could convince me I was wrong about that. Finally, the eye requires what the mind requires: a helpful relationship between content and style.

And you ask a fearless question as to who I think are my readers. I visualize them as myself, my sons, other parents and sons, and then thoughtful people at large. Rereading is desired. After all, anyone can understand this poem. Anyone can read it and, were we a nation of readers, anyone might.

You ask for an attempt at paraphrase. I prefer to try it on a level more general than that of the poem itself. First, the poem by its very method suggests that association and memory are not always random, perhaps never are. To the contrary, they uncover conscious thoughts and feelings. By its content, the poem suggests (to me) that life is loss; that parenthood includes the inevitability of one's own loss as well as the watching of that sense of life-as-loss arrive in the children; furthermore, that man and nature must be thought opposed unless their "joint effort" is seen to be one of change, ageing and death, as well as of birth.

Such a paraphrase is incomplete in itself in general terms and, specifically, omits the naming, the relationships of events and people, the little telling moves (for example, the one correcting our usual impression of a rat as a pet), and the way in which the feelings are shown to persist through changes of time and place. Of course, the paraphrase also leaves out the music, the language, the organization, and the pacing of line and phrase and stanza. Used improperly, the paraphrase allows us to avoid the poem altogether. In fact, this is the most common use of paraphrase. The paraphrase kit comes with thick gloves, a blindfold, a gag and four corks.

How much do I want to tell you about how this poem seems to differ from my earlier poems in quality, theme and technique? You have asked, but our parents told us, "Comparisons are odious." However, my father used to say, about anyone, "He has to make a living too." Therefore, I'll try.

Quality. This poem is as good as many of my poems, better than many, not so good as a few—I think. However, it is as *qualified* as any, which may be what counts.

Theme. The fallibility of the parent, the inevitability of the loss of the parent—these themes have been present elsewhere in my poetry, though not before in the context of these circumstances.

Technique. The poem reads differently from my previous poems. It signals what I hope to be development rather than mere change, and I recognize that it is nowise the poem of metaphysical convolutions I have often written. It *is* a metaphysical poem, to be sure. For myself, I believe the term *metaphysical* applies to any poem I might want to reread. But this poem takes a different path toward its substance, and walks differently all the way. Compared to many of my earlier poems, it is less neat, less "difficult" or dense, more halting, more sentimental, perhaps more humane.

I told my students that I felt I would be a beginner until about the age of forty. I wrote *Gemwood* in 1975, at thirty-seven, and it signals something near a beginning I now see to have been inevitable yet to have depended on the poems which preceded it—a beginning which would not be rushed. That is why I am specially fond of this little ragged piece of saying, maybe a poem.

Marvin Bell was born August 3, 1937 in New York City. He grew up in Center Moriches, on the south shore of eastern Long Island, and studied at Alfred University, Syracuse University, The University of Chicago and The University of Iowa—to which he later returned to teach. He has also taught for Goddard College. Since 1975, he has written an informal column about poetry, "Homage to the Runner," for *The American Poetry Review*. His books of poetry are *Things We Dreamt We Died For*, *Poems for Nathan and Saul*, *A Probable Volume of Dreams*, *The Escape into You*, *Woo Havoc* and *Residue of Song*. A new collection, *Stars Which See, Stars Which Do Not See*, will be published in 1977. He has received the Lamont Award of The Academy of American Poets, the Bess Hokin Award from *Poetry*, an Emily Clark Balch Prize from *The Virginia Quarterly Review* and a Guggenheim Fellowship.

Michael Benedikt

THE MEAT EPITAPH

This is what it was: Sometime in the recent but until now unrecorded past, it was decided by cattle-ranchers that since people were increasingly insistent that "you are what you eat," all cattle on the way to market were to be marked with brief descriptive tags noting the favorite food of each beast, and how much each ate of it. This, it was felt, would both delight the diner and comfort the consumer: people would be able to tell exactly what kind of flavor and texture beef they were purchasing beforehand, and always secure exactly the kind of product most likely to delight their taste (it was something a little like our present-day system of catering to preferences for light and dark meat in chicken). The system set up seemed ideally efficient: first, they attached the tag to each beast on its last day on the ranch, just before the two or three days required for shipment to the slaughterhouse—during which travel time the animal customarily doesn't eat anything, anyway. Once at the slaughterhouse, they carefully removed the tags; and during the slaughtering, duplicated the so-called "parent tag" numerous times, preparing perhaps hundreds of tiny tags for each animal. Directly after, at the packing plant, these were affixed to the proper parts, each section of each animal being separately and appropriately tagged, as if with an epitaph. But something went wrong with this means of augmenting the diner's delight, and of comforting the consumer. At first, quite predictably, the tags came out reading things like "Much grass, a little moss, medium grain" and "Much grass, much grain, generally ate a lot." And this, as one might expect, proved a great pleasure to the consumer. But then tags began coming through reading things like "A little grass, small grain, many diverse scraps from the table"; and "She was our favorite, gave her all we had to give"; and one (featured at dinnertime one evening on national television news) saying: "Goodbye, Blackie Lamb, sorry you had to grow up—we'll miss you." Gradually, despite its efficiency, this system somehow ceased to delight the diner, and comfort the consumer. And this is how the practise of the meat epitaph began to become generally neglected during the course of time; and how people came to eat their meat, as they generally do today, partially or wholly blindfolded.

DRAFT 1

THE MEAT EPITAPH

Sometime in the recent but unrecorded past, they decided that since you are what you eat, before being shipped to market, all cattle will be marked with little tags noting their favorite food and how much they ate of it. This way, with diet as index, people will be able to buy the flavor meat they want. The tags are carefully removed before slaughtering, and at the packing plant

DRAFTS 2 & 3

THE MEAT EPITAPH

[this is what it was:] Sometime in the recent but ~~thus far~~ [up until presently] unrecorded past, ~~they~~ [ranchers] decided that since you are what you eat, all cattle on the way to the market [ought most reasonably] ~~will~~ be marked with tags noting their favorite food and how much they ate of it. This way, ~~with~~ this little diet index, people would be able to tell exactly what kind of flavor they are purchasing, and each time purchase the one that suits them ~~best.~~ ~~A little~~ like our present-day system of dark and light with chicken. The way they ~~do~~ it ~~is~~ to attach the tag on the farm, leave the tag on during the two or three days of shipment (during which ~~the~~ cattle customarily don't eat anyway, ~~you couldn't get in to feed them if you wanted to, crowded in as they are like Jews on the way to slaughter.~~ At the slaughterhouse they carefully removed the tags, and duplicated the parent tag ~~many~~ times, Then, at the packing plant, the various cuts of meat ~~are~~ all tagged individually. ~~It's a little eerie seeing them being shipped away, wearing~~ tages like "Much grain, little grass, ate a lot," "Much grass, a little moss, medium grain." But then tags began coming through reading things like "A little grass, medium grain, many scraps from the table, Goodbye, Blackie Lamb, sorry you had to grow up, ~~and even "Bye Bye old friend, we had six months together at least, grazing underneath the Minnesota stars. Sorry about this, more than I have room here to say.~~" Can you imagine how people felt about ~~finding things like this on their lamb chops~~? This is why the meat epitaph ~~went out of style~~ and why people began to eat their meat, as they do today, partially or wholly blindfolded.

How did the poem start?

The poem started out (and ends) as an attempt to confront directly a contradiction I had long felt: the contradiction resulting from being fond of animals (I have seven cats, for example; or, rather, they have me), and dining on them—i.e., eating meat. I realize that I have cats not cows in the house, but the contradiction, if one is to tell the whole truth, is there; and, I thought, ought to be expressed or confessed in at least one of my poems. I also felt that this troubling contradiction might occur to other people; and so, instead of writing a poem simply recommending vegetarianism in a hortatory way, as if I thought I were alone in being sensitive to the problem—a frequent presumption in the kind of self-righteous political poetry I detest—I went another route. I tried to picture the problem as clearly as possible, allowing the reader himself/herself to either (a) Mend Ways, or (b) accept the fact that he/she is living with guilt, and is going to go on that way. Although (I believe) the latter option is scanted or ignored in conventionally "moral" or prescriptive verse, realistically speaking such a course of action (or rather inaction) is conceivable; and certainly a possibility that needs to be acknowledged in our saintly poetry a great deal more than it has been. Perhaps the ultimate contradiction out of which the poem arises is how a by-and-large impious human can write morally concerned, even ecologically oriented poetry without betraying either the impiousness (or impishness) of the Self, *or* the seriousness of the subject. I suppose the reason why I thought the poem might be *possible* for me, has to do with my belief that though we undermine it all the time, within each human self is a still more humane, kindlier self that the poet might tap—if not bring about—both in himself and in others. In my own case, there has been a certain change; I still eat meat, but a lot less of it, and with considerably less pleasure than previously, as the reader might imagine from the poem itself.

What change did it go through from start to finish?

The changes in the poem were many. After a first attempt at beginning *The Meat Epitaph*, I struck the typescript entirely and started anew, retaining only a phrase or two. I suppose I felt I had leaped into the description of the metaphorical meat-processing with which the poem is concerned far too quickly and evasively, skipping over various horrifying possibilities. The second typescript, the one completed, was begun with a determination to face the necessity of an inventiveness more adequate to the subject, and to follow to the death the implications of what I had begun. This second draft furnishes the thoughtless meat-eater's chamber of horrors more thoroughly.

(*Note:* At this point I should say that I would like to avoid the fallacy of the otherwise esteemed E. A. Poe, who in his essay "The Philosophy of Composition" credited himself with working out all the details of his poems ahead of time. I work mainly by discovering, each poem being an expedition into my unconscious. Although I hope they are present in the final version, there are very few *preconceived* signposts in my poetic territories. For example: in the poem the vision of "Blackie," the pet lamb who is shipped off for slaughter, tagged with a loving background pedigree, came to me suddenly and unexpectedly, as did—following this focusing on a particular side of beef—the final, contrastingly abstract statement about our all having to eat our meat blindfolded. Also, it was only later—after the poem was written—that I realized that the blindfold image that closes the poem has an overtone relating to an execution, appropriate since the "message" of the poem is, in part, that by killing other living beings, we are, at least implicitly, killing ourselves.)

In draft 3, which exists as extensive penciled revisions to typescript 2, the key addition is the phrase "This is what it was." That little phrase sets the tone for the matter-of-fact, even handbook-style treatment that follows, and the direct, colloquial diction I sometimes use in an attempt to bring about an immediate response or Shock of Recognition in the reader. There is no worksheet on file for draft 4, probably because—but for a few words—it is very close if not identical to the poem as it was finalized; and as it appears in print here. In this case—perhaps because of the piousness of the enterprise—the Muse was kind. Usually the struggle is more complicated.

What principles of technique did you consciously use?

Although the prose poem (a form in which I worked exclusively from 1969 to 1974) looks as if it is merely "freely associative," I must paraphrase a celebrated dictum of T. S. Eliot: "No poetry is free for the person who wants to go a good job." Since I want to do this, this poem (as with many of my prose poems) is as relentless in pursuit of structure as I could make it. Specifically, its structure revolves around logic—the element of logic, you might say, carrying the weight of the lyric in certain verse poems, an "out" offered in that genre by the mechanical device of the line break, a logic-breaker that I tend to resist in my own prose poems. *The Meat Epitaph* proceeds step by step, one idea arising from and resting on the next, like levels in a building-block castle (or, perhaps, layers in a painting). All in all, it is for me a question of extending a conventionally accepted "logic" to the point where, in the face of "fact," that logic breaks down and is shown to be questionable—not to mention destructive to the human self—at which point the poem, having hopefully made its point, immediately closes. (There is probably an analogy here to the couplet of the sonnet, and to the formal tidiness it tends to suggest.)

Beyond this specific structural technique, of course, lies the technique of the prose poem generally. Without lecturing on about that subject (I do that a bit in the introduction to an anthology of prose poems from around the world which I've just edited), I should say that this poem is based on the pursuit of a (albeit somewhat muted) metaphor: the contemporaneously popular statement that "you are what you eat." Carefully following the metaphor, however slight, is what for me provides structure in many a prose poem; you might say that I believe it to be the formal nourishment on which the prose poem most decorously and deliciously feasts. Also, the technical aspects that I have mentioned aside, the reader may also notice that although the poem is scarcely strictly metrical, its sentences/tropes are considerably cadenced; and there is also a musical or rhythmical element in the repetition of identical or nearly identical phrases, as the poem develops its theme. Many of my other prose poems, which do not partake quite this much of the handbook approach, and of quite this "flat" a style, often employ internal rhymes and echo metrical or musical patterns much more than did my earlier poems in "free" verse.

One final point about the technique of the poem, as it relates to logic. Like the French Surrealist poets I admire (perhaps more for their advanced philosophy than for their imagistic technique, which has already begun to be a new convention in our time), my use of a relatively relentless logic to undermine conventional logic—and the resulting quality of "the absurd" or "Black Humor"—is philosophical in nature. Perhaps even (if the term is not too pretentious) epistemological. Aside from questioning the assumptions of the kindly but thoughtless carnivore, the poem is an inquiry into the fundamental ideas of "reason" or "reality" we conventionally accept, but which in the end tend to turn on themselves in a way that tends not only to self-destruct them, but us as well. In general, I feel a great severance of cause and effect, a gap between pretensions and realities, in this world, and through the use of logic to undermine logic, that is reflected in my poems.

Whom do you visualize as your reader?

The reader I visualize is the most unflinchingly, self-exactingly intelligent kind of person I can find, whether or not she/he is a poet. My world view is not so pessimistic that I don't believe that there are many such people around today; and that there aren't going to be more of them around all the time. It's just that this will probably take a while. In that sense, my poetry (like all poetry, I would hope) is probably visionary.

Can the poem be paraphrased? How?

The poem itself can't be paraphrased, I expect. With its directness, in both diction and imagery, it is already written in as precise a way as I could write it. The content of the piece is not simply "don't eat meat, it's degrading," but also exists in the gradual building up of the absurd or ironical implications: the dynamics of the poem, the way it moves, is also the content of the poem. Also unparaphraseable, I would hope, is the peculiar tone of the poem, which moves from a seemingly cheery acceptance of things as they are, to a darker humor, and horror at this situation.

As for the specifically pro-vegetarian aspect, any paraphrase would I think not only cheapen, but literally weaken the argument. Even on the political level, how does a perspective really "take hold"? Not through paraphraseable speeches, I think; and not by legal actions either, ultimately (since laws can easily and even whimsically be repealed), but by reference to the original psychic dynamics that produced the political resolution, and which may, if one is lucky, be captured for good in a poem. One wants the poem to be a kind of indestructible building-block—indestructible because whether or not the work is agreeable in the sense of flattering to the reader's (or writer's) ego, it is self-contained, and therefore not subject to the usual processes of obsolescence. Yeats, of course, pronounced the wisest words on this subject, when he said that no apt poem can be paraphrased; and although he was referring to a more obviously "mysterious" kind of poetry than I generally care to practice, the perception still holds true, I think. The deepest "meaning" of a poem is how that poem works; that is what—if the poem is any good—may definitively affect our consciousnesses and consciences.

How does this poem differ from earlier poems of yours?

This poem probably differs from my earlier poems inasmuch as the prose poem differs from the verse poem; or anyway—since the prose poem is too interesting a realm of possibility for me to wish to be the *final* spokesman for it at present—it differs from my own earlier poems inasmuch as my prose poems differ from my verse poems. My two earliest books (in verse), *The Body* (1968), and especially *Sky* (1970), tend to be a bit soaringly optimistic to my present taste (though others have found these books tonally tricky and even "dark" in the extreme). I feel that my recent collections, *Mole Notes* (1971) and *Night Cries* (1976), take into account a wider range of consciousness than the earlier works do, partly because of their refusal of the simply *poetical* or lyrical. So the issue of *comparative* quality does not arise in my mind; and I must say that I give myself no particular moral credit here, since any change may be simply a matter of growing older and perhaps, accordingly, slightly wiser. I see more links than differences; my poems have always dealt thematically with the possibilities of the human animal, against odds (often set up by the same creature), which I continue to conceive of as formidable. To a certain extent, I realize, the implications of that view are socially critical and even political. In short: there is a shift in the prose poems from a lyrical framing of tensions to a bearing down harder on what I believe are the essences of the issues that face us. At this point in my life, not to mention the life of the period, I can trust no other way to go.

Michael Benedikt was born in 1935 in New York City, where he still lives, and was educated at Columbia and New York universities. He has published four books of poems, *The Body* (1968), *Sky* (1970), *Mole Notes* (1971), and *Night Cries* (1976), and has been represented in some twenty-five anthologies of modern U.S. and British poetry. A former editorial associate for *Art News* and *Art International*, he is currently poetry editor of the *Paris Review*. His interdisciplinary interests include the editing of five anthologies of international literature: *Modern French Theatre* (1964), *Post-War German Theatre* (1966), *Modern Spanish Theatre* (1967), *The Poetry of Surrealism* (1975), and *The Prose Poem: An International Anthology* (1976). He has taught at Bennington, Sarah Lawrence, Hampshire and Vassar colleges, and at Boston University.

Philip Booth

DREAMSCAPE

On the steep road
curving to town, up
through the spruce trees
from the filled-in canal,
there have been five houses, always.

But when I sleep
the whole left side of the blacktop
clears itself into good pasture.
There are two old horses,
tethered. And a curving row
of miniature bison, kneeling,

each with his two front hooves
tucked in neatly under the lip
of the asphalt. I am asleep.
I cannot explain it. I do not
want to explain it.

HOW A POEM HAPPENS

How did the poem start?

From the beginning. Always from the beginning, trying to recover the original impulse and move the poem with it. Always, back to the beginning, to be moved by the impulse, to make the poem move.

In this particular poem the title begins to tell.

What changes did it go through from start to finish?

All possible changes that might, as I sensed and tested them, writing and rewriting, enable the poem to move toward its own conclusions. All changes that might both explore those conclusions and, naturally, light their way.

What principles of technique did you consciously use?

None, consciously. No principles as such. A poem consciously principled belongs to a School before it's begun; or ought to be left to poetry workshops: purely an exercise.

Principles inhere: say how a lifetime inhabits earthspace. How a voice gets down on a page is mostly another matter.

A poet in the process of writing need be no more or less aware of "techniques" than a skijumper approaching the lip of a jump. On hills where darkness has closed down early, he has already learned by example, and practiced every possible technique. Readied, he is full of experience and feeling, set to inhabit blank air. What may once have felt mechanical becomes, in process, organic: his form is an event: an act of intensely concentrated motion both grounded in common sense and defying it.

First courage, then skill, then luck. The luck that courage and skill help make. Worrying about a principle as basic as gravity can only bring the poet down hard; tactics become reflex are what accomplish the leap. There's some unspoken poet in every skijumper: who else leans out so far and learns, briefly, even in mid-flight, how to reshape the whole course of his life?

Whom do you visualize as the reader?

One person and one person and one person. Never, collectively, "an audience." Never, as I write, editors. Sometimes, on the far margins of my first feeling, this person or that whose art (not necessarily poetry) has lent courage to my own. But I believe the reader I hope for, reading late by simple light, is bound to be out there: one—or one with another. The person will find the poem if the poem finds the person. Writing, writing, I try only to get back, down, and out to what the world of the poem may come to.

The oldest commandment is still first: Honor Thy Subject.

Can the poem be paraphrased?

I trust not.

Dreamscape is in part about a refusal to paraphrase complex perception, and that part of the poem can probably be "talked about." Around-and-about, which is probably more illuminating than the ways that paraphrase thinks are "direct." Paraphrase, as distinct from close reading, is almost always reductive. A good poem never is: the nature and quality of its concerns are too surely human and too surely eventful. In subtracting the eventfulness, paraphrase discounts humanity.

The recurrences in *Dreamscape* seem to me, long after the fact, to reinforce my emphasis on what may be the poem's pivot-word: "always." Short of the poem itself, what lesser statement might give that word its due, or tell by context its tone?

How does this poem differ from earlier poems of yours?

Quality. Asked to guess, I wouldn't want to confuse the always singular present with the continually plural past. The poems I've earlier written are already a grove: hardwoods and softwoods, evergreens, and deciduous trees of all sizes. This apparently small poem is more likely to be shaded out by new growth than to thrust up through old. But it might seed some strong new roots. I didn't know when I wrote it. I still wouldn't want to pretend to.

Theme. It would take a reader almost as familiar with my poems as I am, and more objective, to judge the growth of my themes. I rarely look back at my earlier books; when I do, I find myself mostly amazed. I am always more interested in what I am writing than what I have written.

Technique. Before I was old enough to be a parent, yet was, I thought that poems like *L, M, O,* were so accomplished that they clearly fulfilled the promise of what a poem could be. Now that I'm old enough to be a grandfather, and am, my belief is in more difficult trusts: the round of enigmas and ambivalences and mysteries that make life the most certain poem of all, the poem I hope my own poems may increasingly honor.

Philip Booth, born in 1925, grew up in New Hampshire and Maine. He received his master's degree from Columbia after graduating from Dartmouth. He taught there briefly, as well as at Bowdoin and Wellesley, before moving to his present position as professor of English in the creative writing program at Syracuse University. He has published five books: *Letter from a Distant Land* (1957), *The Islanders* (1961), *Weathers and Edges* (1966), *Margins* (1971), and *Available Light* (1976). His work has been honored by a Lamont Prize, by Guggenheim and Rockefeller fellowships, as well as by awards from *Poetry*, the *Virginia Quarterly Review*, *Poetry Northwest*, and the National Institute of Arts and Letters.

Hayden Carruth

LONELINESS

An Outburst of Hexasyllables

Stillness and moonlight, with
thick newfallen snow. I
go to the hollow field
beneath the little ridge
of spruces. The snow lies
on the trees, drapery
white and unmoving. I
cannot see any light
from here, no farmhouse, no
car moving through darkness.
A bird makes a sleepy
sound somewhere, probably
a pine grosbeak in the
trees. Often I visit
this place, here where no lights
show, only the cold moon
and the stars, for I have
so long a loneliness
(I think of all my time
compounded with all time)
that often it might cry

if it saw a lighted
window in the night. Now
a little breath of cold
air in the stillness sways
the white trees with a sigh.

*

Between two snow-heavy
boughs, a bright star; perhaps
many stars combined in
one sparkling, perhaps a
galaxy. I look up
to incalculable
space, on which my two boughs
almost close. Somewhere there
a world like this exists,
as beautiful as this,
snow in moonlight gleaming,
yet with no mind. Nothing
on that world knows what is
beauty or loneliness.
Only the snow-draped trees.

*

Moonlight is "reflected
light reflected again
on snow." It seems—no, it
actually is from
everywhere. It casts no
shadow. It is pale and
what is called, with justice,
ethereal; and yet
its brightness is enough
to show up everything,
"as bright as day." But this
is not daylight; it is
the visible aspect

of stillness: the two are
one. See how the spruces
stand in moonlight as in
the silence, unmoving
and soundless, held like that
to be reflectors of
loneliness, the arras
hung in this empty room.
These spruces belong to
Marshall Washer, my friend
and neighbor, whose light I
can never see from here.

*

Cursed, cursed from childhood with
incapacity, with
the vision of the void.

*

Everyone now has thought
how it may be when soon
universal death comes
down the mountainsides, creeps
up from the seas, appears
out of the air like snow,
and how one might escape
in all the multitude
and survive alone. This
is the archetypal dream
or daydream of our years.
That one will be alone,
alone, more alone than
anyone ever was;
no look, no voice, no touch,
no *mind* in all the world.
It might be me. It might
be now, this moment, here.

*

The snow sculpts this object,
a snow-tree, and does it
neither by carving nor
by molding, for there is
a third way nature knows
and a few men besides
(who will not give themselves
to the controversies
of theorists). Rather
this sculpture is made by
the whole of motioning,
all in a concert, which
condenses out of air—
out of universal
substance—the exact form
this tree must take. Never
a flake too many or
too few: it is exact.
All growth is a kind of
condensation, like these
intense words gathering
here. Its exactness is
all that we understand
of perfection. Yet it
cannot last. That dream was
a folly, for the sun's
first minutest degree
of heat at dawn, the wind's
least pressure, will change it
irretrievably. This
snowy spruce is good for
these few hours only, in
a quiet winter's night.

*

This is being alone,
this learning with the years
how exactness fails, how
it must fail always, how
the momentary fit
of mood and circumstance
must necessarily
decay. One consciousness
in the night can never
find another to share
or even know this, this
particular felt hour.
O God, I know you don't
exist, or certainly
you would blast us or lift
us backward into that
simplicity they knew
long ago when people
had someone to talk to.

*

But if it were only
the problem of a new
metaphysics! One could
invent something, almost
anything. Think what schemes
and dreams have served. But I
am here in this real life
that I was given, my life
of a withered tongue. I
brush through the trees, and snow
spills down on me, a chill
colder than the cold. Mad,
maddened, turning around,
I beat the tree with my
arms; unweighted branches
spring upward and snow flies,

a silent fury. Then
I fall back, winded, wet,
snow melting in my shirt;
I stumble in ruckled
snow, all exactness gone,
only the stillness left
in its indifferent
perfection on my ruin;
and I am limp, frightened
of myself, yet saddened
by such futility.
I go away, slogging
in my own tracks that make
an erratic passage
like a wounded bear's, scuffed
over the lovely snow.

*

At home the fire has died,
the stove is cold. I touch
the estranging metal.
I pour tea, cold and dark,
in a cup. The clock strikes,
but I forget, until
too late, to count the hours.
I sit by the cold stove
in a stillness broken
by the clock ticking there
in the other room, by
clapboards creaking, and I
begin to shiver, cold,
at home in my own house.

*

Down in the duckpen they
are moving around in
the moonlight and they are

affected by it, they
gabble, and from time to
time—now—the hen ducks break
into quacking, raucous
in the still nighttime. I
cannot decide if it
is laughter. I cannot
decide if this laughter
is derisive or just
maniacal and sad.

*

I do my work, all night
until the dawn comes, late
in this week of solstice.
Then pink, as I look up,
is the snow out in the
garden, pink is the snow
on the spruces, pink the
immense snowy mountain
across the valley. I
lean on the cold window.
A jay slips down and lights
on the birch, dislodging
drops of snow from his bough.
The moon is a pallid
disk on the horizon,
as if it had been washed
with snow. The world has turned
from night to day, and this
event is still touching
deep sources in me, though
I do not know what they
are. The cold weight of my
body pulls downward and
I feel it as if my

years were heavy, and I
feel a drop of moisture
sliding down my nose, cold
and weighted, until it
meets the glass. I know that
I am a fool and all
men are fools. I know it
and I know I know it.
What good is it to know?
18–19 December 1974

The poem I have chosen for this discussion is called *Loneliness*, subtitled *An Outburst of Hexasyllables*. It was written last winter; my worksheets are dated December 18–19, 1974. On the evening of December 18 I spent several hours in the company of acquaintances, people younger than I whom I liked but did not know well. When I came home I felt that I had been awkward, unable to talk or make a connection; i.e., I felt estranged and also, because this experience was nothing new in my life but something that had recurred many, many times, somewhat bitter. At midnight I sat down and began to write. I worked for a couple of hours on the poem, then went on to the other work I have to do for a living. (I usually work at night.) The next afternoon I went back to the poem again, for about another hour, and wrote two or three additional sections, which were not, however, tacked on at the end but were inserted within the poem and were by way of amplifications. After that I made no further changes. The poem is long, at least as poems go nowadays: 231 lines, in eleven sections.

The way poems occur is important to me, much more important than the way they are written, and I've thought about it a lot. This poem arose directly from my experience that evening, but it has no explicit connection with that experience, which isn't mentioned in the poem at all. Instead, the poem takes off on remembered and projected experiences over many years, experiences of my life here in this particular place. The actions in the poem are those of a single person in his relationship to woods, weather, the night, the snow, a house, etc. All these actions are given a specificity that is fictional in the poem; though all of them may have occurred at one time or another in my life, and though some of them have in fact occurred many times, the unity they have in the poem is invented. And one of the principal episodes, that of the poet leaning against a window and shedding a tear, is totally invented; I have never done that, as nearly as I recall, in this place or this house, though I may have felt like it. Actually I believe this was dredged up from a time more than twenty years ago, when I was an inmate of a mental hospital.

I think of the entire content of the poem as *typical*. It is the type of what does happen. It is authentic because I know the place and time I am writing about, and I know myself. The poem is a complex integration of real and imagined elements, too complex to be analyzed, brought into being by an experience outside the poem itself, a "catalyst"—I believe that's the popular term. And perhaps an added factor of authenticity in the poem is its feeling, which is something I have known all my life, often in extreme ways.

When I sat down to write I wanted freedom, but freedom within a limiting frame. I chose hexasyllables. I don't know why I chose that particular meter, perhaps only because the first line I wrote happened to have six syllables—such choices are often, with me, exactly that arbitrary. But I know I chose the syllabic scheme because I felt it would give me a certain fixed armature to work on, while at the same time permitting great flexibility of phrasing, accenting, etc. I consciously varied the accents, both in placement and in number, from line to line, and I consciously introduced rhymes, half-rhymes, assonances, and other sound patterns as they occurred to me, trying to make the modulations of both rhythm and sound progress in largely cyclical movements, so that they would reinforce the unity of feeling in the poem. But when I say I did this "consciously," I don't mean I bore down on this aspect of the work when I was writing. I was aware of technique, as anyone is who has been writing for more than thirty years, but I was primarily concerned about the substance of the poem, and the language, for the most part, flowed naturally and quickly. In other words, the technique—sounds, rhythms, textures, and all the rest of it—was suggested to me, as it unfolded, by the progress of my feeling, and only the broadest principles were held in my mind as things to be consciously aware of.

One of them, however—a prominent one—was the question of line values. For me the line is the essential unit of verse, and I don't like to see it smudged. This means that although I chose syllabic verse, my lines were not determined merely by syllable counting. Except in special cases, I do not care for weak words and hyphenated words at the ends of lines, a usage that seems to have become habitual among many younger writers. Consequently I tried to make my line breaks work functionally, in terms of both syntax and rhythm. Now when I read the poem to myself I read it with a very slight pause, the least of hesitations, at the end of each line.

The poem has few explicit metaphors, perhaps none. In general I do not care for metaphor, and though I don't rule it out absolutely, I use it sparingly. I try to insist with myself that no metaphor be admitted that is merely ornamental or augmentational. For me both elements of the metaphor—the thing and the thing-to-which-the-thing-is-likened—must be genuinely relevant, necessary to the substance of the poem. Of course this does not mean that the objects in a poem, even a poem with no metaphors, will not assume a symbolic function as the poem progresses. They will, just as words themselves were originally symbols and metaphors when language was invented. And this, I think, is exactly the way a poet should use his own simile-making faculties.

When I was writing the poem I had no reader in mind at all. I wrote it for myself. Of course if I write a poem addressed to a particular person I have that person in mind, inescapably, when I am writing, but otherwise no, I never think about the reader until after the poem is finished, usually some time after. Several days after this one was finished I typed it up and showed it to my wife, who didn't like it (because it made her cry), and to a friend, who said he did. I then sent it immediately to David Ray, editor of *New Letters*, along with some other poems written at about the same time, because I had promised him I would. Usually I hold my poems longer than that.

I suppose now I think of the poem as being of interest to people who have read my earlier poems and liked them. I suppose I have some idea of what sort of people these are, but it is vague and at best a stereotype. I don't think much is gained by talking about it. Of course, like other poets, I always hope my poems will be valuable to people in general, people who are not themselves poets; but it is a forlorn hope.

The poem is simple. It contains a simple action—a little journey, so to speak—which could easily be paraphrased, and I suppose a rough paraphrase could be made of the emotional and intellectual substance of the poem too. But what would be the point of it? The poem really is simple. I can't imagine any literate person failing to understand it as it is written.

The poem does not differ at all, in either theme or technique, from some earlier poems I've written, but it differs greatly from many others. I don't feel a poet needs to confine himself to one method or even to one style—in which I differ from most other poets, apparently. I have used syllabics, traditional meter and rhyme, rough meter, free meter, and I have written some poems with no meter at all (i.e., no real lines), though this last I believe in principle to be wrong. As for quality, I leave that to others. Of course I hope any poem I write is a good one, or at least any poem I complete and publish. But I'm not fool enough to think my hope is realizable. For myself, this poem works pretty well. If I have any anxiety about it, it is that readers who, for whatever reason, do not read it in the spirit in which it was written will find it too simple or self-revealing.

Addendum

Now I've reread what I've written, and I should like to say, briefly, that I don't believe in this way of talking about a poem. It gives the wrong impression. The truth is that this poem, like most of my poems, was written in a state of mind very close to trance. I think people nearer than I am to the neo-Platonic conventions would say it was a trance. I was writing in extreme emotion—agitation, depression, bitterness. The next day this feeling had partly evaporated, but only partly; the sections of the poem I wrote then are the more abstract ones dealing with questions of art and form, but there is enough of the original feeling in them, I think, to make them consistent with the sections I had written the night before. For what it is worth, this is perfectly typical of the way I write: the first trance, then a second lesser one in which amplifications are made. Then after that only slight editorial changes, blue-penciling. I never disturb the structure of a poem once it is fixed, which usually occurs at the poem's inception, and I disturb the wording as little as possible.

I called the poem an "outburst" and that is what it is.

Hayden Carruth was born in 1921 in New England, where he still lives. He studied at the universities of North Carolina and Chicago, served in World War II with the Army Air Corps, edited *Poetry* in the late 1940s, and has worked as a free-lance editor for the past twenty-five years. He has published fiction and criticism and eleven books of poetry; the most recent are *From Snow and Rock, from Chaos* (1973), *Dark World* (1974), and *The Bloomingdale Papers* (1975). He edited *The Voice That Is Great Within Us* (1970), an anthology of American poetry in the twentieth century.

Laura Chester

PAVANE for the Passing of a Child

after the music of Ravel

Possible
that I lift this hand
feel a weight I've never felt there?
Possible
I hold this weight
collapsed   and sunk   and tamed now
feel a flesh so warm gone under
that will not home.
I give her back
for whom I sang
I sing no longer.
Possible
my arms surround
will lay her down this last time
not return—
There was no taming her
but in this claiming of her.
I give her up I hold her here
all that was left to me.
I hold I can not

give her up
I lay her down
my arms fold over.

And then she took her child
and then she laid the child to rest
and then she laid the cover on the child
and then she closed her heart.
And it tore over her.
She turned away to face it
and in the door the light came in
and made a breakfast of her.
It spread all over her.
It sucked and made a vacant space there.
Where there had been a child
a child no longer.
Collapsed in her.
It sucked her fill—
She let the sobs come
take her gut and wrench
the place of blood
where she had spilled   and grown   and swollen
where she had born   and held   and given
what had been pulled from her
what had been torn
was taken.
What had been chance and breath
what had been closer than
her mouth her hope her plea and cry
was aching.

She stood there in the sun
and it disgraced her.

The plate
the cup
the dress the bed and book

turned over.
The toy the finger smudge
the corner
folded.

If sea could tear   and water hold a stone
she'd sink there.
Was told
to let her go—
It was no good—
The light crashed through her.
She meant to force it
swell up and take her too
but something stopped inside
marked off   and framed her.
Before   there was a lingering
and now an outline
a separation.
She was retreating.
The force welled up—
She stopped.
She gave it back.
Refused to nurse it.

The light came on
came on and planted her.
She felt nothing.
The sun rose up
and smeared itself all over her.
But she felt nothing.
The man who stood behind
and placed his hands upon her shoulders—
She felt nothing.
She felt nothing.
The sky that morning flatter than she'd ever known it.

And then she took her child
and then she laid the child to rest

and then she laid the cover
on the child
and then she closed her heart.
And when she turned away
it made a breakfast of her.
It sucked   and made a vacant space inside her.
Where there had been a child
a child no longer.
The blood place wrenched
where she had spilled
where she had born and held
what had been torn
was taken.
What had been breath
her mouth her hope and plea
was aching.

The plate   the cup
the dress the bed and book
turned over.
Held back and gone
her song was sung
the sod was heavy in her.
It could not cover.

TALKING ABOUT IT

To talk about this poem, I have to go back to the evening where the emotion that moved the poem surfaced. We were having dinner with Stan and Anne Rice, and as usual in their company, I was charged up by their intensity but couldn't let myself go. When I'm unable to express myself, incapable of letting friends know what I feel for them, I am anxious to write, and the poem becomes not only an inward communication but a message toward the other.

Several years ago the Rices lost their only daughter to leukemia. Many of his poems deal with this long, excruciating death trudge, but that night after dinner, in just one look from Anne, I recognized the present tense of their tragedy. A young girl from the next apartment came over to play with our boy, and seeing her, Anne flashed as if stunned in memory. Then she looked to Stan for apparent acknowledgment. Some common maternal hurt struck me then and left me in a sad and moody place.

After they went home, I wanted to sit by myself and sink into that feeling, a tenderness cut with sharp cord. I put on the piece of Ravel's music that we had listened to earlier and which had been such a perfect complement to my melancholy, a combination of weepiness and frustration. As the music played, I wrote in longhand, letting the music ground the feelings I had to negotiate, something I had to uncover in myself by assuming her loss as a mother. I don't usually write to music, but this piece sang so perfectly what I needed to express in words, that it helped to guide the flow without interfering.

While I was writing, I was gripped with the fear, that these words spelled out an unconscious wish for the death of my own child. I didn't hold on to that irrational, unbelievable thought, and explained it away as the guilt that writing can bring with it, especially when you absorb someone else's tragedy and assume a very intimate kind of empathy. Only later, after working on the poem, did I see where the real guilt was coming from.

At the time I suspected that I might be pregnant again, and this time it wasn't planned or hoped for. A close friend had just had an abortion, and because of her circumstances, the choice seemed like the only sane decision. I stayed at her place and watched the children while another friend went with her. We were all slightly edgy beforehand, avoiding the seriousness with firm smiles, thumbs up, then see you soon and it'll all be over. But when she returned, her usually radiant face was wrenched with it, her hands pathetically on her son's hair and shoulder; then holding herself in, she sank back on the couch in sobs.

Almost as a sympathetic response, I became certain that I was pregnant too. Being married, my situation was different, and abortion just didn't seem possible as I'd rock and nurse my son, imagining daughter, but then I'd turn off and think, "Grab onto your own life—Don't let this birth happen when it's not what you want." Luckily I had no real need to act or allow.

When I wrote *Pavane*, all of this was the emotional well into which I was lowering my bucket. I wasn't conscious of the abortion imagery as I wrote, though later when Geoff pointed out certain lines "And then she took her child . . . The blood place wrenched . . . It sucked and made a vacant space inside her," the connection was quite clear, and yet initially, I thought of these images in relation to the death of a growing child and how it would rip emotionally at the womb of a mother, cinching the ache of birth and death together.

Perhaps because of the French title to Ravel's piece of music, *Pavane Pour Une Infante Défunte*, I placed the circumstance imaginatively in a French villager's farmhouse, the mother in long layers of skirts, incredulous before the blazing doorway. I didn't give many details to convey that setting, partly because it was not an actual death that I was describing, but the sensation of loss on a simple gut level. Although *Infante* in French means princess, I'd like to think that the same song could have been composed for the loss of any child.

When I first begin writing a poem, the words come quickly and I don't try to censor myself. Then I immediately type up what I have, regaining control for gradual revision, pressuring the poem while trying not to lose that initial blood beat. I type draft after draft almost obsessively until that first soft clay shapes itself into the poem it has to become. Given a resting period of about one week, I am drawn back to the poem with more critical distance and make minor changes, crossing out sections or words that suddenly seem obvious and wrong, altering line breaks so that they are more in tune with the way I'd read the poem out loud, sometimes replacing a phrase with one from an earlier more authentic version.

In the early stage of rewriting *Pavane*, I continued to play the music that had helped stir it. It allowed me to sink back into the same place more easily, and when I rewrite I have to retrieve that original urge, otherwise it becomes mere correction and something vital is lost. True re-vision can be as exciting and "creative" as the first attempt. I love to feel the poem as a malleable substance that I can push and reshape on the page.

While revising *Pavane*, I became absorbed by the repetitions in Ravel's music. I wanted certain clusters of words to come back in the poem as they did in the music, not as a monotonous refrain, but transformed and recalling, a resurgence of familiar sound but in a different wave of intensity. I didn't labor over this idea, it just clicked and allowed me the circling of music which I needed for this mourning song. The internal rhyme, the repetition of "her" and of opening phrases throughout the poem helps to bring out a hymnal gravity.

> And then she took her child
> and then she laid the child to rest
> and then she laid the cover on the child
> and then she closed her heart.

I also wanted to get at the psychological syndrome that occurs when we try to digest a shattering life event by going over and over the details. Because the last line in the poem admits to this kind of repetition, it could lead the reader back to the beginning of the poem, or at least allow a resonance.

I don't try to write in terms of symbols, but sometimes when I try to figure out why I said something the way I did, an object will take on greater import, and I'll try to understand the meaning symbolically. The sun in this poem first seemed to be a ridiculing sensual presence—it told the woman that Nature was unaffected. But then more dramatically, it came to represent for me a masculine deity that the woman could not believe in or tolerate. The husband behind her seems to be in alliance with this force and that makes her even more solitary. This masculine force plants and takes away without reason or pain, while the woman in defense is forced to shut off her anguish, refusing to feed her own lament.

> She stopped.
> She gave it back.
> Refused to nurse it.

These lines seem to put hands up, in short gesture. The contrast between her state of numbness, "She felt nothing," and the encompassing urge towards acceptance found in the alternating lines, which are long and round in sound, is extended in the next stanza, until it seems that her sorrow is blocked. The ending of the poem breaks down this mind set, and in a sense releases her to accept her sorrow.

I think this poem presents a wide blank horizon, even though the details called up are common objects, recognizable as the stupid kitchen clock. Shock of familiar objects signals a more actualized bereavement. The plate cup dress bed book are so simple, so much of the child, that they have to be single syllables. Language is reduced to the reality of "things" in their places, things which in their significance, appear so much more alive without the living presence of the child.

> The plate
> the cup
> the dress the bed and book
> turned over.
> The toy the finger smudge
> the corner
> folded.

The way I wrote this stanza was most influenced by the pace the music took at one point. When I'd read it out loud, the music in the background made me step carefully, slowly touching down on each word.

My poems don't usually like comma punctuation. It's annoying to me visually, but I do put considerable tonal importance on the place I cut a line. It's as important as a gesture of paint on canvas. I want a subtle tension to gather so that the last word in a line pulls back, then gives in to the following line.

I think the vague quality of this poem lets the reader connect a personal experience to the universal human element of loss. The poem doesn't need me or my unique history. And yet when I go back to this poem, distant from the emotion that bore it, it takes me right back there, building up to the point where it says

> where she had spilled   and grown   and swollen
> where she had born   and held   and given
> what had been pulled from her
> what had been torn
> was taken.

That part always gets to me, and I think it's because, here especially, I enter into my own feminine, deepest sense of loss.

Laura Chester was born April 13, 1949. She has always thought of Oconomowoc, Wisconsin, as "home," although she has lived in New Mexico, Paris, and now Berkeley, where she and the poet Geoffrey Young edit a new poetry press *The Figures*. Together they co-authored a book of poems, *The All Night Salt Lick* (1972), while travelling in Africa, and edited thirteen splendid issues of the magazine *Stooge*. Other books by Ms. Chester include *Tiny Talk* (1972), *Nightlatch* (1974), *Primagravida* (1975), and *Proud & Ashamed* (1977). One of the collective founding members of the feminist poetry magazine *Best Friends*, she has worked for the publication of other women writers, co-editing *Rising Tides, 20th Century American Women Poets* (1973). She was the recipient of the Kappa Alpha Theta Award for Poetry, and the Steloff Poetry Prize. Presently, she is caught up in the deluge of a second novel.

Norman Dubie

MONOLOGUE OF TWO MOONS, NUDES WITH CRESTS. 1938

Once, Lily and I fell from a ladder
And startled the white geese that were
Concealed in the shadows of the house, and
I wrote much later that the geese
Broke from the shadows like handkerchiefs
Out of the sleeves of black dresses

At a burial. When the matron was sick
It was work to carry the powders
On blue paper and the clear water
With a spoon into her large, cold room.

In the evenings we would look out
At the spruce trees. It was wrong to have
Visitors. It was wrong those clear nights
To remember that boys were out on the hills
Falling onto sleds or into their grey baskets.

We were two young girls with black hair
And the white cones

Of our breasts. Lily said, "I will put
My hand, here, on you and follow the rib, and
You can put your hand, here, on me,
Up the inside of my leg."
We spent that Christmas morning pressing
Satin skirts for the boys' choir. We take
Butter away from the closet.
We take the lamp away from the green
Cadaverous child who is not ours.

I have a little violin pupil who eats
Bread in cream.
We love the details mice leave in flour.
The ways the clouds
Are low like before a storm in early summer.

Lily slept with a Jew once in Vienna.
I opened my hand that morning
On a milk-jug that had frozen and cracked
On the doorstep.
Yesterday, I saw the perfect impression
Of a bee in asphalt. It was under a shade tree.
Lily said, "I will kiss in the morning
Your mouth which will be red and thick
After sleep." She has left me
For a banker she met in the gardens.
The gas-jets are on: they are
Like fountains of the best water. I am

Remembering the vertical action of two birds
Building a nest. It's in Munich and
Both birds are dark and crested,
But the female, I think, is the one whose
Nesting materials are all wet things:

Twigs, leaves and an infinite black string.

DRAFT

MONOLOGUE OF TWO MOONS, NUDES
WITH CRESTS, 1938.*

~~For Natalie & J.~~

Once Lily and I fell ~~together~~ from a ladder
And startled the fat geese that were
Concealed in the shadows of the house. ~~I said~~
~~The white birds broke like handkerchiefs~~ → And I wrote much later that the ~~white~~ geese broke from the shadows like handkerchiefs
Out of the sleeves of black dresses

At a burial. When the matron was sick
It was work to carry the powders
On blue paper and the clear water
With a spoon into her large, cold room.

In the evenings we would look out
At the spruce trees. It was wrong to have
Visitors. It was wrong to remember
That boys were out on the hills,
(Those clear nights,) falling onto sleds
Or into their grey baskets.

Two young ~~women~~ girls with black hair
And ~~secrets:~~ the white cones → She said,
Of our breasts. "I will put my hand,
Here, on you and follow the rib, and
You can put your hand, here, on me;
Up the inside of my leg."
?# → We spent that Christmas morning pressing white
Skirts for the boy's choir. We take

* The original manuscript is in the University of Iowa Libraries, Iowa City.

Butter away from the closet.
We take the lamp away from the green
Cadaverous child who is not ~~sleeping~~. ours.

We love the details mice leave in flour.
The way the clouds
Are low like before a storm in early summer.

Lily slept with a Jew once in Vienna.
I ~~cut~~ opened my ~~wrist~~ hand that morning
On a milk-jug that had frozen and cracked on the doorstep.
~~I ate the milk avoiding the glass.~~

Keep | I have a little violin pupil who eats
| Bread in cream.
Yesterday I saw the perfect impression
Of a bee in asphalt. It was under a shade tree.
She said, "I ~~have~~ will kiss~~ed~~ in the morning ~~the strong red~~
~~Muscle of Lily's rectum.~~" (What?)

"your mouth which will be red and thick after sleep."

She has left me
For a ~~gentleman~~ banker she met in the gardens.
The gas-jets are on ~~all around me:~~ they are ?
Like fountains of the best water. I am

~~Hungry for strawberries. I am not in the least~~
~~Sleepy.~~
Remembering the ~~strong~~ vertical ~~movements~~ action of two birds
~~Over~~ Building a nest. (In Munich) They are both dark and crested
But the female, I think, is the one ~~who nests, not believing~~
Whose materials are all wet things: twigs, leaves and some string. ?

Strange + page!

Ending! Wrong!!!!

This poem began as a fragment of another poem which borrowed for its title from the title of a Paul Klee pen and ink, *Two Aunts: Nudes with Crests, 1908.* This fragment began with the image of the geese from line 5 of the finished poem and never progressed past the image of the boys falling onto their sleds, line 15. The fragment was abandoned even before I had any clear sense of who it was speaking through the poem.

Several days later I sat down to write again and began with the image of the geese, now, treating it as a diary entry belonging to some woman who would have been in her late twenties at the start of World War II. I decided then that she would speak throughout the poem of an unsatisfactory love affair with another woman, Lily. Even though the speaker of my poem by the final draft was nameless, in earlier drafts she was addressed by Lily as Nora. It will be convenient for me to refer to her, the speaker, as Nora.

I was able to write the poem, I think, for a very simple reason. When I began the poem the second time I treated the image of the geese as something Nora remembered as having written down in a diary, that very same passage I remembered as having been written down by me in the hopeless fragment I had discarded. Suddenly Nora and I had something in common, not just an experience but a *recorded* experience; accidentally this woman whom I had created shared with me a pre-creation memory. I honestly believe I wrote this poem just for Nora; she was a reality for me living outside my poem. From the beginning of the second stanza on, it was effortless for me to imagine her sitting in a chair in her white kitchen with all the gas jets open hurridly remembering things from her life just at that moment that she was ending it. The poem has a simple plot: Nora and Lily were servant girls in the same house, they worked for a sickly woman, and as mere girls they formed an alliance that was both practical and sexual. Lily was more confused about the relationship than Nora, and Lily was also the more aggressive of the two. Lily, if we believe Nora, was a flirt and she finally deserted Nora to marry a wealthy banker. Nora is inconsolable and kills herself.

There were only minor revisions of the poem after the poem had clearly become a monologue. The two little seductions or speeches Lily makes were originally more explicitly sexual and less tender. And the choice of verbs changed. These decisions were made to a single point: Nora's voice had to seem both passive and yet excited with clear detail. The passivity, as with Paul Valéry's gaff for Flaubert, is the very vehicle for the making of the poem. The poem is meant to work with principles of ordinary speech and not seem that poetic. The stanzas are built like paragraphs and the basic instinct is toward the sentence rather than the line. The poem is a monologue. The prose quality of the poem is violated only at the very end with the things/string couplet, but this couplet as a device is subverted by the final stanza break which is meant to distance the rhyme. The couplet is used, I guess, for its authority.

And finally, about this image of nest building at the end of the poem; the materials for nest building are usually the remains of something else. Nora knows that for us it is almost expected that we build out of destruction and that this is also the way of our natural world; anyway this is an image surrounded by the prospect of change, seasonal for the birds, real and circumstantial for her: it is her last conscious thought before death and is a small inauguration of our Second World War.

Norman Dubie was born in 1945 outside Websterville, Vermont; he grew up in Maine, New Hampshire, and Vermont. He has degrees from Goddard College and The University of Iowa. He has taught at The University of Iowa, Ohio University, and Arizona State University. He has published three books, *Alehouse Sonnets* (1971), *In the Dead of the Night* (1975), and *The Illustrations* (1976). He lives with his wife, the poet Pamela Stewart, and their daughter, Hannah, in Tempe, Arizona.

Richard Eberhart

A SNOWFALL

As the snow falls I brush it away
With a delicate broom so as not to use a shovel.
Every hour I go out to the long walk,
Conquer the new swirls and pile as if persistence
Were a virtue to keep up with nature.
If I did nothing I would be snowed in.
Some slumberous thinkers think this the best, January.
Let three feet fall, stay indoors, go to sleep,
Luxuriate in sleep like the groundhogs and gray squirrels.

There is something in me to test nature,
To disallow it the archaic predominance,
And if the skies blanket us entirely
With a silence so soft as to be wholly winsome,
(This beguilement of something beyond the human)
I have enough in me to give affront
And take my thin broom against the thick snowflakes
As a schoolmaster who would tell the children
What to do when they are getting sleepy and lazy.

I now make my predicament equal to nature's.
I have the power, although it is timed and limited,
To assert my order against the order of nature.
The snowplows begin to take away the snow,
Flashing big lights in the middle of the night.
They, corporate, have the same idea that I have,
Individualist, not to let nature better us,
But to take this softness and this plenitude
As aesthetic, and control it as it falls.

Hotel Chelsea #1026
222 West 23 Street
New York, N.Y. 10011
March 14, 1975

Dear Alberta Turner:

Here are musings anent your Questionnaire. I am sitting here in New York on a raw day before the Ides of March and am recalling my latest poem written in Hanover, N.H., a month or more ago. I am writing this without the text to hand. The poem is entitled *A Snowfall.* It was written after the beginning of a snowfall, for mysterious reasons never fully understood, and has the distinction of being the poem of mine soonest selected for publication after birth. I sent it to the *Atlantic Monthly.* They usually ponder a long time, usually return work, but this poem was accepted immediately and should appear soon. Born one day, it was almost accepted for publication the next, give or take a few days. I rushed a copy to Chatto & Windus, London, to see if it could be entered in my new *Collected Poems 1930–1975.* Perhaps there will be more birth throes here, it may not make it. (Also Oxford University Press, NYC.)

Poems should be read in relation to other poems of the poet. This poem is one of several which came whole, was born whole. That is, it was unpremeditated, came spontaneously, and was written in a mood of calmness and control. I like the old word "inspiration," which is unpopular today, which suggests also "expiration." The ideas come in and the ideas go out while the poem is being written or born. Form is dictated by mood or state of being. The form of this poem was natural to it. I do not believe in automatic writing, by possession, but there is something magical or trancelike, or breathless (see above: in-between) sometimes in the writing of poetry. Many poems demand and receive short or long-time revision, but this one did not. It came off whole, a complete experience. I changed no word, but am indebted to Peter Davison at the *Atlantic* for his brilliant suggestion of putting one line in parentheses. I readily accepted this emendation as I did a suggestion to change "but" to "and" in the last line as there had been a "but" up the page a bit. Collaboration on such critical aids may be more valuable than trying to improve your lines by taking thought. I always believe in the sacredness or special quality of the creative time or onset and have not been addicted to changing lines because of my strong belief in the power of the imagination when the creative drive and mood is on. Why is there not a fifty-fifty chance of making a poem worse by tinkering with it in cold intellect? Why do we assume that we can make it better by taking thought? This is not to say that I have not taken and do not take much thought after the writing of a poem. It is necessary to look them over coolly, critically later; often I make changes, hoping they are for the better. There are poems and poems. I repeat that this poem was a whole-born poem and needed no changes, yet received beneficial changes from a sensitive editor.

I think I write to the poem itself, not to any particular audience. I must assume an audience of intelligent readers. I do not assume a specialized audience or elitist group, that is, not only professors.

There was only one draft of this poem. It was written probably in less than half an hour. The poem grew and developed as it came all the time with a sense of control and power, also ease and restraint, a balance of harmonies.

On lineation this is all mysterious. I write some poems with preconceived architectures. Some poems are *a priorily* structured. If you will read all the poems of a poet you will see what range and strategies are employed. You ask about rhythm, metaphor, and so forth. All I can reply of this poem is that it is on a real subject really treated and I have to say that, probably, it represents a totality of my consciousness at the time of writing. It is what I call a whole state. Probably one's entire life goes unconsciously into the making of a poem, so that it is inevitable and could not be other than it is. The poem is an expression of your whole being at the moment of vision, the time of writing. All the physical manifestations of the poem, the diction, linguistics, technicalities are natural to the self from long years of being and writing. It is the thrust, the brunt, the meaning of the poem that is paramount when utterance is made. All poems may be both seen and heard. I do not feel that they are only for the eye or only for the ear.

A Snowfall is about man's relation to nature, which he can never get away from. It is a meditative poem, a contemplative poem. It takes a stand for trying to do something about nature, sweeping away snowflakes as they fall so as not to be snowed under. It is not a moralizing poem (I am still thinking of it from memory without the text to hand) but suggests an analogy with what we are up against by being alive. I suppose it calls for order against disorder. Individualist man tries to control nature. Can he? The poem was prompted by the gentleness and seeming innocence of the snow, its wordless-verbless silence, its reality seen as aesthetic, perhaps a suggestion that this is illusion before dark realities. There may be a balance of tensions. Man can whisk away the snow, that he can do, but nature will always control him.

Yours sincerely,
Richard Eberhart

P.S. I found a copy of the poem, went out on 23rd Street and had a xerox copy made (the shop was closed against marauders), and feel that reading the poem is a better experience than reading the criticism. The poem is simpler, more gently persuasive, and is immediately communicated. The prose talk about poetry is thick, in some way clogged. Creation comes first, criticism second. It used to be a joke decades ago that if students read the notes to *The Waste Land* enough they would not have to read the poem. This is a reductio ad adsurdam but dangerous to contemplate, destructive. Criticism should be constructive, helpful, but it never can come up to the mystery of poetic creation.

Richard Eberhart was born in Austin, Minnesota, in 1904. He was educated at Dartmouth, St. John's College, Cambridge, and Harvard. During World War II he served in the U. S. Naval Reserve and subsequently as an executive of The Butcher Polish Company, as Consultant in Poetry at the Library of Congress, 1959–1961, and has been poet-in-residence, now Professor Emeritus, at Dartmouth since 1956. From 1930 to the present he has published more than a dozen books of poetry and verse drama, for which he received, among others, the Bollingen Prize, the Pulitzer Prize, the Shelley Memorial Prize, and the Fellowship of the Academy of American Poets; his *Collected Poems, 1930–1960* (1960) and *Fields of Grace* (1972) were nominated for the National Book Award. The most recent and complete collection of his poems is *Collected Poems, 1930–1976* (1976). In 1976 he also published *Poems to Poets* and *To Eberhart from Ginsberg.*

Russell Edson

COUNTING SHEEP

A scientist has a test tube full of sheep. He wonders if he should try to shrink a pasture for them.

They are like grains of rice.

He wonders of it is possible to shrink something out of existence.

He wonders if the sheep are aware of their tininess, if they have any sense of scale? Perhaps they just think the test tube is a glass barn . . .

He wonders what he should do with them; they certainly have less meat and wool than ordinary sheep. Has he reduced their commerical value?

He wonders if they could be used as a substitute for rice, a sort of woolly rice . . .?

He wonders if he just shouldn't rub them into a red paste between his fingers?

He wonders if they're breeding, or if any of them have died.

He puts them under a microscope and falls asleep counting them . . .

ON *COUNTING SHEEP*

It would be foolish of me to claim to be an expert on Edson's work. Writing it does not make the work any more open to me, perhaps less so than anyone else. I approach my work as a *reader*, rather than as a writer writing it. Each of my pieces is written without premeditation or expectation. For one thing, if I have an idea what I shall be writing about, such as this little article, I am bored and blocked from the *secret message*; I want to follow the writing as a reader; which is to say, I am as surprised as anyone might be as the writing begins to come out of the typewriter; the mysterious *other* life begins to send its message. It is also necessary not to have a literary expectation, but to enjoy the special reality on its own terms.

This piece, *Counting Sheep*, is one more of the experimental scenes that I have been writing all along of that other life, in an ongoing series of make-believes.

The first line, as with all of my pieces, suggested itself; and of course without my having an idea what would follow it, or what the line meant in the first place. But I have come to recognize that there is no point in trying to force a *starting* place. The trick is to be on station, and to wait, even if it takes hours (most times minutes). The *reality* appears in typewritten form as from no particular place: *A scientist has a test tube full of sheep.* What this means at the time, or even now, I don't fully know; but instinctively I know that it is *authentic*, and that the other life that we all know in our sleeping and daydreaming is once more available.

As I work I recognize something in this first line that is both quaint and horrible. The idea of tiny sheep is quaint. But that they are so out of scale to their normal environment is grotesque. And I see that I have committed myself to something horrible because I have believed the first line.

As far as I understand it, the second line comes obbligato to the first, it attempts to repair the loss of scale that the sheep have suffered, as the scientist *wonders if he should try to shrink a pasture for them* (the sheep). The speculation on shrinking so large and indefinite a thing as a pasture is the departure into a horrible madness that is almost silly. The tininess of the sheep causes them to be faraway; they are isolated, as it were, in the distance of scale: death in life, which is worse than actual death.

The scientist sees that they are *like grains of rice*, that they have lost their sheep, or animal, definition, and have been reduced to greyish white grains. They have not only been made tiny, but they no longer look like sheep!

The scientist *wonders if it is possible to shrink something out of existence*; he would like to shrink the sheep entirely out of his own awareness, but within the terms of his experiment. He could of course flush them down a toilet, or destroy them in many other ways. However, he, like the sheep, is lost in the context of the shrunken possibility. If he could shrink them out of existence he would, in a sense, not be destroying them, but bringing them back to a condition of pre-existence. In other words, there was a time when the sheep had no existence, and then at a certain point in time they began to manifest out of a small fraction of the biological *sheep presence*. What he would do, while being rid of them, is to once more return to them the possibility of normal existence; the open chance of pre-existence.

This is of course quite impossible, shrinking them out of existence, or renewing their time in terms of birth and re-existence. The situation can only advance, he cannot go back.

Next he must try to re-endow these *grains* with some awareness of their own existence, as he *wonders if they are aware of their tininess*; he concludes this speculation with *Perhaps they just think the test tube is a glass barn*. Although they are confined by their absurd smallness from the real world, the further confinement of the test tube may be a source of comfort. For in the real world they have always been confined in the human enclosure; they are still being looked after, as it were. And they are once more sheep, and not just simply tiny objects that look like rice.

Now that they are re-established in their sheepness the scientist can start to think about the human use of sheep, which, for the most part, is commercial. Since they have *less meat and wool than ordinary sheep*, he wonders if he has *reduced their commercial value*? Which is of course silly, since the scientific achievement, however horrible, of shrinking biological entites would far outweigh his absurd consideration of their meat and wool. And of course he is trying to sound to himself like a man rooted in the world, a man of practical and mercantile concerns.

This does not work for long, the sheep once again collapse, in his awareness, to grains of rice. He tries to see commercial value in this, as *he wonders if they could be used as a substitute for rice, a sort of woolly rice. . . .* The notion of taking a fair sized animal and reducing the animal down into a substitute grain of rice in the attempt to retain some commercial value, or even, perhaps, some novelty, or in the idea that someday rice might be less available than sheep, is quite beyond description in its absurdity. I hope the surface humor suggested by these turnings is not lost on the reader.

Then, in a new key, with an almost careless brutality, *he wonders if he just shouldn't rub them into a red paste between his fingers.* We realize suddenly just under the nondescript grainlike appearance of the tiny sheep there is a redness of flesh and blood, that just the slightest pressure of human fingers would burst and smudge into a *red paste.* This is the kind of viciousness that comes of despair; and the kind of ecstasy of cruelty that has its target in the self.

Of course the scientist does not destroy the tiny sheep. I, the writer, would not have permitted this; although, as I have mentioned earlier, it is not my job to interfere, but rather to read as the piece unfolds.

In the last moments of the piece he again wonders if they are continuing, in spite of their distance from this world, a somewhat normal existence, *breeding* and *dying.* But to see them intimately, to count them, he must put them under a microscope. Tiny things are the same as distant things, and both rendered to our visual scale with lenses. As he looks at them under a microscope he is looking into the distance.

At the end is the cliché of counting sheep and falling asleep, albeit this time tiny sheep under a microscope; and these tiny sheep are no less mental and removed from surface reality than the sheep that one might count in a sleepless bed. This also gives a shammed *literary* ending to the piece, and defines it as a make-believe.

I chose to write about this piece because it seemed simpler than many others. But I realize that this analysis seems hardly literary, and of course it isn't, in the strictest sense. I am more interested in emotional formations, entities that have a compact psychological life of their own, such as dreams. Yet I hesitate to say *such as dreams,* because I have no use for loose, dreamy writing, without image or focus.

As far as I can make out, this piece is a mediation, or rather, the *shape* of a meditation upon which surface pictures and speculations play. We realize that what we see is not the reality, as the light from a star is not the star itself, but indications of the other life produced in a theater of make-believe. All we can really bring to paper is a vague description of the mind drifting through its own interior; in a sense all else in any work of art is the impurity, the contradiction that makes it the human expression.

Russell Edson lives in Stamford, Conn., with his wife, Frances. He handset and printed his first pamphlets and is also a printmaker (woodcuts and etchings). Recently he won a Guggenheim Fellowship (1974–75) in "Creative Writing in Poetry."

His books include *The Very Thing That Happens* (1964), *What a Man Can See* (1969), *The Childhood of an Equestrian* (1973), *The Clam Theater* (1973), *The Falling Sickness, 4 Plays* (1975), *The Intuitive Journey and Other Works* (1976), and *The Reason Why the Closet-Man Is Never Sad* (1977).

Peter Everwine

ROUTES

I

Sun drops below the elms.
Moon comes along
and freezes the wheels of the street.
In her room my mother shakes out
her road of dark colors
and knits the first step.

My window faces the funeral home.
When the exhaust fan
starts to hum
something is flying, something
is leaving at the level of the trees.

II

I enter a street
where the sun is falling.
I look over my shoulder
and follow a thread that was my coat.
At its end is a vacant room
and a little bench of sleep.

I sit down quietly.
A few others arrive,
their eyelashes shining like crystals.
One coughs in a cloud of incense.
One closes his silver telescope.

A lost town circles overhead in the dark.
The houses hang out their lanterns.
On a blue bike
I race the shadows of the trees.

*1** *Routes* partly grew out of a visit home after years of absence—"home" meaning the place where I grew up. I remembered then a special night sound—the exhaust fan that enters the poem—and what it had evoked. This image became a focus for the poem, a condensation of events and feelings, a bridge to my own travels. It is the kind of connection that often moves me toward writing.

2 It's difficult to remember how the poem evolved. I usually get rid of drafts; my own way of composition is somewhat obsessive and leads to using up a fair amount of paper. I place no value on the waste. The poem was written and revised over several days, doggedly, and remained fairly close to the original impulse. I can say this much:

The opening three lines came from a fragment I had jotted into a notebook. They entered *Routes* along the network of connections, unbidden and unresearched, as if they had been waiting for a context.

At one stage I wrote a short sequence that brought in members of my family: a grandfather, an aunt, etc. But they seemed too "local," pushing me into more realistic conventions, more information. These figures gave way to the more ambiguous ones in the second section, kinship by metaphor as well as by blood.

* These numbers roughly correspond to the numbers on the Questionnaire on page 21. —ED.

The poem did not seem to move until I utilized a two-part structure. I was not after linear progression. The structure had to accommodate ellipses and images that dissolved into each other. I wanted the poem to feel suspended, protean.

And reading what I've just written, I'm aware that nothing here conveys the groping and hesitation that was, in fact, the process of writing.

3 Without denying the importance of technique, I'm not very conscious of it when writing. For one thing, I should hope that technique involves flexibility rather than a fixed body of principles. Certainly I'm not deliberate about matters such as alliteration, consonance, etc. The state of being attentive, of following words and phrases, leads to what may later be isolated as elements of technique. Some form of association is at the heart of matters, and this occurs on many levels. My own language patterns now are rather simple, as at one time they were not, but I would like to believe that my work issues from formal awareness. Sometimes I think technique is mostly a matter of avoiding whatever commits the poem to behaving in a predictable way.

As for voice and rhythm: Most discussions of free verse are impractical, many are not even readable. Probably every poet has a characteristic energy to his voice, modified by the demands of any given poem. The way one "hears" rhythm being adjusted over the spectrum of the poem—its speed, timing, recurrence—may not reside in pure choice, and may be a personal characteristic that is discoverable in areas other than writing.

4 The role of the reader is rather hypothetical. I like the sense of privacy and solitude in writing poems, of being in intimate touch with my own selves. A reader implies what is public. I think one may revise a poem with a greater sense of the reader, and this suggests a higher degree of manipulation. But some elements of a poem may remain relatively private, even mysterious, without collapsing the work into obscurity. In any case, I'm not arguing for self-expression or the snobbish purity of art, only that the mode of address is indirect rather than direct. The words go out to someone. Also to no one.

On a more practical level, I do have a few old and close friends to whom I show my poems, and I trust their critical intelligence almost as much as I do their enduring sympathy.

5 Paraphrase tends to turn every poem into weak allegory. It summarizes, or states an idea or proposition that can be detached from the poem. It probably provides a comfortable feeling of clarity or purpose, especially for rather direct poems. But mostly it simply abandons the poem and steps out into the one-dimensional world of clichés and ad men and reducing salons. If a poem is memorable it creates itself over and over again in its own saying.

6 I've written poems that are clearer than *Routes*, poems that stay closer to their occasions. I'm less and less interested in certain ways of narrating and informing. One desires to break away from personal limits and formulas that proved adequate. I don't know how good a poem *Routes* is; I like it because it still retains for me something of that desire. Next month I may decide this is another illusion.

Peter Everwine was born in Detroit in 1930 and grew up in western Pennsylvania. His published work includes *In the House of Light* (1970) and *Collecting the Animals* (1973) which won the Lamont Award. He teaches at California State University, Fresno, and currently is a Guggenheim Fellow.

Robert Francis

SILENT POEM

backroad leafmold stonewall chipmunk
underbrush grapevine woodchuck shadblow

woodsmoke cowbarn honeysuckle woodpile
sawhorse bucksaw outhouse wellsweep

backdoor flagstone bulkhead buttermilk
candlestick ragrug firedog brownbread

hilltop outcrop cowbell buttercup
whetstone thunderstorm pitchfork steeplebush

gristmill millstone cornmeal waterwheel
watercress buckwheat firefly jewelweed

gravestone groundpine windbreak bedrock
weathercock snowfall starlight cockrow

A fascination with words, single words or groups of words, has been the origin of a number of my recent poems. *Hogwash*, for instance, and *Condor* (Candor).

I became so fond of the strong character of solid compounds ("backroad," "stonewall," etc.) that I made a list purely for my pleasure. In time I wanted to make a poem out of these words, fitting them together like a patchwork quilt. In so doing I saw I could paint a picture of old-time New England, a picture moving from wildwood to dwelling, outdoors and in, then out and up to pasture and down to millstream.

At the time of writing I was exploring a technique new to me, which I call "fragmented surface." By this I mean a poem made up not of sentences but of short phrases, grammatically unconnected but emotionally focused. This poem of solid compounds differs from the others by consisting of single words rather than short phrases.

Feeling the need of some formality in such an informal procedure, I decided to have just four words to a line. Thus, without being quite aware of it at the time, I was making another "word-count" poem, word-count having been an earlier exploration of mine.

For years I had been thinking about the concept of silent poetry or silence in poetry. In this poem by simply presenting words without talking about them, I felt I was gaining a certain silence. Hence the title.

Here, then, is a poem that happens to unite four poetic interests of mine: word-count, fragmented surface, silent poetry, and words themselves as one source of poetry.

Robert Francis was born in 1901, grew up in Massachusetts, and received his bachelor's and master's degrees from Harvard. He has been a teacher of various sorts off-and-on, but is now simply an independent writer. He has published many poetry books: *Stand With Me Here* (1936), *Valhalla and Other Poems* (1938), *The Sound I Listened For* (1944), *The Face Against the Glass* (1948), *The Orb Weaver* (1960), *Come*

Out Into the Sun (1965), *Like Ghosts of Eagles* (1974), and *Collected Poems: 1936–1976* (1976). He has also written a novel, *We Fly Away* (1948), his autobiography, *The Trouble With Francis* (1971), and *Memoirs, Frost: A Time to Talk* (1972). He has recorded *Robert Francis Reads His Poems* (1975). He has been the recipient of major poetry awards and fellowships for the past thirty-five years.

Stuart Friebert

THE APRON

The man's been pitying himself all Sunday long,
first he went down cellar to oil the generator,
see what the potatoes were doing, then he took
a few baits from the tackle box, paint wearing,
hooks falling off. When he put the last fish of
the season back into the water it sank down to
the bottom, left a long streak of blood behind.

He dragged the boat to the car, in the mirror
the lake was gray and thick. He put his foot
on the gas, it was like stepping on the woman's
apron, a pleasant apron with flowers and teacups
all over. The kettle was singing. And steaming.

When the man gets home there's nothing at the end
of the stringer in his hand, when the child runs
between the man and woman he makes strange sounds
they can't understand. When they put him to sleep
in a clear glass bed they look in from all sides.

This poem is much less dense, less complex than the body of my work, but I've chosen it because I can discuss it easily. It began the way most of mine do: some nagging event in my daily life knocks around in me, trying to connect with what I call my symbol system—that is, those images and ideas, mostly in fragment form, that I've been carrying around a long time and that never seem to increase or decrease. They are notions I seem to have been born with, much like genes. I need to deposit them somewhere, on something, and see if growth will start. Sometimes, these prefigured forms seek out an historical subject, or someone else's story. Then the poems that result are generally not successful. Accomplished perhaps, but lifeless to me. My best work, I think, results when I find (unconsciously) the right subject matter to mate with the genelike materials.

In the poem at hand, I'd spent quite a fitful Sunday, a day when I'm particularly vulnerable. Waiting for Monday, my favorite day. Things around the house always seem to need attention on Sundays, and I take a swipe at them—oil the generator, check the potatoes. . . . Another way of saying I'm trying to take care of my family, insure their well-being. This is a huge theme for me, in some poems I'm repairing our roof, in others gluing a chair, or carrying a mattress across a field, carving a chicken, or helping my children bury their cat: little acts that lead to enormous conflicts later. One things always leads to another when I start something my heart's not in, and I quickly look for rewards: right near the furnace was my baitbox. I'm not sure what came first, the box or my desire to get away fishing. Actually, more things than the generator and the potatoes were in trouble, but there I was, snatching the baitbox and getting the hell out of another bad Sunday. And feeling a kind of guilt for rewarding myself too soon for the little I did, hence the punishment of having the fish I catch, or release to catch another year, sink to the bottom.

The metaphorical substratum has already begun to alter the text: self-pity, physical decay, seasons ending—I've (unconsciously) pre-selected details one by one to fit these themes and altered them in turn to heighten the narrative (my baitbox isn't old; the season didn't end that day; the boat's light, it was not dragged; the lake was not "gray and thick"). By and large the poem still bears with the actual events of that Sunday until the moment, "he put his foot/on the gas." At this line, I sensed the end of the outer story was near, that the limits of the actual experience were drawn, and felt a need to look in another direction (what is the poem really about?). When the actual event I'm tracking dies out, a different form of the imagination takes over, helps me discover what else has been going on, makes me stop the outer story, veer off to what I call the inner story. I can't say how I know "he put his foot/on the gas" is when I leave the straight narrative, I just sense it strongly.

Now I took a long time hitting on the emotionally logical extension, the link to the inner story: the apron. Some might call this image surreal. I think that's not helpful. Nor is it mere metaphor, to illumine an experience. I think it has more to do with that childlike ability to connect wildly disparate objects in an emotional release: stepping on the apron is not really like stepping on the gas, *except* for the jolt; the jolt of stepping on the gas *on that day* was connected for me with stepping on an apron, though I leave it to you to make the connection work. I pray you do, but it's yours to make. Structurally, I try to prepare you for the leap, not internally within the metaphorical possibilities, but through the "syllogisms" of the sentences; and by giving you: generator, potatoes, baits, fish, blood, lake and mirror. And hoping you add them as I do. Remember that intelligence-test question, "Which of these items doesn't belong in the following list?" Well, that's the test I use in revision, Can all these things be accounted for emotionally along the way to the apron?

Once I got to apron, I began to see how intensely domestic the poem was trying to be, a veritable discourse on my family life, which I write of again and again. Part of me felt, like a Romantic, that the fragment shouldn't be extended, the text should end with the connection: stepping on the gas-apron, provided it was deepened by the patterns on the apon, say, and the return to the family from a misguided journey. But I wanted to stay with the domestic scene longer, to locate this family more precisely, to see whether or not I'd dug up enough materials to reconstruct the ruins. I always try working beyond the point the text seems complete, just in case I may have missed something. And this time I found the text extending to the child between the people. At first it seemed like the old threesome, with possible overtones of a tale, or fable (is the glass bed from Snow White?). Then I realized that the child was a kind of equivalent for the activity of fishing that separated the two people. Possibly injured but not dead like the fish, asleep but very much alive (my treasure was at home all the time?). Finally, I began to see the home as a kind of aquarium which contained all the sustenance, if restricted, that I was looking for outdoors. Now, while writing this, I remember a poem I wrote ten years ago. Originally called *The Kitchen*, I remember changing the title to:

THE AQUARIUM

My wife's eyes bloom
in the cave. My sister
sinks past on a painted
body. My father plays
poker, his mouth
itching with deceit.

I caress my mother's
sweet ribs, whisper
she mustn't worry, I'm
not going to change
the water.

She relaxes, like my
wrinkled children beside
me, we swarm to the other
side of the glass.

As for technique: I came to poetry slowly. A math and chemistry major, with a side trip through German, I had almost no background in English literature (some say, "How lucky, you don't have to crawl over Eliot"; others say, "My God, you mean you never read . . .?"). At any rate, I've never been conscious of technique as such, and only one issue seems to matter most in this whole area: sentence to sentence relationships. Like my Hungarian tailor of a grandfather, I look at them the way he'd run fabric through his fingers for tears and snags. I run the material through by lengths. The poem is typical of most of my recent work: I've been trying to work against an earlier tendency to use more and more effects, go wall to wall with blazing colors. By keeping things low-key, with a kind of flatness. I want to see how quiet I can be without your drifting off; but I also want to see how fast I can be without your just skimming: how telegraphic, how abbreviated the journey can be without losing you (now you're in the cellar, whoops, now you're on the lake, whoops, now you're back home, what happened?). The themes are old favorites: family, fishing, going out and coming back with nothing much to show, a laying away for the night, a little mumbling, but then, always, a moment of watchful concern for signs of life. While I never have anyone in mind as an audience, when I write there is a kind of internal argument going on with the people in my poems. Is my story, my account, fair to them? Or do I just use them in my little dramas? I'm trying less to say: Hey, I need you in this poem, come here! And act more as if I were just directing, with little personal (but much aesthetic) stake in who gets to do and say what. My poems go through three to five main drafts, with side trips to see if other poems may be off to the side. Always within a week: I find I can't lay anything aside longer than that. The whole process seems very much like the kind of fishing I do. First, I make a long cast, let the jitterbug lie on the surface while I light a cigar, then slowly work the bait back in. If something strikes, it's all in how you set the hook. When you get it back to the boat, try to get it in as fast as you can, no fancy stuff now. When it stops flopping, get out the tape, see if it's a keeper. If it is, ask yourself: Now how did I catch that fish?

Stuart Friebert was born in Wisconsin in 1931, did a Ph.D in German Literature at the University of Wisconsin, spent some years in Switzerland and Germany, taught at Mount Holyoke and Harvard before going to Oberlin College where he directs the creative writing program and is co-editor of *Field.* His published books of poetry include: *Dreaming of Floods* (1969), *Calming Down* (1970), *Up in Bed* (1974), *Stories my father can tell* (1975); and in German, *Kein Trinkwasser* (1969), *Die Prokuristen kommen* (1972), *Nicht Hinauslehnen* (1975), and a collection of short prose fiction: *Der Gast, und sei er noch so schlecht* (1973).

Gary Gildner

THEN

In the village the children
were what they always had been—
a girl wanted to be a nurse
or a dancer, a boy wished for a horse
or an elephant up in his bed.
Autumn got chilly, winter hard
and longer than dreams, but dreams
came back, slippery and quick
as minnows. And spring—
spring made you stop, look,
and fall from the sky
for keeps. You had a tadpole
and the whole day . . .
One summer, tasting the salt
on your lips, you promised forever—
and the cricket's song was long and full
before it got slimmer and quit.
But the road and the river
were what they always had been,
and your heart would not break, not ever.

1 It was raining. I was sitting in my studio at Yaddo watching the rain against the pine trees and thinking about some lines I had written toward a long poem about the track, and then about a two-year-old filly named Mocha Bear, with Mary Ann Dotter on top, and why I had not bet her. I had looked at that horse under the maple trees, looked at her being saddled, watched her in the paddock and I watched Mary Ann parade her in front of the grandstand. Mocha Bear, I thought, you are a beautiful nag. And I was all set to go place my bet, feeling that excitement you feel when you know something is right (also I have been partial to women jocks ever since August 22, 1973 when Robyn C. Smith brought a filly named Bel Sheba around seven furlongs at Saratoga, leading all the way, her hair let loose from under her cap and streaming and I thought if I touched it I would burn my hand)—when she took off running toward the starting gate set up on the far side of the track, and I wavered—thinking she will have run her race, she will tire—wavered and changed my mind and bet some horse who finished God knows where and whose name I have forgotten. Mocha Bear, of course, won and looked beautiful winning and looked as if she could have run without effort forever. After a while I started to write and most of *Then* appeared. Perhaps the horse in the poem came from my daydreaming about Mocha Bear.

2 Near the bottom I crossed out "quit" and wrote in "went away" and then went back to "quit." I guess the poem went through a dozen drafts in which I tried out slight variations here and there, but I kept going back to the original I wrote while the rain came down.—Except for lines 18 and 19. When they got in I let them stay.

3 Technique, for me, comes down to this: the lines have to feel right to the story—not too fast, not too slow.

4 Whom did I visualize as my reader? No one I can name.

5 I would not feel happy paraphrasing this poem.

6 How does this poem differ from my earlier poems?
(a) In quality? I can't answer.
(b) In theme? I have a number of poems which have come from looking back, and this is another.
(c) In technique? My technique, as always, is to make the thing feel right.

Gary Gildner was born in 1938 in West Branch, Michigan. He grew up there and in Flint and attended Michigan State University. Four collections of his poetry have been published: *First Practice* (1969), *Digging for Indians* (1971), *Nails* (1975), and *Letters from Vicksburg* (1976). He has also edited, with his wife Judith, *Out of This World: Poems from the Hawkeye State* (1975). He has received the Robert Frost Fellowship, two National Endowment Fellowships, and the Theodore Roethke Prize. Gildner is a contributing editor of *New Letters* and a member of the Associated Writing Programs editorial board.

Louise Glück

THE GARDEN

1. The Fear of Birth

One sound. Then the hiss and whir
of houses gliding into their places.
And the wind
leafs through the bodies of animals—

But my body that could not content itself
with health—why should it be sprung back
into the chord of sunlight?

It will be the same again.
This fear, this inwardness,
until I am forced into a field
without immunity
even to the least shrub that walks
stiffly out of the dirt, trailing
the twisted signature of its root,
even to a tulip, a red claw.

And then the losses,
one after another,
all supportable.

2. *The Garden*

The garden admires you.
For your sake it smears itself with green pigment,
the ecstatic reds of the roses,
so that you will come to it with your lovers.

And the willows—
see how it has shaped these green
tents of silence. Yet
there is still something you need,
your body so soft, so alive, among the stone animals.

Admit that it is terrible to be like them,
beyond harm.

3. *The Fear of Love*

That body lying beside me like obedient stone—
once its eyes seemed to be opening,
we could have spoken.

At that time it was winter already.
By day the sun rose in its helmet of fire
and at night also, mirrored in the moon.
Its light passed over us freely,
as though we had lain down
in order to leave no shadows,
only these two shallow dents in the snow.
And the past, as always, stretched before us,
still, complex, impenetrable.

How long did we lie there
as, arm in arm in their cloaks of feathers,
the gods walked down
from the mountain we built for them.

4. *Origins*

As though a voice were saying
You should be asleep by now—
But there was no one. Nor
had the air darkened,
though the moon was there,
already filled in with marble.

As though, in a garden crowded with flowers,
a voice had said
How dull they are, these golds,
so sonorous, so repetitious
until you closed your eyes,
lying among them, all
stammering flame:

And yet you could not sleep,
poor body, the earth
still clinging to you—

5. *The Fear of Burial*

In the empty field, in the morning,
the body waits to be claimed.
The spirit sits beside it, on a small rock—
nothing comes to give it form again.

Think of the body's loneliness.
At night pacing the sheared field,
its shadow buckled tightly around.
Such a long journey.
And already the remote, trembling lights of the village
not pausing for it as they scan the rows.
How far away they seem,
the wooden doors, and bread and milk
laid like weights on the table.

1 This poem began with its last section, which was written to fulfill an assignment. For the past four years I have been a member of an informal workshop; it is our habit to devise assignments. I like to work this way. Because I am allowed to consider the poem at hand an exercise, my heart is somewhat lightened and my paralyzing fear of failure diminished. *The Garden* was begun in response to an assignment less explicit than most of ours: to write a poem about fear.

2 The original poem, *The Fear of Burial*, did not change a great deal. Nor did the sections which followed change significantly, within their boundaries. But my concept of the poem changed several times during the three months spent writing it.

Almost immediately after writing *The Fear of Burial* I wrote *The Fear of Birth.* I had never before written companion poems. For me the impulse to write is usually spent in a brief lyric. I had never extended, never built upon, a poem, mistrusting the reverence for size that pervades our culture.

I thought those two made something finished. Then, three weeks later, I wrote *The Garden*, which seemed to willfully attach itself to the others. For a while afterward, for the space of a summer, I thought I'd use the three together, with *The Garden* placed between the other two, the obvious placement of a second, an intruding, voice. I was still writing with unprecedented fluency at that time and, in regard to this poem, not feeling the sense of depletion I wake to when something is finished.

I wrote *The Fear of Love* deliberately, with great confidence. I had the other three; I thought this one would be gravy if it turned out well. It *was* gravy. After the celebration I realized I had written myself into a corner, that this fourth section, if I chose to use it, dictated the poem's form far more rigidly than had any previous combination. Clearly a fifth piece had to be written to balance *The Garden.* This section, *Origins*, was hardest of all to write, despite the fact that I like writing to specifications. The benign aspect of the workshop imperatives was lost in that the poem couldn't be scrapped. Writing *Origins* involved a kind of revising almost totally unfamiliar to me: I had never revised by adding, only by paring away.

Once the piece was assembled, the individual sections were pruned here and there. Initially I had wanted each section to be capable of standing on its own. After several workshop sessions I came to feel I couldn't have both independent poems and a coherent longer work. Sections one, three, and four had rather operatic terminations. These were all right when the poems were read separately. But in the longer work they impeded movement. I jettisoned three stanzas. From this point all editorial adjustments were made in the interest of the long piece.

3 I used no principles of technique consciously.

4 I see the members of my workshop as my readers. I need them; their responses instruct me.

5 This question puzzles me. Anything that has been understood can be paraphrased. But the paraphrase, however sensitive, will not contain the poem's suggestive silences.

Believing in this process as a tool, I still resist paraphrasing my own work. That act seems to dignify the paraphrase, to set it up as an acceptable alternative to the poem. Nor would I have the same mind furnish both text and illumination.

6 I chose this poem because I wished to be represented by it. My choice implies my opinion of its quality, relative to the rest of my work.

Its length sets it apart from my other poems.

Louise Glück was born in New York City in 1943 and raised on Long Island. She attended Sarah Lawrence College and Columbia University. Her awards include grants from the Rockefeller Foundation, the National Endowment for the Arts, and the Guggenheim Foundation. She has taught at Goddard College, the University of North Carolina, and the University of Virginia. She has published two books: *Firstborn* (1968) and *The House on Marshaland* (1975). She lives in Plainfield, Vermont.

John Haines

AT WHITE RIVER

We drove south from Burwash Landing
that blue and gusty day.
Close by the White River delta
we stopped to read a sign
creaking on its chains in the wind.

I left the car and climbed a grassy bluff,
to a grey cross leaning there
and a name that was peeling away:

"Alexander Clark Fisher.
Born October 1870. Died January 1941."

No weathering sticks from a homestead
remained on that hillside,
no log sill rotting under moss
nor cellarhole filling with rose vines.
Not even the stone ring
of a hunter's fire,
a thin wire flaking in the brush.

Only the red rock piled
to hold the cross, our blue car
standing on the road below,
and a small figure playing there.
The Yukon sunlight warming a land
held long under snow,
and the lake water splashing.

From the narrow bridge in the distance
a windy clatter of iron—
billow of dust on a blind crossing,
but a keen silence behind that wind.

It was June 4, 1973. I was forty-nine.

My ten-year old daughter
called me from the road:
she had found a rock to keep,

and I went down.

FIRST DRAFT JUNE, 1973

The cross At White River *The river drains*

climbed to
Came to
I saw
High on a *grassy* . . . .bluff
at the end of Lake Kluane
A white cross. . . leans /*hangs* *painted wood*
and a name in black
Isak
Erik Issacson - 1946 - Thorgeson
No house, site of a cabin
cellar - fenceline /no farm
no. . . history swaying in the wind
/swinging
/ creaking /air

John Issakson
Alexander Clark
Fisher
Born Oct. 1870
Died Jan. 1941
a thin wire
flaking in the brush

Only the red rock piled
to prop the cross, my blue car
on the road below
the blue lake water ~~milky~~ lapping with silt
a narrow bridge, windy clatter, distant
and dust lifting from the river bars
Beat a silence behind ~~the~~ that wind. /delta
It is June 4, 1973. I am 49
My ten year old daughter
calls from the road –
[that she has found. perfect . . stone / rock
And I start down. / keeping

they built this road,
and the war close
then as now
working on the road
operator / surveyor
scanner of dust
Immigrant / watcher
and the long ice
counter / floes
of moonlight / fog

your bones. . .?
she has found a
shining rock
a stone to keep
rock

SECOND DRAFT JULY–AUGUST, 1973

AT WHITE RIVER

High on a grassy bluff / I left my child behind
at the end of Lake Kluane
where the W. River clears
I climbed to a white cross / leaning there
and a name in black / painted in black
Alexander Clark Fisher
Born/ October 1870 / Died Jan. 1941.

weathering
ghost of a farm
a thin wire flaking in the brush

No house — log wall rotting site of a cabin
hole/cellar ... fenceline or farm
no history – a shingle swaying in the cold air

Only the red rock piled And the Yukon / far sunlight of the Yukon
to prop the cross, ~~my~~ our blue car / in the sunlight / the forest around
standing / on the road below

the lake water lapping / milky/silt / upon a winter shore
the narrow bridge in the distance
a windy clatter in the steel
and dust lifting \ blowing from the river bars
But a keen sielnce/behind that wind

It is June 4, 1973. I am forty-nine.
My ten year old daughter
calls from the road — / to me
she has found a rock to keep
And I start down.
went

At the end of Kluane Lake
where the White River empties
in the blue of the lake,
I left the road and car and child

THIRD DRAFT FALL, 1973

AT WHITE RIVER

High on a grassy bluff / I left the road –
at the end of Lake Kluane
where the White River empties /flows, drains /I parked

and climbed to a grassy bluff to a white cross leaning there

I climbed to a white cross a grassy bluff /leaning on the sky
leaning there,
with ~~and~~ a name painted in black.
Alexander Clark Fisher.
Born October 1870. Died January 1941.
No house to be seen. . .
no logwall rotting in the moss,
nor cellarhole giving back a /blank stare
no fenceline, the weathering ghost
of a farm,

a thin wire flaking in the brush.
Only the red rock piled
to ~~prop~~ hold the cross, my blue car
standing on the road below; / and the hills Brown in early summer
the ~~cool~~ chill Yukon sunlight
lake water rippling silty/milky / milky Blue
the small figure there
the narrow bridge in the distance / blew down
a windy clatter of iron,
and dust blowing. . / crossing /and dust over the crossing
but a keen silence behind that wind. /and dust made
blind the crossing
It was June 4, 1973. I was forty-nine.
My ten year old daughter
called to me from the road—
she had found a rock to keep.
And I went down.

FOURTH DRAFT DECEMBER, 1974

Here—where the White River stains the depth of the lake

Present Tense?

AT WHITE RIVER

South of Lake Kluane
where the White River empties,
staining the blue, / with silt
~~I left the road, my car and child,~~ / and the road goes east
and climbed a grassy bluff
to a white cross leaning there / freshly
and a name painted in black: / peeling in black
with a name

"Alexander Clark Fisher.
Born October 1970. Died January 1941."

vastness
square
garden
No grey weathering ghost of a farm / Juniper / absence
spoke from that hillside,
no logwall rotting ~~down~~ in the moss, / under

nor cellarhole filling with rosevines,
post or fenceline,
a thin wire flaking in the brush. stanza break
Only the red rock piled /car or child?
to hold the cross, my blue car
standing on the road below, bending
a /~~the~~ small figure playing there; /beside it
the cool Yukon sunlight
and the lake water splashing.
From the narrow bridge in the distance
a windy clatter of iron;
billow /a ~~figure~~ of dust on a blind crossing,. ./filling the land
But a keen silence behind that wind.
the hillside that — more vastness
It Was June 4, 1973. I was forty-nine.
My ten-year old daughter
called to me from the road—
she had found a rock to keep,
[And I went down.
drop a space

DISCUSSION OF *AT WHITE RIVER*

1 I began this poem in early June, 1973. I was on my way south by car from Anchorage to California, traveling with my ten-year-old stepdaughter, Karen. Near the south end of a large lake in Yukon Territory we stopped to look for mountain sheep on the slope above the highway. I left Karen by the car and climbed some distance up a steep bluff, where I found the cross with its name and dates. I don't recall now if the cross was visible from the highway. It appeared to have been recently painted and lettered. There was nothing to indicate why anyone had been buried in that spot, at the edge of the Kluane Game Refuge; no sign of human dwelling, not even, as the poem says, a section of fence wire. I thought the man might have been an early settler in the area, or perhaps someone who had worked on the highway, but I was only guessing. The incident of the grave marker itself in that remote place, far from any town, was enough to set off my imagination. The name and the dates, the very starkness of the information, seemed vaguely significant to me. And I was getting close to my own fiftieth year.

2 I think I may have written something in one of the notebooks I habitually have around, either then, or later on that evening when we camped. The earliest things I have are some scribbles on a sheet of looseleaf paper, noting details of the place and the dates. Much of the fifth stanza and the last half-dozen lines of the poem are already there. It was a matter thereafter of deciding how much else I wanted to say, and to find a satisfactory way to begin the poem. Several other handwritten and typed pages add bits and pieces to the poem. Some of this work may have been done in California that summer or fall, or possibly early the following year in Seattle, where I had gone to teach. But it was not until early in 1975 that I felt willing to risk the poem to public view. I read it at the conclusion of a reading I gave at the University of Montana in February. I had to ad-lib a few things as I read it, but the audience seemed to like the poem. I later brought a version of it into my graduate workshop to see what the students thought of it. Several of their comments were extremely helpful, particularly respecting the opening lines.

As nearly as I can tell now, the poem has gone through six or seven drafts. I am still not quite satisfied with a few things, especially the first three or four lines. I was unsure how soon to introduce the figure of my daughter. As it stands now, she does not come into the poem until the fifth stanza; originally I had mentioned her in the very first.

3 My sense of any poem's structure is usually and initially intuitive. I nearly always have a strong feeling for the potential visual shape of the poem on the page, some sense of how long the poem ought to be, and whether the lines are to be long or short. I base my sense of line primarily on the structure of phrases and clauses, and on the cadence of my own thinking and speaking voice. It becomes a matter of shaping these to the requirements of the individual poem. Some poems seem to fall naturally into short lines, into brief and more or less regular stanzas. Others want to sprawl a bit. Usually the first line or two in a poem gives me a clue—that is, the first line or two that I write. This is all worked out on the page and in my head as I go through different drafts. Sometimes the poem changes radically in the process, but I often find my original conception holding up pretty well. Long practice at writing poems, I suppose, has given me sufficient precedent to work from, but every poem is a new beginning. It had better be, or I will run the risk of repeating myself, something every writer tends to do anyway.

I cannot offer any strict principle of composition. If one exists in my poems generally, it is this: the substance of the poem, the *idea*, always suggests a certain *form*, visual and aural, a certain figure in time and space. My work then is to define this figure as well as I can, to discover and reveal the essence of the emotion, or idea.

In this case, I wanted above all a strong suggestion of the place, a vastness and emptiness, in which the cross and its words, the road and my car, the bridge, my daughter and myself, all took on the importance of things seen in a certain isolation. I took some of the tone of the poem from the words on the white cross, the matter-of-factness of them, the exact kind of information they gave, and which I repeated in the single line near the end of the poem. Possibly some of the most authentic lines in the poem are in the sixth stanza: I felt keenly the silence behind that wind, and wanted to say something to fill it.

The spacing of the poem on the page is important; the grouping and breaking of the lines emphasize movement and meaning. For example, someone in the workshop suggested that the last line of the poem be dropped a space below the final stanza. I thought this a very good idea. I think any poet has an understanding that certain things should occur in a poem in a certain order, and that other things ought to be withheld. As an instance of this: I do not say in the poem that my daughter climbed the bluff to see the cross and have her picture taken. This happened, but it was not the kind of information I wanted in the poem. Neither do I say anything about the cross being freshly painted and lettered. I decided to leave that out. The task of any poet, or artist, is to shape reality, not to copy it, and thereby to create a new reality: one that did not exist before. I know of no rule one could follow in this. Either you have an instinct for it, or you do not. Perhaps it is primarily a dramatic sense, similar to what a playwright or a film director might have.

The line breaks, the stanzas, and all the rest are there first of all to help me, the poet, understand the poem better, and then to help the reader respond to it. Certain accidents of diction (not really accidents, perhaps, but things unconsciously provided for) always occur in a poem: repetitions of sounds, rhymes and near rhymes. For example: "fire" and "wire"; "snow" and "below"; "there," "car"; "iron," "nine," "down"; "land," "blind," "wind." I let these things happen, mostly by attention to the sound of it, without letting the rhyme become too obvious. The poem ought to be read aloud, and indeed I intend all my poems to be read aloud, since I speak them aloud as I write them. An attention to syllables, to vowels and consonants, seems to me immensely important. Again, there are no rules to follow, only the poet's ear and the power of emotion that drives the language.

Other things might be noted: the movement of the poem, climbing at the beginning, and coming down at the end. Point of view: the things one might see standing in *that* place at that time. And all this, however worked out, must seem inevitable or the poem will go for naught.

4 As in most of my poems, the audience, or the reader, is that "imaginary interlocutor" Osip Mandelstam once described. An ideal reader, or perhaps some part of myself I can speak to with assurance and familiarity. Some recent poems, however, have been addressed directly to individuals—one of my step-children, or another person. This is something quite new, or at least a kind of poem I haven't attempted for many years. I am not sure what to make of it, but it seems an important change. This doesn't happen in *At White River*. Here the audience is: Anyone willing to listen.

5 The poem might be paraphrased as follows: traveling in a remote area, the speaker in the poem finds a grave marker, a cross with a name and some dates. These, and the landscape he sees around him, signify a world in which human effort is without lasting significance. The land is vast, vast as a continent, and strangely empty. Sights and sounds emphasize this—a loneliness, a remoteness perhaps from his own humanity. The dates on the cross remind him of his own age, relating him in some obscure way to the person memorialized on the cross. And then the voice of his daughter recalls him to the present: *she* has found *something*. It is significant that at the end of the poem he goes *down*, down to rejoin . . . the living.

6 *At White River* seems less concentrated than some poems I have written. It takes a bit more time to get where it is going. On the other hand, it seems consistent with its own terms. In theme, in landscape and mood, it is similar to other poems I have written, particularly about the North. But the figure of the child in the poem, and the fact that I appear to be recalled by her to some human duty, seems to set the poem apart. Possibly this marks a change in attention or orientation, as several other poems I've written recently seem also to do. As to quality, it is too soon to judge that. I like the poem.

One further comment. I find surveys like this interesting, and the questions occasionally force me to think about details of poems I might not otherwise confront. At the same time, I am bothered by the tone of many of the items on the checklist. They have too studied or contrived a meaning. It is difficult for me to imagine any worthwhile poem coming from (conscious) attention to all these things. Granted that any poet will in some way be paying attention to many of these things in actual composition, too much thinking about what he is going to do in a poem may rob the poem of mystery and surprise. In fact, I think that too much of this kind of thing might end by drying up some of the sources of poetry itself. There *is* a way of talking about poems that adds to and deepens them, that explores the world of thought and experience from which the poems emerge, and without attempting to reveal too much. In discussing my own poems, I try to do this, aware that the poems may be saying things I never thought of when I wrote them. I need to concede a considerable area to what I don't know and can't know, and perhaps don't wish to know. Only to understand in a way I do not quite understand.

Postscript

Preparing a folder of recent poems for a reading, I again confronted a vague dissatisfaction with the opening of this poem. Perhaps it was a matter of wanting to feel firmly placed there, at that instant, with no loose ends of arrival. It seemed to me also that I needed a "we" at the beginning of the poem, that the "I" was too isolated. One or two other things seemed worth bothering with. My use of so many color words in a short space might be distracting, and "peeling in black" began to seem a little odd to me. Hence the changes in the first half dozen lines of the final version here.

Inevitably while sorting details, crossing out words and making new tries at old ideas, I wonder if the expenditure of time and energy, the space it seems to demand in my life, is really justified. Surely there is something else I might be doing. Then, closing off that disconcerting vista, it does seem that the effort to be exact, to render an honest account, means something after all—to myself, of course, but in terms of life generally. The language asks of the person who uses it a certain rigor and honesty, and all the more so in a time when language commonly is misused and debased. Experience itself asks this honesty of any artist, whatever his medium of expression.

Not all poems require the continual revision that this one has; some are written with relative ease in a short time. But many of the poems that have pleased me most were finally resolved by this patient, at times exasperating, attention to details of experience, small clues of feeling that often seem about to disappear entirely.

John Haines was born in 1924 in Norfolk, Virginia. The son of a Navy man, he grew up "on the road," on the east coast, in California, the Pacific Northwest and the Hawaiian Islands. He served in the U.S. Navy during World War II. In the late 1940s and early 1950s he studied painting and sculpture in Washington, D.C. and New York City. He homesteaded in Alaska from 1954 until 1969. He received a Guggenheim Fellowship in 1965–66, and a National Endowment Grant in 1967–68. He has published four books of poems: *Winter News* (1966), *The Stone Harp* (1971), *Twenty Poems* (1971), and *Leaves and Ashes* (1974). He has taught at the University of Alaska, the University of Washington, and the University of Montana. He is now working on a new book of poems and has been awarded an Amy Lowell Scholarship to study in Europe for a year.

Donald Hall

THE TOWN OF HILL

Back of the dam, under
a flat pad

of water, church
bells ring

in the ears of lilies,
a child's swing

curls in the current
of a yard, horned

pout sleep
in a green

mailbox, and
a boy walks

from a screened
porch beneath

the man-shaped
leaves of an oak

down the street looking
at the town

of Hill that water
covered forty

years ago,
and the screen

door shuts
under dream water.

Let me try to answer you. First of all, I will deal with a poem called *The Town of Hill.*

The poem started with a few notes taken when I visited my old family farm in New Hampshire, perhaps in the summer of 1970 or '71. Hill is a town in New Hampshire. It used to be an old town, now flooded for a flood-control project, and now is a new town. When I was a child, I visited the old town shortly before everything was removed from it. (Not everything was removed. But the people were, and movable houses were.) I didn't go there in 1970, but I remembered the town, and took a few notes about a town under water.

What changes did the poem go through?

I cannot really answer this. It went through three years of intensive work, with lots and lots of changes. I've got all the copies of it somewhere or other. It was shorter to begin with, then it was longer than it is now, what is the middle was once the ending, and so on and so forth. I kept thinking I had finished it. I would work on it one morning, feel enthusiastic, tell Jane how good it was, and a day or two later I would see that it was not. I showed it to Jane and to Greg Orr (with whom I've been working a lot, the last three years) over and over again. I sent various versions of it to various friends.

It was a poem which went back to an earlier style. I don't think it looks much like the other poems, but it is a poem that is greatly dependent on, and interested in, its own sound. It is Goatfoot and Milktongue—and probably more Milktongue than Goatfoot. And in a way I think that's what it secretly is about. About life before birth even, or perhaps very early on after birth. But I'm not *sure* what it is secretly about, not yet. That usually takes me a few years. I mean, a few years after the poem's finished.

It arrived at its present state about a year ago. Lately, when I read it, I begin to wonder about one or two words in it, so it may go through some more changes. And of course in the meantime I have no idea whether it's any good or not. I hope it is. I have real hopes for it sometimes—but I don't *really* know. I do "really" know, I think, about a few poems, as recent as eight years old, or as old as twenty-five years old. I know about a lot of them that they are no good. I think I know about a few of them that they are good. But this one is far too new for that kind of knowledge.

What techniques did you consciously use?

None. I mean, I am constantly aware of assonance, of syntax, etc. But I didn't consciously use any principles of technique. Come to think of it, I don't know what "principles of technique" would really mean. Unless it meant something like meter, and this poem is not metrical.

Whom did I visualize as my reader?

Robert Bly, Galway Kinnell, Jane Kenyon, Gregory Orr, Louis Simpson, and Thom Gunn.

Can the poem be paraphrased?

Not really. That is, of course, one could substitute prose for the poetry, simply using Thesaurus "synonyms" for each of the words. But a paraphrase usually involves the translation of the irrational into the rational—if there *is* anything irrational—and in this poem, I don't think that the time-switch could be paraphrased *out*. Therefore, the mystery which exists in the plot would not be translated. Of course, the sound would be lost, the images manhandled, and other usual effects of paraphrase would indeed succeed.

How does this poem differ from earlier poems of yours?

I've already said that I can't tell how it differs in quality. In theme, I think perhaps it is part of a return to the past, and a re-examination of the past, which I have talked about earlier, but which this poem may well try to be deeper at. In technique, as I explained before, it is in one way a reversion to an earlier technique. (When I began this poem, I had been spending a certain amount of time writing prose poems, in which attention to Goatfoot and Milktongue was minimal. Plot was important. Some logopoeia, some phanopoeia, but damned little melopoeia. And I was yearning for the old mouth-feel.)

As to the paragraph that follows these six questions, of course, the article in *Field*[1] is something I am consciously referring to. I guess the interview in *Ohio Review*[2] has something to do with some of these questions.

Checklist

1a. It began as a few words, connected with the town itself. And I felt that there was something to pursue, some quarry to be hunted, if I pursued the implications of these words in this rhythm.

1c. Frequently, in late stages of revision, which is to say maybe the last two years of work on a poem, I argue with my friends about it when they are not there. They include the people I visualized above as the reader.

2a. I suppose the poem went through 50 or 60 drafts.

2b. Sometimes I would do a draft a day, or perhaps 3 or 4 pages in one day. Other times I would not work on it for a month.

2c. It shrunk, and it expanded.

2d. The structure changed. I didn't know how to end it. The part about the "man-shaped leaves . . ." was the ending for some time. Other things that ended it have now disappeared.

2e. I don't really know what the theme is for sure.

2f. I don't think the tone changed.

1. *Field*, no. 9 (Fall 1973).
2. *Ohio Review*, Spring 1974.

2g. The early lines describing the town under water became set fairly early, probably within the first two or three months of writing it, and never changed, or changed very little. Because they were fixed. Because they were almost the *given*.

2h. Connotation and sound.

3a. Alternative lineations are possible, but this is the best one I can arrive at for the sound by itself—which is one separate thing; the sound as reinforcing sense, or enforcing sense for the first time—but which can exist only if the first conditions are met. Sound as rock.

3c. I didn't think of any rhythmical principle. I never do. That is, iambic is *not* a rhythmical principle! As many rhythms are possible in iambic as are in free verse, as syllabic, accentual, etc.

3d. No principles for assonance, etc. Just delight, excitement, etc.

3e. I would prefer this poem to be read aloud, *by me.*

3f. About the principles of metaphor and so on. I come to realize that most of these questions embarrass me because I don't think I'm the one to answer them. I think that they *imply* that I know more about my poem than somebody else would who is reading it. I don't think I do. I think that authors have in fact a considerable reason to lie to themselves about what they do and why they do what they do. So I don't trust what they say. And I apply these principles of distrust to myself. I didn't consciously apply any of these principles.

3g. I do have pre-conscious standards about rhythms, and about diction. These pre-conscious standards derive from my love of Ezra Pound, Keats, and great poets.

3h. Toward the end, I became aware that I was writing a single sentence, and became interested in the problem of my syntax. But only after I was doing it.

3i. No reference or allusion. I know people don't know what a "horned pout" is, but I don't care.

It has taken me a bit of time to get back to this letter! In the meantime, the poem has come out in *American Poetry Review,* so you can see it there and I don't have to look around for a copy of it. Also, seeing it in *American Poetry Review,* I am assailed with doubts about it. I think it is possible that by striving to go back to an early style, the really mouthy style, I have limited it in some way or other. Robert Bly keeps saying that it's what is behind that screen door that is really interesting. I think maybe the other poems—the ones I'm writing now in looser, longer lines, with repetitive rhythms—maybe these poems are what is behind the screen door. One always hopes!

3j. By what principles did I structure the poem? Improvisation. I kept changing the organization of things. Certainly it is in some sense psychological. Certainly the various orders were not thought out ahead of time, but improvised, looked at, rejected, tried again, etc.

3k. Did I seek an open-ended conclusion? I sought a conclusive ending, but not a conclusive ending intellectually, really a conclusive ending rhythmically, and in sound. I wonder now that I picked the word "dream" for its assonance, and am stuck with it as intellectual fingerpointing!

3l. The persona is always me. Except that a poem is not a person. And, therefore, I'm rejecting the question.

3m. I did not use cliché in writing this poem deliberately. If there are clichés in this poem, they are the fault of my wicked self.

3n. Appeal to the eye? As it happened, the poem began to make this spacey, skinny thing, and I liked that. But I did not look forward to it.

3o. I cannot describe the tone particularly. The poem is to a degree nostalgic. The poem seems also somehow or other runic. But maybe I flatter it.

5 If it cannot be paraphrased, it simply cannot be paraphrased. Why do I have to give a reason? Earlier, perhaps I answered this, when I said that you could only paraphrase the irrational by another parallel irrationality, or some such thing. That is, I don't think you can explain it *away* in rational terms.

6 If a person had no experience, I wouldn't attempt to help him read this poem. I would try to help him to read poetry. I would tell him, for instance, that he should not ask for a poem to do any particular thing. I would ask him to relax and listen and float. I would ask him to allow himself to associate. I would ask him—as I would ask anyone about my poems—not to translate but to listen. Most people read poems as if they were reading French badly, translating it into English as they went. To read the poem, you must *stop* paraphrasing, stop "thinking" in the conventional way, and do some receiving instead.

Donald Hall was born in 1928, went to Harvard, Oxford, and Stanford, and taught for some years at the University of Michigan. He has published six books of poetry, including *The Alligator Bride* (1969) and *The Town of Hill* (1975). He has published and edited twenty-five other books—biographies, juveniles, anthologies, encyclopedias, literary criticism, and pornography. At present he is living in New Hampshire.

James Baker Hall

THE SONG OF THE MEAN MARY JEAN MACHINE

Strapped to the roof rack of her
silver mint Carrera: a surfboard
and a bobsled and boxes of live
pheasants and rabbits for her hawks.
It's the Mean Mary Jean Machine,
the green flag on pride, a one-lady
field guide to Western birds!
She wears a crocheted white wool
cottage industry Guatamalan power
hat, and a cottage industry purple
cotton Guatamalan power shirt,
and her custom yellow shades are
perched on the power hat like
a Gold Eagle's eyes. On the seat
beside her, two Russian Wolf Hounds,
and in the back, in custom leather
tote bags, a black M-4 Leica,
a one-eighty Blad, and a big mean
peregrine on its perch.

Whoooeee!
Here she comes, shooting the California
mountain passes on her way to her song!
This lady's lyric is in the point spreads,
somewhere between a redtail on a bunny
and a goshawk on a jack! She's up
to her bumpers in leaf mould, and
getting it on up to the brag!
At her
ten-dollar-a-head concert they sell
stickers that say DON'T SHOOT HAWKS
and THE MEAN MARY JEAN MACHINE—
all
the money marked for Bangladesh.
She feeds more hungry people
than the church.

Call it whatever,
it's a kind of paean, the American
love song of the Mean Mary Jean Machine.

On the way to my first hawking meet, in California, I saw an enigmatic bumper sticker which read, *the Mean Mary Jean Machine;* and I had a good time with it. At the meet, which brought together several hundred southern California hawkers for a weekend, I found myself in one of those wonderfully rich little worlds, like weight-lifting or space exploration or scholarship or stock-car racing or photography or tournament tennis, a whole subculture of shared passion and expertise that promotes its own language and customs. I saw dozens of people and situations that fascinated me, among them one hawker who drove a red Porsche 356C which had been done over inside to make room for his birding gear, a perch for his falcon in place of the jump seat; and a chic young couple who, in addition to several impressive falcons and hawks, had a Gold Eagle on display outside their Winnebago: the woman, with long blond hair and tailored suede bell-bottoms, handsome after the ways of a Marlboro ad, appeared at one point, surrounded by the envious, walking a Saluki. Half the people there had cameras, some more than one, most of them far more sophisticated than their owners would ever have any practical use for. I was struck over and over again by how American it all was. Most of the people there appeared modest enough in their means, if not in their souls, given to old pickups and vans rather than Porsches and Winnebagos, and only a few seemed defined simply by the glamor of the sport; but there they all were with the leisure and the inclinations of an aristocracy—though not the heritage. Their passion for reducing the birds to sport expressed something of our disastrous relationship to the natural world, that compulsion to manipulate and dominate that leads us to bulldoze whatever gets between us and our ends. For whatever ugliness I found there, though, the meet was charged with that undeniable vitality that attends people when they are where they want to be and are doing what they know how to do, and even the suede bell-bottoms and the chic dogs were redefined by it; I was, then, more inclined to marvel at their sources of nourishment than to quarrel with them, which means that I was moving into instincts that I've learned to trust. My experience tells me time and again that awe is the only truly moral and simply life-enhancing emotion that I know well; most of the writing that I have done that pleases me seems an effort to find or create some kind of paradigmatic order among an assortment of marvels.

The point here is: all day bits and pieces were jumping off of what I saw and heard, and were grabbing me. At any given time my head and notebooks are full of such details, snippets of language, anecdotes, ideas, perceptions: they are like so many free-floating metal shavings in want of a magnet. The writer in me has among his resources a kind of specialized junk collector who gathers all manner of stuff with only a vague idea what it is good for; he's like a child who needs a parent's imagination to know what to do with his energy.

On the way home I saw a car with a surfboard and a bobsled on the roof rack, which struck me as pure southern California sociology; and as I was winding back down toward San Diego, a silver Porsche 911 jumped up in the rearview mirror and was past me in a rush that brought to mind James Dean and left me with that exhilarating surge of power I always feel when a jet starts down the runway or when the green flag goes up on a tight pack of modified stocks.

The next thing I knew I had a magnet: the idea of a rock singer. Although I had long been fascinated by the world of rock music, it had never occurred to me that I would ever feel cocky enough to write about it; who would dare try to match such a superb work of the imagination as Mick Jagger or the Beatles? But suddenly a lot of the day's shavings began moving on one another; I remembered an in-group conversation I'd overheard that day about the difference between a redtail on a bunny and a goshawk on a jack, and those shavings started pulling others in from all over, things I hadn't thought about for days, weeks, months. *Up to her bumpers in leaf mould* had been hanging around for a year waiting for its occasion, and *getting it up to the brag.* The phrase *California mountain pass* (which had always been intimidated by the crowd of flashier notions) stepped forward and with a flourish set the scene. In La Jolla, where I'd been spending a lot of time, there are as many lovingly preserved C-series Porsches on the street as VW bugs, and I had been following the classifieds daily whenever I was there, entertaining myself at breakfast with fantasies of owning exactly the right kind of car, and with the in-group language in which many of the ads were written. Suddenly I had my Porsche, and I was on the trip that would say something of what wanting one might be all about. I knew then that the poem would take the shape of a character sketch, a form that I had used several times before, and that, assuming that I could bring Mary Jean alive, everything would hinge on what she and that whole rock scene had to do with at least some of the rest of the world. Although my own Guatamalan hat and shirt fit Mary Jean perfectly, I wasn't comfortable having my things mocked until the language got vital enough, the tone rich enough to assure me that they would not be simply mocked. With the likes of Mary Jean, so this poem would have it, feeding hungry people is wired to the same circuit that makes her a tweeter of chic paraphernalia; the way that the poem sees her suggests that if it weren't for the energy she gets off her mean self-indulgence her song wouldn't make the money it takes for her to outdo the church when it comes to Bangladesh. Once I was confident of rendering that essential moral complexity, not just naming it but making it come alive in the details and diction and rhythms of the poem, I felt free to dance with her: I gave her my black M-4 Leica, and she came back with a telephoto Hasselblad and custom leather camera bags, extravagances I am unable to own on my own. We were dealing with one another, hip to hip, eye ball to eye ball, and it was getting interesting. There, off the blind side, were those fashionable yellow goggles, perched on our hat like a Gold Eagle's eyes, just as sexy as I had always known they could be!

Although I've considerably simplified the whole process, and left out all the important fiddling that goes on with words and rhythms, I think that I've given a more or less accurate impression of how this poem came into being. The reason I selected *The Song of the Mean Mary Jean Machine* for this occasion was that I *could* give such an account. The origins and execution of most of my poems, at least the ones I like best, are characteristically far too complex and obscure to account for. There is little in this poem, for instance, that got turned up by the evolving process of writing it; it was more pieced together out of existing stuff than created, more edited, in a sense, than written. I would guess that that has something to do with the poem being no better than it is. It wasn't an act of discovery, but rather a challenge to express something that I already knew, and is thus cut off from the mystery of things. It goes to work with the assumption that it knows the final truth about its subject—which can only mean that the subject is perceived in a very limited way. Except for the ending, which seems to me too abrupt—the poem's proportions want another item to go with feeding more hungry people than the church—*The Song of the Mean Mary Jean Machine* pleases me well enough: it says something worth saying in a fetching way. But it lacks the ambition that would give it a chance for Mary Jean to be an emblem for more than just other people like her. The awe in it, constantly undercut by the irony, isn't the kind of awe that awes; it might nourish the social being and correct a too-simple moral bookkeeping, but it is not going to nourish the soul. A better poem, by going deeper, into what is beneath the social and the moral and the psychological, would balance silence against its need to talk, would have what it does know poised delicately by what it doesn't—have in it an awareness of the ineffable.

James Baker Hall was born in 1935 in Lexington, Kentucky; he studied at the University of Kentucky and at Stanford University. His poems, stories, and articles have appeared in the *Hudson Review, Sewanee Review, Field, Esquire, Saturday Evening Post,* and elsewhere; he has published a novel, *Yates Paul, His Grand Flights, His Tootings* (1963), a chapbook of poems, *Getting It On Up To The Brag* (1975), and he edited and wrote the principal text for the recent Aperture Monograph, *Ralph Eugene Meatyard.* After years of odd-jobbing and teaching on the west coast and in New England, he returned to the University of Kentucky in 1973, where he teaches writing.

Michael S. Harper

GRANDFATHER

In 1915 my grandfather's
neighbors surrounded his house
near the dayline he ran
on the Hudson
in Catskill, NY
and thought they'd burn
his family out
in a movie they'd just seen
and be rid of his kind:
the death of a lone black
family is *the Birth*
of a Nation,
or so they thought.
His 5′4″ waiter gait
quenched the white jacket smile
he'd brought back from watered
polish of my father
on the turning seats,
and he asked his neighbors
up on his thatched porch
for the first blossom of fire
that would burn him down.

They went away, his nation,
spittooning their torched necks
in the shadows of the riverboat
they'd seen, posse decomposing;
and I see him on Sutter
with white bag from your
restaurant, challenged by his first
grandson to a foot-race
he will win in white clothes.

I see him as he buys galoshes
for his railed yard near Mineo's
metal shop, where roses jump
as the el circles his house
towards Brooklyn, where his rain fell;
and I see cigar smoke in his eyes,
chocolate Madison Square Garden chews
he breaks on his set teeth,
stitched up after cancer,
the great white nation immovable
as his weight wilts
and he is on a porch
that won't hold my arms,
or the legs of the race run
forwards, or the film
played backwards on his grandson's eyes.

COMMENTARY ON *GRANDFATHER*

Family background

Much of the early information alluded to in the later (and final) version of *Grandfather* came directly to me through my father, who was born and raised in the town of Catskill, New York; 1915 was his birth year, he the second of five children who survived, and his recollections in part were consummated in the writing. My grandfather worked on the boats that ran from New York up the Hudson River; he worked as a cook and waiter, and moved to Catskill to work in a concession during the high season. After an accident in which he lost an eye from an exploding bottle, he was offered a settlement in cash or the running of the dayline concession in Catskill; he settled on that concession as a means to buy his own business. The family had a tradition of independence; my father's grandfather walked from the South to New York at the end of the Civil War, and bought the house on "Sutter," and much of the storytelling, over many years, included salient episodes on race relations, American history and politics, the economics of the Hudson River, the entrepreneurial limits for black men in the '20s and '30s, railroads, under and above ground, those itinerant progressions from slavery to freedom, games and family mores, folklore and music. My grandfather was an amateur musician and made his own instruments; it was said he could play anything with strings, and though untrained, used his talents during the depression to feed his family. He lost his business in the early '30s and went to work again on the boats up the Hudson River. He was my first clear image of an heroic stance against adversity; I was often sent to my grandparents to do errands for them on weekends, a pretense whereby I could sustain a continued connection with the lineage of my father. It was through my grandfather that I came to realize the stature and importance of my own father, and the poem is more for my father than for any other family member, because he preserved the images of my forebears so clearly in mind, though he did not dwell on them: he was their embodiment and their legacy.

The writing of the poem

I have always been a poet who had a pattern for a poem at conception, a means of balancing form and content in formal rather than traditional lines; the original pattern was the ballad form, because it is economical and dramatic and does not require too much right-sounding rhyme; so I left the poem for some years. I began to ponder the balance between *art* and *life*, what elements of both were necessary to tell a story, a story that I knew well, and which exacted the price of simplicity and straightforwardness in the telling? I had seen D. W. Griffith's *The Birth of a Nation* in a college film survey course, and I was angered at the showing, at the false weight given to elements of the Civil War and its aftermath that I had known from childhood; I was appalled at the instructor's failure to focus on the moral elements that were obfuscated by the film's technical advances, as discussed in a linear survey history-of-film approach, and at the ignorance of my fellow students about the real nature of the Civil War and Reconstruction. I returned to another showing of the film, some years later, to test my recollections. I wrote the poem in one sitting, about five or six drafts, over a whole day, and changed only a word or two thereafter.

Michael S. Harper was born in 1938 in Brooklyn, New York, where he attended public schools; his family moved to Los Angeles in 1951. He wrote plays and short fiction for creative writing classes, worked as newspaper distributor, lifeguard, postal clerk, counselor, and in 1961 spent a year at the University of Iowa's Writers' Workshop. After teaching in Portland, Oregon, Hayward, California, and Urbana, Illinois, he now teaches and directs the writing program at Brown University. He lives with his wife and three children in Massachusetts. Publications include: *Dear John, Dear Coltrane* (1970), *History Is Your Own Heartbeat* (1971), *History as Apple Tree* (1972), *Song: I Want a Witness* (1972), *Debridement* (1973), and *Nightmare Begins Responsibility* (1975).

Phil Hey

OLD MEN WORKING CONCRETE

won't be rushed; will take
their own sweet time.
Now and then, will stop
for snuff (reaching in
the pocket where the circle
of can has worn a circle
in the cloth); and then
get back to work, mix mud
and fill and walk that barrow
back and back and back.
Soon enough the slab end
takes shape. The one man
on his knees with a float
checks it with his eye
stopping time and again
to run his striker saw-wise
and level across the top.
Soon enough it gets long;
smooth with broad swings
of trowel it gets long.
Finally they stop the mixer.

One trowels out the last space,
one works the edger.
Done, they stand back.
They look one more time.
It's good. Yes sir, it's good.
They talk. They dip snuff.
They are happy.

SWEET TIME: WORKING A POEM

I hadn't written in a long time, and despaired of ever writing again. But the concern at the moment was not writing. My friend Bill needed help with his garage floor. He'd had a heart attack, so his friends helped out: George, Al, and me (the only one under sixty). All retired but me; all working with their hands all life long, but me. We did it, we finished more than Bill hoped we would. He was proud of the floor, deeply moved by friends happy to do so much for him. So was I.

So the poem was not begun, in a sense: it was there complete in the experience, needing not so much invention as transcription. Or so it felt, and still does. There are few things more beautiful than old men working. They don't have to; it becomes a point of honor to show the mastery of years working with hands. Supernal patience wins out, the joy of being with the thing worked, of seeing yourself reflected in the work. And of knowing that the work will outlast you, if you do well; and being happy about that too.

The poem did not write itself. It demanded a kind of faithfulness to the experience, a sense of working in language somehow like the sense of working with concrete. Only enough to make it firm and level; unspectacular: strong, without decoration. From first word to completion, perhaps twenty lines of description were eliminated; the poem ended up less colorful and less narrative than when it began (which was by a rapid dumping onto the page of all associative materials, images, names, etc., roughly in the order in which they had been noticed).

But how is the sense of the poem the sense of the experience? I knew (want to say, anyone would know) that

won't be rushed; will take
their own sweet time.

has to be the first two lines. Young men sweat and curse under work; old men retired savor it. Something perhaps to keep, lovingly, from thinking how much is past and how little left; but in any case, savor. Time is sweet when you feel the purpose in your hands again. As time should be sweet and purposeful in the movings of this poem. There is no specific prosody behind this poem; it seeks the motions inherent in the experience. There is a coherence in the way sounds occur in my writing, a subdued but constant repetition and near-repetition; but no more planned or preordained than the phrases of a good jazzman, I hope. Thus I do not directly believe that "the sound must seem an echo to the sense." There is a sense of rhythm larger than any body of sounds one could use mimetically (and thus nothing of "slap and scrape of trowel" or "rough wash of mixer"). In its place, a kind of cadencing, that is, ways to keep the words flowing, or to modulate or stop their flow—ways the sounds, phrases, lines, grammar show the ear how to hear, the mouth how to speak. In a poem it should be immediately obvious to a sympathetic oral reader. At the end, for example, everything conspires to end. Anticlimax in ideas. Short sentences of flat sounds. Full pauses.

But never these aside from some sort of immediate concern with the things said, as if it were the most ordinary prose. I like poems that at once (1) offer an experience which is the words, and (2) indicate an experience of value independent of any poem whatever. But poems are not consequences of judgment. One experience calls another experience into being, and the latter is a poem. Richard Palmer (*Hermeneutics*, Northwestern University Press, 1969) says that truth is "the dynamic emergence of being into the light of manifestness." All language, all craft, goes to make the experience manifest; not only the experience of working concrete, or of old men, but of seeing, of finding all this to be fascinating. I would be a Whitmanlike observer, knowing that observing itself is real experience.

And who to read it? Anyone, I hope; but mostly, a reader no respecter of cultural fashion. I seek to be neither old nor new in style or subject, but to work finally from my own sense of style and experience. I don't know that other poets are either interested or impressed. Readers who like poems such as this one seem to be a little more willingly innocent than most poets or scholars. A reader would have to at least be open to the possibility that old men working concrete are beautiful, that unspectacular style can be most appropriate and good. And that many poems now written are a kind of vitiated, obscure mush in both senses of language and experience; and that I will not let mine be, regardless. I am honored that David Evans and E. V. Griffith (two fine editors) like some of my poems such as this one. I would love to hear from someone who couldn't stand the poem.

Or from someone who wanted to know what it "means." I would rather write a good clear poem than a bad one that could be analyzed all day. (Agreed: there are great poems that could be analyzed all day. But analysis never improved any poem.) In short, I can hardly bring myself to believe that a paraphrase is either needed or valuable, that it would be significantly more clear or understandable than the original. If one is needed, consult a book on how to finish concrete.

Do not consult a book on how to finish poems, however. I have tried very hard to study both technique and poetics so that I could put all away, and write each time as if I had never written before. I see this poem as similar in theme and technique to several others (Midwest life and language; sorry, both coasts, if I haven't entertained you); perhaps slightly better than some. How should I know that? But judgments like these are always retrospective, somehow not lived.

Still. All poetics is a Procrustes bed. If a poem is good, it is more than anything like it, more than anything said about it: almost too much of experience to be as mere as words. And yet, miraculously, it is.

See also: comments with poems in *New Voices in American Poetry*, and "Letter to Any Young Poet," *Oakwood*, I; English Department, South Dakota State University, Brookings 57006.

Phil Hey was born in 1942 and has been growing up ever since in Illinois, Wisconsin, and Iowa. He was enlightened at Monmouth College, and the universities of Iowa and Wisconsin. He has worked as a pinsetter, fry cook, and tuba player; he now writes and teaches writing at Briar Cliff College, Sioux City, Iowa. Published *In Plain Sight* (1974); received Edwin H. Gardner Award, 1968.

Donald Justice

FIRST DEATH

June 12, 1933

I saw my grandmother grow weak.
When she died, I kissed her cheek.

I remember the new taste—
Powder mixed with a drying paste.

Down the hallway, on its table,
Lay the family's great Bible.

In the dark, by lamplight stirred,
The Void grew pregnant with the Word.

In black ink they wrote it down.
The other ink was turning brown.

From the woods there came a cry—
A hoot owl asking who, not why.

The men sat silent on the porch,
Each lighted pipe a friendly torch

Against the unknown and the known.
But the child knew himself alone.

June 13, 1933

The morning sun rose up and stuck.
Sunflower strove with hollyhock.

I ran the worn path past the sty.
Nothing was hidden from God's eye.

The barn door creaked. I walked among
Chaff and wrinkled cakes of dung.

In the dim light I read the dates
On the dusty license plates

Nailed to the wall as souvenirs.
I breathed the dust in of the years.

Twice I went round the rusty Ford
Before I tried the running board.

At the wheel I felt the heat
Press upward through the springless seat.

And when I touched the silent horn,
Small mice scattered through the corn.

June 14, 1933

I remember the soprano
Fanning herself at the piano,

And the preacher looming large
Above me in his dark blue serge.

My shoes brought in a smell of clay
To mingle with the faint sachet

Of flowers sweating in their vases.
A stranger showed us to our places.

The stiff fan stirred in mother's hand.
Air moved, but only when she fanned.

I wondered how could all her grief
Be squeezed into one small handkerchief.

There was a buzzing on the sill.
It stopped, and everything was still.

We bowed our heads, we closed our eyes
To the mercy of the flies.

DRAFT

```
The morning sun rose up and stuck,
Sunflower strove with hollyhock.                1

Shadows shrank, and then the shade.
I hid myself, I was afraid.                     2

I ran the worn path past the sty.
Nothing was hidden from God's eye.

The barn door creaked. I moved among
Chaff and wrinkled cakes of dung.               3

there
And / as I read off [all]
In the dim light I read the dates
From /On the dusty license plates               4
```

Nailed to the wall ~~as~~ for souvenirs.
I breathed the dust in of the years. 5

climbed
I sat upon the running board
Of the long abandoned Ford. 6

Indoors, under dampened cloths,
Women's eyelids moved like moths.

~~Clifton~~ The neighbor paused behind his plow
To draw one arm across his brow.

I could watch grandfather whittle,
Pause, and let fly the golden spittle.

On a campchair in the shade
I read of Robin and his maid,

And I watched grandfather whittle,
Pause, and let fly the golden spittle.

Shadows shrank & then withdrew.
What was there for a child to do?

Sat at the wheel & felt the heat
Press upward through the springless seat. 7

I could have driven anywhere,
Anywhere but out of there. 8

First Death developed consciously, so far as the development was conscious, out of no more than a feeling many poets must have conditioned themselves to respond to—the generalized desire simply to be writing a poem, any poem. Having been sick for some months, I had not been writing and was, perhaps, beginning to feel guilty. A first worksheet shows that I was typing out tetrameter couplets about nothing in particular. Since it is not my usual practice to *type* a first draft, I suspect that I was merely practicing, trying to warm up, not feeling altogether responsible for what my fingers might find to say. Ultimately, about halfway down the first page, I typed a couplet or two about something, about something specific and real: raindrops caught in a spiderweb on a back porch. I knew which porch that was—my grandparents' porch, on a farm near Tifton, Georgia, some time in the early thirties. (The detail was not to survive in the poem.) I rationalized the process by supposing that, while my conscious mind was attending to details of rhyming and metering these couplets about nothing, my unconscious had been freed to rove and dive until it came up with a fragment of memory, entangled with associations rich, for me, in feeling and significance. Why I was writing couplets at all I cannot remember. I had never published a poem in such couplets; indeed, I had not tried rhyme for years (except in a libretto that year for which the composer had requested rhyme), and I had never rejoiced in rhyming, being less than adept at it. I do recall feeling then that most poets were tending to write more and more sloppily and that some attention to the strictest formal etiquette might check that inclination insofar as I shared it. Nor did I wish simply to repeat myself, to write on and on of the themes and in the manners of *Departures,* the book I had recently completed. I would try to be new, at least for myself, by returning to the old—old form, old subject.

It is rare for a poem of mine to go through an orderly succession of drafts, versions which begin at the beginning and go right through to the end. The four or five drafts usually required in such cases are quickly done, and with pleasure. A different pleasure comes from the kind of work this poem involved, the pleasure resulting from care and labor, as in making something with tools in a manual training class or putting up a house of cards. Each line and, in this poem, each couplet had, it seemed, to be shaped into something close to its final form, or at least made to fill up its imagined place with more or less the right meaning, before I was ready to continue. Although there are no drafts except for very late ones, I can count thirty-four worksheets. Unhappily, long periods elapsed between intervals of work. If I started the poem some time in the summer of 1973, as I believe I did, and made substantial progress on it then, getting through much of the first two sections, I did not resume serious work on it till June, 1975. I was not sure how long the poem would or should be—couplets have a way of running on and on—but I did see it early as falling into parts (if not pieces), and once I had more than enough for the first two sections down on paper, it seemed that one last section, something conclusive, should suffice. What—I must have asked myself, on coming back to it—what more conclusive than the funeral itself? (The first funeral I had ever attended.) In this sense the poem expanded, grew, was added on to. But in other ways it just as clearly shrank, the first section from twenty or more lines to an exact sixteen, and similarly throughout. And if I had vaguely imagined a poem that might re-create the Georgia summers I had passed as a child—a part of my own lesser *Prelude*, so to speak—, a poem of no fewer, surely, than two hundred lines; if, indeed, I must have written that many lines for it (though I do not wish to count the worksheets to verify the number), it nevertheless ended as a mere forty-eight, not a documentary of all that those Georgia summers had been, but an edited cinema of three days remembered from one summer only.

In the nature of the case, the structure, this once, did not much change, except for the fixing of the exact number of lines for each section. The theme changed only in being narrowed down and focused on my grandmother's death and my reactions as a child to that shaking, though common, experience. The tone, unfortunately, did undergo some modification. I had wanted from the first something childlike, folklike, near primitive, feeling the couplet to be a fit vehicle for such a tone, and that tone to be in keeping with both the subject and, as might be remarked of a fiction or memoir, the child's point of view. The first two lines, I felt, set the tone I wanted to maintain. But I could not maintain it, despite effort. In what follows there is a growing self-consciousness, perhaps some reminiscence even of the handling of this particular verse line from Milton's great pair of poems, but I hope not so much as to spoil completely the innocence from which it started. The first two lines of the poem, then, are the unchanged lines, the model lines. Only slightly changed were the "witty" line about the Void, the lines about the hoot owl, and the final couplets of the first and last sections. Everything in the second section was considerably revised and may yet be further, since signs of the trouble which that part gave me still seem all too visible. Most of the revisions seem to have been made for the sake of coherence—narrative, stylistic, and especially tonal.

The meters require little explanation and, in my view, no defense. The tetrameter couplet is a more flexible instrument than generally acknowledged, and the line itself may crop up anywhere from ballads to Milton. Its particular adaptation here is the one which allows you, depending on whether you regard the line as iambic or trochaic, to drop or to add a first syllable; in other words, the first foot is free. In *L'Allegro* and *Il Penseroso* this slight admixture of freedom opens the line to grace, beauty, and delight, and in this respect suggests the attractive waywardness with which the line is treated in many ballads. Wishing to keep the tone casual and unsophisticated, in tension with the apparent severity of the couplet, I was happy to find a handful of inexact rhymes. The metaphor, what there may be of it, is conventional or so simple as to escape notice. It seems to have become virtually a principle with me—in practice if not yet in theory—to use literal details so that they imply metaphor. Summer heat is equivalent to intense misery: temperature becomes metaphor. When the child in the poem touches the dead horn of the old Ford and the mice scatter, the paradox of creatures responding to silence as if it were a sudden frightening noise is, I suspect, metaphorical, an attempt to render the child's projection of his own terror onto his surroundings. As for language, anything that is not simple, not obviously rooted in the child's sensibility, is most likely to be traced to the oppressive influence of the religion which afflicted that sensibility (as in lines 8 and 20). Against custom, including my own, I was willing to admit here and there certain old-fashioned "poetic" devices, such as inversion ("by lamplight stirred"), easy enough otherwise to get around, on the grounds that they reinforced the tone I was after. I was trying to write a poem, not an exemplary text on how poetry ought to be written now or in the future.

The order of the poem is chronological, a narrative with a beginning, middle, and end, and with no more ellipsis than common in narrative, yet selective rather than accumulative, more like a short story than a novel.

I wanted a big ending, quietly done. The boy in the poem is myself, but myself at seven, which gives me the illusion of distance I prefer to work with. I had, as usual, no particular audience in mind, but readers certainly, nameless readers. And for once, this was a poem I would have been glad to have my mother read, but she died before I finished it.

The outline of the poem is easy enough to paraphrase, and paraphrases that do not wallow in prolixity are of outlines only. Paraphrase: (1) A boy sees his grandmother die and is terrified by the mysteries and customs surrounding the death, feeling himself alone in a hostile world. (2) He hides himself away from others and attempts to know the past, to master it and escape from the present through an act of make-believe. (3) At the funeral he feels oppressed by the heat, the rituals, and the inefficacy of religious consolation. Such a paraphrase necessarily leaves out what I trust may seem the magical reality which comes about through the more detailed rendering and more substantial ordering required by the poem, though some of what is lost might be restored by expanding the prose commentary. (With a "creative" critic something might even be added.) What would be lost forever if only the prose commentary survived would be the pleasure (if any) of the meters and rhymes themselves and whatever effects of coherence, compression, and point their binding force had led to (or not prevented), all of which ought to have helped *fix* the poem, as the right solution fixes the snapshot. The reader would have lost the chance to experience the event for himself. I would have lost my own pleasure in having put the poem together in this way, in having made something, this.

The poem is not at all obscure, I think, and should give no one trouble on that score. How good or bad the poem may be is another question, one I cannot answer. For one thing, it is new. For another, it is unlike other things I have written. For the time being, I do like it. I like it because it records something otherwise lost.

Donald Justice was born in Miami, Florida, in 1925, studied there and at the universities of North Carolina, Stanford, and Iowa, and has since taught in many schools. Currently he teaches in the poetry workshop at Iowa. His first book of poems, *The Summer Anniversaries* (1960), was the Lamont selection for 1959. He has published *Night Light* (1967), *Departures* (1973), and edited *The Collected Poems of Weldon Kees* (1975).

Shirley Kaufman

DINOSAUR TRACKS IN BEIT ZAYIT

for Iris and Michael Wade

How there is anything so old
we can't imagine
anyone not there
to see them

three fingers
out of touch with each other

scars under my sole
like an old cut starting
to hurt again

when I put my foot
over his foot
I move in the same direction.

*

Everything dies in its own language
even before we find the name
and we remember only
what we can put together

what do I know about
pain in the bones of an old man
or those feet
always having to risk how far to go.

*

Next to the broken stones
in a small clearing
the sky is pale
as if it never got over the long night

and the white dust that gathered
where they fell
comes like sleep over my eyes

if I keep walking over the earth's rim
I'll disappear.

*

In less than the time it takes
to get from one life to another
we move closer together

I want to say to you
where are the children

the wind can't get in
where our shoulders touch.

*

Someone is digging next to her front door
she is planting a rose garden
her spade hits rock
she scoops the earth away
uncovering footprints

she thinks about everything
under her going
somewhere it doesn't arrive

at night when everyone's sleeping
she hears the silence of the world.

DRAFT

DINOSAUR TRACKS IN BEIT ZAYIT

What I'm amazed at is the print
like scars on the back of a giant hand
three fingers out of touch
with each other

that there is anything so old

all this time who would have thought
they were under us
going somewhere they didn't arrive

when I step into one
I move in the same direction
his stride was not much longer
than mine.

PAGE FROM JOURNAL

Your feet hurt
your tail is dragging in the mud
there's a light up ahead
that turns ~~in~~ (out) to ^ (bea) disaster
It wipes you out
something like that.

Dust. Sand. *Rain* Millions of years
Someone is digging next to his ~~house~~ *front door*
He is planting a rose garden
His spade hits rock
He scoops the earth away
What we ~~remember~~ *stand watching* is the size, their deep *wavering in the ~~ancient~~ stone* / *all that is left*
If my ~~feet~~ *foot* grows stems
in three directions ~~they~~ *it* will
fit ~~a~~ *the* dinosaur's prints
His stride is not much longer
than mine. A 7 foot man
would make it

Act.5
dream → *Outside Jerusalem*
In the town of the house of the olive
we follow the tracks
the bones of my feet are ~~growing~~ *changing*
making a house. They smooth
the sand into a floor.
They stand over it to keep the wind out
they know what's coming.
But nothing helps. They ~~know they~~ are perishable

they too are perishable the only dif. is they know

1 The poem was started by my seeing the dinosaur tracks. Strong visual experiences are frequently where poems begin for me. I had been living in Israel for about a year, with four months away to teach at the University of Massachusetts in Amherst. The first part of my life in Israel was overwhelmed by the October war and the change in my personal life, break-up of a long marriage. When I returned after teaching in New England, I was impressed, as I always am, with how old everything is in this part of the world—the weight (historical) of each stone. The other most impressive thing is the landscape, which especially struck me after the lush greenness of New England. The hills around Jerusalem are bare (except for a small pine forest recently planted), and you can see the remnants of ancient terracing, the whole thing falling away to the east into the Judean wilderness, desert, dust. Beit Zayit is a small village just outside of Jerusalem where our friends Iris and Michael Wade have their house. The Hebrew name for the village means "House of Olive," and there are very old olive trees all over the place. Olive trees live for hundreds of years, very gnarled and twisted, and go on bearing fruit forever. Our friends had been out of the country for two years, and when they returned to their home, which they had leased in their absence, they learned that tracks of dinosaurs had been discovered in the village. A neighbor was digging by her front porch one day to plant a rose garden, and suddenly, a few feet down, her spade hit bedrock. When she cleared some earth away, she discovered these strange prints petrified in the stone. Experts were called in from the university who verified that they were the footprints of dinosaurs. The village of Beit Zayit decided then to buy the property from the people who were living on it and create a public park, clearing away all the earth that buried the rest of the footprints. The people refused to move, and there was a long struggle; money had to be raised, another home built for them, etc. Their original home is now a small clubhouse, and the tracks are exposed for anyone to see, covering quite a large area. The footprints all move in the same direction. The village wants the government of Israel to take it over and build some kind of shelter over the prints, perhaps charge admission to the public. But the government has more important things to do right now, and so the prints are completely exposed to the rain and winter snow and very hot sun. They will be worn away with time. Iris told us all this, and another little story. When she came home to Israel and saw the dinosaur tracks, she said to another neighbor, "Isn't it wonderful to have dinosaur tracks in Beit Zayit!" The neighbor, a very practical old lady, said, "What's wonderful about it? I was digging in *my* garden and found lots of the same footprints. I covered them up right away. Do you think I want all that commotion in *my* place?!"

So the poem started with Iris and Michael telling us about the discovery and then taking us to see the footprints. We couldn't resist stepping into them at once, fitting our feet to the dinosaurs' feet. The distance between them is about the distance of the stride of a very tall man—they must have been about seven feet tall. My husband had to stretch his legs a little to get from one to the other.

Thinking about what this part of the world was like that long ago (no people, no Israelis and Arabs fighting!), the vastness, the silence, I began to want to write something. I never write my poems imagining the reader. I write them for myself—to get down on paper something strongly felt which is completely unformed and undefined at the beginning. I began the poem with the five lines that start the last section: "Someone is digging . . ." Only I wrote, "Someone was digging . . ." It wasn't too long before I realized that I didn't want to write a narrative poem, that there would be only related fragments, and that the beginning would be the end. Because the thing I felt almost immediately was my link with the dinosaurs, all of us becoming extinct at some point in time. And who would discover *my* footprints millions of years from now? And in what kind of world?

I realized that these weren't very original thoughts, that if the poem was to succeed I would have to get my feelings into it, not any ideas that tended to get in the way. This is another way of saying I usually have to control my mental processes when they interfere from time to time while I'm writing the poem, to let it just *happen*.

2 There were several drafts. I still have a draft of the first section that I discarded at the end for the final version, so I'll include it. But that's already greatly refined. I work a lot on most of my poems. I wrote this one over a period of several months, putting it away for weeks at a time, and then taking a fresh look at it, and changing lines, words, each time I came to it fresh. This is my usual way of working, and it takes me a long time to finish a poem.

The structure never changed, though originally there were three or four (I forget now) longer sections. Lately I prefer asterisks to numbers between sections of my poems, because I don't think of the separate parts as falling into any consecutive sequence. They are, rather, different ways of looking at the same central theme. It would be nice to print them in a circle with the title in the center. Still, as I'm working, a strong sense develops in me of where the poem should begin and end. And this had to begin with my amazement at seeing the prints. What happened between the old version and final version is that I didn't have to spell the amazement out quite so literally. I wanted to suggest it without hitting anyone over the head.

The changes that occurred as I worked on the poem were mainly in the arrangement of lines and the line breaks, sorting out what went where. This is also typical of the way I work.

Changes also take the form of sharpening the individual images. Sometimes they arrive in a rather vague way, and I see later how to make them more intense. An example of this is the last stanza of the first section:

> when I step into one
> I move in the same direction

became in the final version:

> when I put my foot
> over his foot

I wanted to re-experience the tactile sensation.

Then you might look at what happened to the "scars." I began to feel that the back of the giant hand was too cute, too invented, though it came easily enough. This is a problem I have to keep fighting in my work. It's too easy for me to find a felicitous phrase and get carried away with it. And I have to force myself later to ask how honest it is. Again I wanted to get the tactile sensation, so came back to my own foot, away from the fantasy about giants.

So the changes are first order, then line break, then tightening of images. In all my poems. I always am aware of the sound and rhythm, and make the changes only when reading the entire poem through each time to see how the total rhythm accommodates the change. I usually do this out loud.

3 I've answered most of the questions about technique already, I think. When I arrive at the final breaks in line, stanza, and section, they seem to me inevitable. In the process I experiment with many alternative breaks, but when I get it the way I want it no alternative seems possible. I can't explain it logically.

My rhythmical principle is my own speech rhythm, my own breath. Assonance, alliteration, consonance are second nature to me by now. I hardly think about them, except when I'm stuck for a word. I chose "cut" in the first section because of "foot." But "p*ain in* the b*on*es of an *o*ld ma*n*" just happened, because my ear is tuned that way by now.

I'd like this poem to be read or heard—I don't care how.

I have no hesitation to use obscure references or allusions in a poem if they work in the poem. Like the story about the woman planting the rose garden. No one would know that this is really how the tracks were discovered in Beit Zayit. But it doesn't matter.

I would prefer to write my poems with more open-ended conclusions, and I struggle to avoid tying things up in a neat package. But I don't think this turned out as open-ended as I would have liked.

The persona in the poem is myself, and that's the way I almost always write.

I made no conscious attempt to appeal to the reader's eye. I can't describe the "tone" of the poem. I said it started with amazement. But it moves on from there to something more troubled.

4 I imagine as my reader everyone who reads contemporary poetry—no newspaper readers generally! On the other hand, I read this poem to a gathering at the United States Cultural Center in Jerusalem—many people who do not read much poetry. For them it was interesting to hear my reaction to a wonderful thing in their midst.

5 I wouldn't want to paraphrase any of my poems. If I could paraphrase a poem, I wouldn't write the poem. A poem is more than its occasion/idea. If it's a successful poem. Feelings can't be paraphrased or even defined most of the time.

To help a person read this poem who has had no experience with poetry written since World War II, I would tell him most of what I have been writing on these pages, especially giving the background for the poem, and then explaining how it grew out of my sensory awareness while standing in the footprint of the dinosaur. And how our feelings are irrational and unconnected, and only the poem as a whole can begin to make the connections.

6 How is this poem different from earlier work? I think I am moving in a more open direction, less organized, letting my incoherence spill over (if it will make some "sense" in the end). I've stopped using commas, except when their absence would cause misunderstanding, and I use periods sparingly—a sense I have of the running together of my thoughts and my breath. I would like to be able to present the *process* of feeling my way through a poem as it occurs more than I have in the past—instead of adding it all up afterward.

I don't know about the rest. . . . I take my themes where I find them.

Well, there it is—off the top of my head. Or, in this case, under the soles of my feet. I didn't think I would write so much. And that makes it all seem a bit pretentious. After all, it's just another poem. I take poetry very seriously. But the way we're rushing toward oblivion these days, it might be better not to take *oneself* so seriously!

Born in Seattle, Washington, in 1923, **Shirley Kaufman** received her B.A. degree from UCLA, and her M.A. from California State College at San Francisco. She is the 1969 United States award winner of the International Poetry Forum for her book *The Floor Keeps Turning*. Other books are *A Canopy In The Desert*, Selected Poems of Abba Kovner, translated from the Hebrew, and *Gold Country* (both 1973). She has taught in the Poetry-in-the-Schools program from the time it began in San Francisco in 1964. She now makes her home in Jerusalem (with annual visits to the U.S.A.) where she continues to write and to translate contemporary Hebrew poetry.

X. J. Kennedy

CONSUMER'S REPORT

They don't make things like they used to.
—American proverb

At meat, or hearing you deplore
    How soon things break, my mind salutes
John Dowd, who brought by rolling store
Horse radish to our kitchen door
    He'd make from cream and home-ground roots.

My God! the heat of it would burn
    Right through your beef and knock your tongue out.
Once for a snowsuit I'd outgrown
Came so much free stuff in return
    It smoldered down and ended flung out.

Why did he wear that look of pain,
    Strangely, although his trade kept thriving?
They said the fumes get to your brain.
One day he came back with a cane
    And someone else to do the driving,

But ground right on with open eyes
    And, grinding, stared straight at his killer.
I bet theirs took them by surprise
Though they could see, those other guys,
    The guys who used white turnip filler.

Let me quote a remarkable statement by a poet on the subject of his working habits. Wordsworth made it to Alexander Dyce, who put it into his *Reminiscences:* "When I compose a poem I generally begin with the most striking and prominent part; and if I feel pleased with my execution of that, I then proceed to fill up the other parts."

The apparent drabness of that account of the poetic process, the seeming crassness of proceeding "to fill up the other parts," invites misinterpretation of Wordsworth's statement. To people who detest stanzas and rime-schemes, a familiar received idea is that the form of a formal poem is a boring old jug that formal poets fill with just any old guck they have handy. But Wordsworth, if I read him right, isn't talking about form. (Is it necessary, any more, to dispute that familiar received idea? A poem, whether its form be open or closed, isn't written in order to pad it out. To try to do so would be like trying to fall in love with whoever conformed to a certain chest measurement.) No, Wordsworth refers, I believe, to the truth that poems tend to enter the world by their most astonishing parts. Often, a poet bothers to finish a poem only for the sake of containing those first-born, unlabored lines. In order to deliver the rest of the poem, the poet may have to bear down on it. For in any poem much longer than a haiku, a prominent moment can't stand alone. Such a moment usually has to be led up to, or down from. Evidently, the rest of the poem won't be so intense, so splendid. In a way, that's an advantage: for if every part of a poem were equally prominent, there would be no prominent moments. We can except that handful of sublime lyrics that are, miraculously, intense throughout: Blake's "Tyger," Hopkins' "Windhover."

Let me add a small *me too* to Wordsworth's statement. *Consumer's Report*, which happens to be a formal poem, was a breech birth. The first thing to protrude was its bottom stanza. Then I had to urge forth the rest of it. That last stanza seems to me now quite the best of the four—the most lively with hints, the most readily speakable. The first and second stanzas aren't anything special—just good competent workaday hack poetry—but they're necessary to prepare for stanzas three and four. I like poems that improve as they go along—not that there can't be poems that begin magnificently, then fall off in intensity:

> At the round earth's imagined corners, blow
> Your trumpets, angels, and arise, arise
> From death, you numberless infinities
> Of souls, and to your scattered bodies go . . .

What do you bet that those lines dawned first, and then Donne had to fill up the other parts with white turnip?

Unlike most things I write, that are rewritten at greater length than they are written, this one emerged in very nearly the same way it now remains. The final stanza arrived one morning while I was lying in bed. Later, as I was picking up fallen branches out in the back yard, more lines insisted on coming. I made up the first three stanzas while sitting on a pile of brush, then had to go indoors to fix them in writing. I can hold about twenty unwritten lines in my head before the damned thing spills. They stay there because their rimes, meter, and stanza help hold them together. That's one good thing about writing old-fangled stanzaic poetry—for your first draft, you don't need paper.

Strongly impelled and yet loosely defined, that's an emerging poem—like a burst of buckshot. And what prompted that final stanza to begin with? An urgent memory from childhood, from the days of the National Recovery Act. Legions of the jobless sold homemade products from door to door; among them, one man in particular—John Dowd—stands out for me. (There were people selling home-hooked rugs, hard candy, ocean fish—and if you too were strapped for cash you could barter with them. That's what my mother does in the poem: she swaps an outgrown snowsuit for some horse radish.) In life, his name was Jones, but I changed that for fear the reader would think I invented it. Turning Jones into Dowd may have been suggested by the stock market crash of '29: a fall in the Dow-Jones averages. Now Dowd/Jones's product was homemade horse radish so reeking and fierce and pure that in time he went blind from making it. Perhaps he was a fool—still, I admire his integrity.

In a sense, John Dowd was the ideal poet whom all of us lesser poets yearn to be: the poet whose each work is wholly inspired and unflaggingly high in intensity. Now if Dowd had written poems instead of making horse radish, he would have written nothing less than "The Tyger" and "The

Sick Rose," or "Hurrahing in Harvest" and "The Windhover"—the kind of poem that knocks your tongue out. He wouldn't have had to fill up the less prominent parts, unlike us poor working poet-stiffs who can't swing more than a prominent line or two, not being steady tenants of the divine madness.

As title and proverb may indicate, John Dowd, in his insistence on quality, is a vanishing kind of American. That's the main theme of the poem: devotion to excellence. But there are further themes to find, if the reader wants to. Dowd lost his eyesight from staring at roots within his grinder; but he also stared at Death, that lethal vegetable. (Rereading the poem, I imagine Dowd's death as some hideous fume-surrounded personification of the Spirit of Horse Radish. But there is no need for the reader to imagine that.) An ordinary man, Dowd foresaw his death and still continued working, feeding his kids and obtaining snowsuits for them; and by doing so, he attained a bit of tragic dignity. Some Yiddish writer put it well: there are people who deserve a medal just for getting up in the morning. Blind though Dowd became, yet he saw more clearly than some who see—those "other guys," those merchants of the shoddy. (I don't regard us inferior poets as such slippery operators. Us working poet-stiffs are doing the level best we can. At least we aren't trying to gyp the consumer. So what if we don't write any pure "Windhovers"?) Those other guys, the con men, die from car crashes or from mixing pills with their drinks or from sudden heart attacks. Unlike Dowd, they don't ply their trades in despite of the universe. Their deaths, like their lives, are strictly run-of-the-mill—just so much adulterated horse radish.

X. J. Kennedy was born in Dover, New Jersey, in 1929 and now lives in Bedford, Massachusetts. He teaches at Tufts. *Nude Descending a Staircase* (1961) was his first book; his recent books are song lyrics, *Three Tenors, One Vehicle* (with James Camp and Keith Waldrop, 1975); poems for children, *One Winter Night in August* (1975); and a textbook, *Literature* (1976). *Breaking & Entering,* selected poems, appeared in England (1971). With Dorothy Kennedy, he published *Counter/Measures* (1971–74), a magazine of new poetry in meter and rime. He has been given a Guggenheim Fellowship, a Lamont award, and a Shelley prize, shared with Mary Oliver.

Peter Klappert

O'CONNOR THE BAD TRAVELER

The more I chew this stuff
the bigger it gets.

I thought Men think
with their heads and suffer from claustrophobia:
I will think with my tongue, I will
find my truth in the elaboration of lies,
I will dig through with this *lit*tle trowel
to the land of sweet meats where my mother hums
and waits by the four rivers
to bathe me in primary light.
And do you know
where my tongue led me? Into
Cholera, Dysentery,
Typhus. Oh, I've traveled
like the Guinea worm—the Fiery Serpent of
the Bible, if you didn't know it—and grown
three feet and miserable in a human form.

So I awoke in a perpetual drizzle
in the country of Neurasthenia, bordering
Catatonia, where the occupants are all slaves
without masters. "Here," I said, "My passport,"
and showed them the medical record
scribbled over my body like a bungled
account book: one lung
in debtors prison, a belligerent liver
suing for divorce, a stomach
argumentative as a nest of pelicans
and my heart a claimant in bankruptcy.
But no one would look at my passport.

"The permanent condition of mankind"
said Ahab, "is sordidness." For who knows
how hard the worm bites?
                                        Lay away some
honey on a back shelf, a crock of
rich old bellywash like mead, small morsel
of something good, that never happened,
against the grieving of the locusts on the corn.
That's my song: a couple of mouthfuls of air,
a serenade, by bulblight.

NOTES ON *O'CONNOR THE BAD TRAVELER*

I start most often with a swatch of *language* or with an *image* that, for whatever reason, holds my attention. I do not start with an *idea*, a *theme*, or an *abstraction:* one finds out what he is doing in the process of doing it, and one seldom knows if he's been to a plateau, an alp, or a cesspool until the trip is over. But often a poem starts with a *mood.* Indeed, moods are the primordial mess and are anterior to poems the way gasses were anterior to the Earth.

I find some poems arriving in *voices.* Some part of the psyche splits off and becomes an autonomous personality with its own vocabulary, mannerisms, physical characteristics and obsessions. *O'Connor the Bad Traveler* is spoken by such a mask or persona: Dr. Matthew Mighty-grain-o-salt Dante O'Connor, the character in Djuna Barnes' novel *Nightwood.* O'Connor is an American Irishman who came to France in The Great War and who has lived in Paris (where the novel takes place between 1920 and 1934) most of the time since. He is Tiresias come to life as a credible twentieth-century figure: an openly homosexual, unlicensed "gynecologist" with a sweeping knowledge of the seamier regions of history, psychology, and culture; a torrential raconteur who holds court in a café across from St.-Sulpice and who will embroider anyone's story; a kind of defrocked priest who has, in Eliot's words for him, a "helpless power among the helpless." It is O'Connor's *voice* that fascinates me, the *language* and *images* he uses, as well as the image of O'Connor himself.

I first read *Nightwood* in 1970, wrote a ten-page poem in reaction to it, tinkered at the poem off-and-on for about eight months, and finally junked it. I retained a vague intention of doing something with the novel, however, and in 1971 or '72 typed out nine pages of fragments from the poem and loosely related journal entries. At the time I was thinking in terms of a series of poems by or about the characters in *Nightwood*—and in fact wrote one such poem, *Nora's Journal.* But by March 1973 I had settled on O'Connor as the speaker, and Paris during the 1939–40 "Phoney War" as the setting, for a poem of perhaps forty pages. I had read a number of novels, autobiographies, and histories related to Paris in the '30s, as well as books on the psychology of violence, and gradually all these materials began to come together. In June, at The MacDowell Colony, I continued to do background reading; I kept a pad at hand for anything that might trigger O'Connor's voice. In July I went to Paris, like James Michener establishing "locale"—and spent two weeks sick in bed. On returning I went to Yaddo, where for the first week I experienced an almost neurasthentic blocking of the faculties: whether reading or writing I could not comprehend units longer than one sentence. The condition passed and my stay turned incredibly productive. I did the first draft of *Bad Traveler* and began to envision a very large collection of separate monologues by O'Connor. Then there was another interruption, from October until April 1974, when I did almost no work on the poems. That April, after being fabulously ill with some sort of flu, I went to Florida to recuperate at a friend's home. It was there that *Bad Traveler* took final form.

The point of all this chronology is that this poem is but one in a long sequence, and that the sequence has been slow to evolve. (It is also that I worked on *Bad Traveler* after two periods of illness, a fact reflected in the imagery.) The sequence now stands at over 100 pages and will probably go ten or twenty more; its most recent working title is *The Idiot Princess of The Last Dynasty.* Although *Bad Traveler* may not be stylistically representative of the whole, it does illustrate one way I have worked and am working from accumulated scraps.

I started at Yaddo by reading through typed pages of poem fragments, notebooks, and my Commonplace Book. This last is a huge collection of quotations and snippets from things I read, anything from single words to long philosophical and descriptive passages. I no longer have the evidence, but I suspect I wrote a number of related passages and bits of fact on a yellow legal pad, hoping something would coalesce. Actually, two poems developed simultaneously, and leftover material turned up later in other monologues. What follows, however, is only the material I believe went into *Bad Traveler.*

From the early group of fragments that went into *Nora's Journal* (1972) I took "The more I chew this stuff, the bigger it gets." From the notebook kept at MacDowell and in Paris (1973) I took:

> Serenade by bulblight
>
> what is the body [but] a bungled account book,
> a defendant and claimant in bankruptcy.
>
> The country of Neurasthenia bordering
> Catatonia, a country of slaves
> without masters
>
> the hearts that beat in broken bodies

I have probably forgotten a number of things I took from the Commonplace Book, but here are a few roots as they appear in the CPB:

What am I? A way of breathing. That spondee is himself.

Yeats said of one of his poems: "I made it out of a mouthful of air."

Lewis operated from (did not necessarily hold), a view of life.
—Hugh Kenner, *The Pound Era*

The liar was finding his truth in the elaboration of his lies.
—Jean-Paul Sartre, *The Words*

I asked him why he thought the whites were mad.
"They say that they think with their heads."
—C. G. Jung, *Memories, Dreams, Reflections*

"Do you believe that white people think with their heads?"
"No, they think only with their tongues."
—Miguel Serrano, *C. G. Jung and Herman Hesse: A Record of Two Friendships*

Guinea worm is "the firey serpent" of the Bible
excreta illnesses: dysentery, cholera, typhoid
the black fly, simulium, causes "river blindness"
Guinea worm grows to three feet in the human body
—Claire Sterling, "Superdams," *The Atlantic Monthly*

Although I cannot find the page(s) on which this and other material was collected, I do have three sheets from a legal pad on which I was trying to find the connections I sensed were there. One, in blue ink, contains a fragment that later went into *Bad Traveler;* the rest of the page contains first drafts of the poem which evolved at the same time. The other two pages are in black ink and contain various first drafts of *Bad Traveler.* All the pieces for that poem have been numbered to suggest a possible ordering. Although I see relations between these pages and the snippets from notebooks and CPB, most of the more promising material has been written for the first time, much the way someone not working from notes would generate a rough draft.

At this point, within hours or days, I went to the typewriter. I used to keep a poem in longhand until the desire to see it typed became unbearable, but recently I find myself working at a machine much earlier. On the other hand, when I reach a real impasse or am making major revisions, I very often go back to working longhand. This typescript hung around until I took it up in Florida in April 1974. I have subsequent typed versions dated 7/10/74, 9/74, 11/16/74, 11/25/74 and 2/7/75. These are what survive of perhaps forty drafts.

I'm not sure when I first saw *Bad Traveler* as a single poem rather than a section of a longer monologue, but the handwritten version becomes simpler, more syntactical and more self-contained in each typescript. New lines and transitions were added longhand or in a machine; gradually the visual form emerged through trial and error. I revise exhaustively: the change of a colon to a period sends me back to the typewriter to see how this shifts the kinetics of the whole. Each revision enables me to hear unrecognized or unexploited sounds and rhythms, and only when I can remember most of the lines exactly as they are written do I begin to trust a piece. I used to scan or count stresses or count syllables, but I rarely do so anymore except to resolve some knotty problem of rhythm or visual arrangement. For all the mystical theories of prosody, the tools of scansion available to the poet are fairly primitive. I am more inclined to trust the ear of memory. Moreover, except in the formal poems I have done, I find the words and the order of the words are established before I have settled on a "shape."

Visual arrangement is an attempt to find an appealing abstract design which best reflects the rhythm, tempo and tone of voice of the poem while pointing to certain doublings within the language. This is at best a compromise, for there are things one can do orally which cannot be conveyed in writing and, conversely, there are layerings of meaning or assocation one can suggest on the page but not outloud. For example, the italicization of the first syllable of "little" (line 7) is an attempt to imitate a specific, conscious and slightly sarcastic verbal mannerism which probably remains unclear just the same. For example, the enjambement of lines 3 and 4 seems to me to contain ironies which cannot be conveyed in performance, since to come to a full stop at the end of line 3 would make nonsense of the sentence; nevertheless, visually "I thought Men think" becomes a unit by itself, suggesting "I thought men think but I was wrong, and I was wrong because men do not think and therefore I was not (am not) thinking."

I honestly do not know how consistent I am in using principles of composition. Certainly the compromise between eye and ear is not always the same kind of compromise. Every poem makes its own peculiar demands. Still, I will try to list a few principles by which I generally work:

1. The poem must have an interesting start; the title and first line are the bait.

2. As many lines as possible should be engaging verbal units out of context: Do the words make unusual noises? Do they conjur a momentary image different from, but related to that of the poem as a whole? Do they make new images or metaphors by putting together in one line parts of other images or metaphors? Do they pose a paradox or seem to contradict the sense of the syntax of which they are a part? Do they work with or against the action by tripping the reader into the next line, coming to a full stop, etc.?

3. The succession of lines should do some of the above without busying-up the page too much, without botching the rhythm, and without needlessly obscuring the syntax.

4. Words at the beginnings and ends of lines often receive extra visual and oral emphasis, though they may not if the enjambement is mainly intended to keep the reader moving down the page; in any case, articles, conjunctions and prepositions should almost never end lines.

5. The preposition "of" makes a weak beginning or ending for a line, although often enough one must choose one position or the other.

6. Metaphors linking an abstract and a concrete noun with "of" are best avoided.

7. Since most poems approximate speech or thought, and since people rarely speak or think with semicolons, semicolons are best avoided.

8. Commas can often be omitted from the ends of lines.

9. Despite the implications of the last two points, most poems benefit from extremely careful and precise punctuation; our language has wonderfully subtle conventions for conveying shades of meaning, tempos, tones of voice and degrees of emphasis. It seems silly not to use them. At the same time, it is best to simplify punctuation as much as possible without losing precision, and sometimes it is best to omit all marks.

10. Choosing a word is like choosing a tie: however attractive it is by itself, it may clash with the ensemble. Then there are times when one needs to be flashy or vulgar.

11. Don't explain away a line which has an authority of its own, even if the line may puzzle the intellect—i.e., don't write for people more interested in understanding a poem than experiencing it. This is not the same as being willfully difficult or obscure, which is merely tiresome.

12. The poem must of course end, but it needn't end with a punchline. The conclusion should lure the reader back to the beginning.

13. Every poem should be capable of performance, nothing just for performance. The process is a dynamic tension, an interplay, a competition between eye and ear.

14. Finally, Time is the greatest reviser of all. I am rarely in a hurry to see a poem in print, and I find that at least half of my revising happens unconsciously or semiconsciously while I am away from the page. Pound said, "As anyone who has ever made a good job of anything knows, the last 2% of excellence takes more time than the other 98%. That's why art and commerce never savvy one another." I do not understand poets who publish Tuesday's poem on Wednesday and write eight poems a week—Sunday being long enough for two. I do not believe that the first words out of one's mouth are the truest words. I don't believe the people who do.

The following specific comments on *Bad Traveler* are merely hunch. I have selected four stages of the poem, which for clarity I will designate *Notebook* and *CPB* (the materials collected on that hypothetical sheet of legal paper), *A* (the third and last handwritten draft, 8/73), *B* (the second typed draft, 8/73), and *C* (the completed poem, 2/75). Line references are to version *C*. There were, of course, many other stages of revision.

1-2	Notebook	The more I chew this stuff, the bigger it gets
	A	The more I chew this stuff the bigger it gets. I thought "Men think
	C	The more I chew this stuff the bigger it gets.

This sentence probably first caught my attention and sent me looking for "this stuff." Since two poems came out of the assembled salvage, I guess I didn't know whether "stuff" referred to words, lives, loves or something else. Often the first lines are moved or removed, but here they survived exactly as written, with the paradoxical part on line 2 for emphasis and surprise. My reasons for suspending "I thought Men think" have already been explained. The quotation marks were removed, finally, because in another part of the sequence I need to distinguish between O'Connor recalling thoughts and recalling conversation, and I want punctuation consistent throughout the poems.

3-4	<u>CPB</u>	I asked him why he thought the whites were mad. "They say that they think with their heads." "Do you believe that white people think with their heads?" "No they think with their tongues."
	<u>Notebook</u>	The country of Neurasthenia border- ing Catatonia, a country of slaves without masters
	<u>2nd hand- written draft</u>	I thought 'men think with their heads and ~~get~~ ~~vertigo~~ get claustrophobic, so I will think with my tongue for I believed my little trowel...
	<u>C</u>	I thought Men think with their heads and suffer from claustrophobia:

The *Notebook* lines may have suggested the extension of the *CPB* quote. "Vertigo" suggests pride and is wrong for the meaning here; "get" is less precise than "suffer." Line 4 ended with a semicolon until 7/10/74, but a colon (which is a mark of anticipation rather than separation) is more appropriate grammatically and also moves the reader more rapidly to the next line,

5–7 CPB

```
The liar was finding his truth in
  the elaboration of his lies.
```

A

```
I will think with my tongue, I will
  find
truth in the elaboration of lies, I
  will dig
through with this little trowel (in
  my mouth) to the land
```

C

```
I will think with my tongue, I will
find my truth in the elaboration of
  lies,
I will dig through with this little
  trowel
```

All of lines 5–10 went through many changes. The fragment from Jung and its extension in Miguel Serrano's memoir quickly tied up with the Sartre quote. Moreover, since Jung and Blake are associated in my mind, I was led to an image of Blake's Beulah, the state of childhood innocence, in lines 8–10.

8–10 A

of sweet meats where my mother hums
  and waits
to bathe away the coal dust in the
  six rivers
of primary light. ~~But I can see now~~
  ~~all men~~
~~dig with their tongues~~

to wash me behind the
ears in the six rivers
of primary light

B

to the land of sweet meats where my
mother hums
and waits (by the ~~six~~ 4 rivers) to
bathe me in ~~the six rivers~~
~~of~~ primary light.'

C

to the land of sweet meats where my
mother hums
and waits by the four rivers
to bathe me in primary light.

"Sweet meats," more emphatic and more sensual as two words, was written that way from the start. "Coal dust" was again suggested (however unconsciously) by Blake, but it was not part of my image of O'Connor. I was thinking there are six primary colors (*A*), was "corrected" and changed the number to four (*B*). Of course there are only three primaries, as I eventually realized, but I opted for "four rivers" because that number suggests the Jungian/Blakean quarternary and the harmonious interaction of Thinking, Feeling, Sensation, and Intuition. This decision was confirmed for me, very much later, when I recalled the four rivers that flowed out of Eden. (Genesis 2: 10) The cancelled line in *A* was heavy-handed and worse, undercut O'Connor's peculiar claim to accomplishment.

11-14 CPB

excreta illnesses: dysentery,
cholera, typhoid

A

& what did I get for ~~the~~ my
trouble?
Dysentery, Cholera, typhoid, ~~excre-~~
~~tory diseases~~ a medical record
scribbled over my Body like a
bungled account book

& do you know where my tongue lead
me?
Into the kingdom of Cholera, the
dynasty
of Dysentery, the Tyrrany of typhus;
oh I've ~~grown~~ travelled

& what did
my trouble
get me?—

Dysentery, Cholera,
typhoid
& other diseases of
the excreta
A medical record
scribbled

B

And do you know
where my tongue lead me? Into ~~the~~
~~kingdom~~
~~of~~ Cholera, ~~the Dynasty of~~
Dysentery,
~~the tyranny of~~ Typhus. Oh, I've
travelled

C

And do you know
where my tongue led me? Into
Cholera, Dysentery,
Typhus. Oh, I've traveled

Of the various transitions in *A*, I settled on the least rhetorical and most off-hand. A suspended line seemed right from the beginning, since a stanza break would suggest too much of a stop: O'Connor is pausing briefly and reflecting on the previous image, which prods him into the question. Line 11 is broken to give the line a little momentum and to suggest the colloquial "don'tcha know." The attempt to make diseases into countries (*A*) was a discovery suggested by alliteration and visual resemblances: Kingdom/*Cho*lera, *Dyn*asty/*Dysentery*, *Ty*ranny/*Ty*phus. But in typing *B* I realized that simply capitalizing the diseases makes them look like countries. Besides, alliteration is an easy device and the repetition of the motif three times is excessive, indeed preening. The enjambements in 12–14 keep the reader moving and throw added emphasis on the diseases. "Oh, I've traveled," set by itself, momentarily suggests a man bragging.

15-17 CPB

Guinea worm is "the firey serpent"
  of the Bible...
Guinea worm grows to three feet in
  the human body

A

like the Guinea worm—the firey
  serpent of the Bible
if you didn't know it—~~thrived in
 the excreta~~
grown to (a miserable) three feet
  in the human body.

B

like the Guinea worm—the firey
  serpent
of the Bible if you didn't know
  it—and grown
~~a miserable~~ three feet (& miserable)
  in the human body.

C

like the Guinea worm–the Fiery
  Serpent of
the Bible if you didn't know
  it—and grown
three feet and miserable in a human
  form.

I want "Guinea worm" and "Fiery Serpent" linked visually as well as grammatically; putting the serpent in caps and using this spelling, I hope, enhances its mythical stature. Moving "the Bible" to the next line had the added advantage of highlighting "the Bible if you didn't know it" and also enabled me to get "and grown" out to the end of the line where it might better suggest "and groan." "Human body" became "human form" both to echo Blake's "human form divine" and to make a series of slant-rimes: worm, grown, form.

18 So I awoke in a perpetual drizzle

I can think of no guidelines I use for stanza breaks except the obvious (formal conventions, transitions, emphasis, a change of voice or rhythm or point of view, etc.). This break was added late; it gives a shove to a new movement which continues through line 29.

19-21 Notebook The country of Neurasthenia bordering
Catatonia, a country of slaves
without masters

B in the Country of Neurasthenia
bordering
Catatonia, where the natives (occupants) are all slaves
without masters. No one wanted my
passport (looked at/would look
at)

C in the country of Neurasthenia,
bordering
Catatonia, where the occupants are
all slaves
without masters. "Here," I said,
"My passport,"

Though only slightly altered from the *Notebook*, the passage doesn't come into the poem until *B*. Odds are I intended to use it all along, saw a place for it in *A*, and didn't bother to write it in. But I often go back through old journals looking for a missing piece for a poem; that may have happened here. The *Notebook* version has an ineffective repetition of "country." "Natives" was not accurate—anyone in the state of neurasthenia is a naturalized citizen—and I find "occupants" suitably odd and impersonal. "Bordering" is in a border position between lines, which position is enhanced by the comma, and which comma represents a pause that I hear in any case. The enjambement "slaves/without masters" throws emphasis on both halves. The change at the end of line 21, between *B* and *C*, varies the style of the poem by introducing a bit of quotation, and that gives new impetus to the line. It also brings O'Connor forward as a character in his own narration.

22-29 Notebook

what is the body [but] a bungled
  account book,
a defendant and claimant in bankruptcy.

the hearts that beat in broken
  bodies

A

a medical record
scribbled over my Body like a
  bungled account book,
a heart like a defendant in bankruptcy, ~~liver~~ one lung
in debtors prison, a ~~liver~~ belligerent liver
suing for divorce...

B

the medical record scribbled over
my body like a bungled account book:
  one lung
in debtor's prison, a belligerent
  liver
suing for divorce, a stomach
  ~~screeching~~ (argumentative as)
~~like~~ a nest ~~of hungry~~ pelicans,

and my heart a defendant (claimant)
  in bankruptcy.
                    (Here's my passport,
                      I said
tried to   and ~~showed them~~ the
  show them   medical
                    record scribbled over
                    my body like a
                    bungled account Book)

<u>C</u>

and showed them the medical record
scribbled over my body like a
  bungled
account book: one lung
in debtors prison, a belligerent
  liver
suing for divorce, a stomach
argumentative as a nest of pelicans
and my heart a claimant in bankruptcy.
But no one would look at my passport.

There is a second version of the catalog of bodily ills in *A* (not reproduced here), and most of the major revisions have occurred by *B*: some similes become metaphors; the similes and metaphors are assigned their organs. "Bungled" in the *Notebook* suggested "scribbled" (*A*) as an almost palsied extension of sounds, and they in turn led me to "belligerent" and "pelicans." This last is funnier and more grotesque than "birds," and "hungry" as a modifier for "pelicans" seems to me redundant. I can't hear pelicans "screeching," but I can see them being argumentative. "Defendant" is not accurate: the heart is a "claimant in bankruptcy" because the body can no longer meet the heart's demands. The enjambements in lines 24–26 are arranged so that, in addition to the syntactical sense, one gets "account book: one lung," "a belligerent liver in debtors prison" and "a stomach suing for divorce." Visceral anarchy. But the following lines are arranged phrasally to quiet things down before the next stanza.

30-32 <u>first long-hand draft</u>

The permanent condition of mankind,
  said Ahab,
is sordidness. ~~& there is no escape from pain~~
for who knows how hard the worm
  bites?

<u>B</u> & <u>C</u>

"The permanent condition of mankind,"
said Ahab, "is sordidness." For who
  knows
how hard the worm bites?

I want the blunt hopelessness of Ahab's statement accentuated by a stanza break. I do not know if this is, indeed, a quote from *Moby Dick*, though I seem to recall it. Usually I will go to great pains to check facts and don't know why I never have here. Nevertheless, I would not change these lines if I discovered they are not in the novel. The canceled abstraction in the first draft is implicit in the line that follows.

33-37 <u>C</u>

Lay away some
honey on a back shelf, a crock of
rich old bellywash like mead, small
  morsel
of something good, that never
  happened,
against the grieving of the locusts
  on the corn.

These lines also started in the first longhand draft. They went through a great many changes while I was trying to get the taste sensations right. I wanted to suggest simple pleasures without violating O'Connor's ironic character, and this was finally achieved, I hope, by combining "honey," "crock," "mead," "morsel," and "corn" with "bellywash," "something good, that never happened," and by breaking line 34 to suggest "crock of shit." For a long time I wondered if the poem would support the archaic and rhetorical "against the grieving of the locusts on the corn"; finally I decided that, tempered by the last two lines, this vision of an historic blight upon the human condition was the right follow-through to Ahab's statement—and it is consonant with O'Connor's style in *Nightwood.*

37-39	CPB	Who am I? A way of breathing. That spondee is himself. Yeats said of one of his poems: "I made it out of a mouthful of air."
	Notebook	Serenade by bulblight
	A	So this is my song: a couple of mouthfuls of air a serenade by bulblight
	C	That's my song: a couple of mouth- fuls of air, a serenade, by bulblight.

After the fulsomeness of lines 33–37, the poem needs this sardonic and Senecan ending. "Bulb light," written as one word, becomes also "bul-blight": the bulbul is a Persian songbird, which may make O'Connor a blighted Nightingale. The comma in the last line was added in February 1975, as a result of listening to myself read the poem outloud.

There are, of course, many other observations I might make. I have not quoted every stage—even every stage I have copies of—and I have not mentioned each detail of the finished poem, although every detail ought to have involved a conscious or semi-conscious decision at some point. I have said little about sound patterns and rhythms, which I believe are questions of the poet's ear and happen, at first, without premeditation.

Even years later one notices effects he was not aware of. And I do not know if these notes jibe with a reader's experience of the poem. They only express what I think I *was* doing and what I hope the poem *is* doing. No reader will sense all or even most of the allusions and "suggestions" mentioned—a reader who did so would be a grinding pedant, a book-duster, and I'd rather not meet him.

Who then is the audience? Really, there are two quite different audiences. The first is O'Connor's, at the *Café de la Mairie du VIe*, and it comes into *Bad Traveler* only in the overall context of the sequence. Indeed, this poem, by itself, has none of the formal characteristics of a dramatic monologue.

The second audience is any reader of the poem. I'm afraid I don't worry much about who that reader may be. As I've said elsewhere, if someone comes up and complains "I read your poem ten times and I don't understand it," then perhaps the poem works. If it had enough interest, enough music, enough resonance to make someone want to re-experience it ten times—well then it can't be a total failure. But of course one hopes for more than that. If the title and first lines are the bait, the first readings should seduce the reader into a structure of shifting perspectives where each successive experience, however long one remains in the poem and however often one reenters it, is a new experience. I do not write primarily for fellow poets or students or critics, and I have been gratified in the past by the diversity of people who have said they liked my work. On the other hand, I do not write for people who do not read contemporary poetry; I can't imagine many situations in which I would try to explain or justify a poem to someone who reads only best-sellers. The ideal reader, I guess, would be one who loves language, who is attracted by the mystery—the unparaphrasability—of successful poems, and who believes in the basic, decent, high-minded (but not necessarily humorless) seriousness of art, even as he loathes the pomposity of saying so.

Peter Klappert was born in 1942 and spent the best part of his childhood in Rowayton, Connecticut. After studying at Cornell University, he took an M.A. in Renaissance English Literature and an M.F.A. in Poetry at the University of Iowa. He has taught at Rollins College, Harvard University, and New College (Florida); he is currently Writer-in-

Residence at the College of William and Mary. He won the Yale Series of Younger Poets competition with *Lugging Vegetables to Nantucket* (1971) and recently published a second collection, *Circular Stairs, Distress in the Mirrors* (1975). He has received a National Endowment for the Arts creative writing fellowship and been in residence at Yaddo, The MacDowell Colony, and the *Fondation Karolyi* in southern France.

Maxine Kumin

HOW IT GOES ON

Today I trade my last unwise
ewe lamb, the one who won't leave home,
for two cords of stove-length oak
and wait on the old enclosed
front porch to make the swap.
November sun revives the thick
trapped buzz of horseflies. The siren
for noon and forest fires blows
a sliding scale. The lamb of woe
looks in at me through glass
on the last day of her life.

Geranium scraps from the window box
trail from her mouth, burdock burrs
are stickered to her fleece like chicken pox,
under her tail stub, permanent smears.

I think of how it goes on,
this dark particular bent of our hungers:
the way wire eats into a tree
year after year on the pasture's perimeter,
keeping the milk cows penned

until they grow too old to freshen;
of how the last wild horses were scoured
from canyons in Idaho, roped, thrown,
their nostrils twisted shut with wire
to keep them down, the mares aborting,
days later, all of them carted to town.

I think of how it will be
in January, nights so cold
the pond ice cracks like target practice,
daylight glue-colored, sleet falling,
my yellow horse slick with the ball-bearing
sleet, raising up from his dingy browse
out of boredom and habit
to strip bark from the fenced-in trees;
of February, month of the hard palate,
the split wood running out,
worms working in the flour bin.

The lamb, whose time has come, goes off
in the cab of the dump truck, tied to the seat
with baling twine, durable enough
to bear her to the knife and rafter.

O lambs! The whole wolf-world sits down to eat
and cleans its muzzle after.

I will try just impressionistically now to talk about *How It Goes On* got written, with one eye on the questionnaire and one eye on the checklist.

The poem was initiated by a fact: I had of a pair of lambs (Southdown ewes, named Gertrude Stein and Alice B. Toklas), and the older one strangled to death in a freak accident, leaving this one to be disposed of somehow before the winter snow. Up until the very last worksheet the poem was called "The Lambs." This was the theme, but the simple narrative did not seem to be enough to sustain the poem, nor indeed suit my very dark and depressed mood of those winter months. Thus the poem began—it was to be a poem of lambs, of going off to slaughter, and I had intended to make a parallel with the suicide of a close friend. I couldn't do it. It didn't work; the two sets of facts refused to intersect in a sensible way and eventually I discarded everything but the first two stanzas and the ending and put the poem away.

I don't remember how long after, but certainly several weeks, I picked up the worksheets again and began fiddling—you might call it free associating—and what came back into my consciousness was the terrible memory of the slaughter of the wild horses in Idaho. I suppose you might say that for me animals in general and horses in particular represent a kind of lost innocence in our technological society and they often stand as a symbol for mute suffering. And little by little the other details arrived and were fitted together to prepare for the ending, those last two stanzas, which I had had from the very beginning. As is so often the case, the ending seemed quite clear to me before the poem was properly begun.

The poem went through about twenty drafts, if you can call each addition and subtraction on a fresh piece of paper a draft. There's always a lot of material that doesn't fit in and has to be pulled out of the poem. I don't think I ever consciously use anything that can be called a principle of technique. It is hard to answer a lot of the items on the checklist because these items seem to me to presuppose a much more conscious process of creation than I am aware of. Indeed, I am afraid to inquire too closely because I don't want to meddle with whatever it is that happens, whatever it is the muse brings forth. Obviously, though, I rely heavily on free association, trying to let everything come that will come and then building around selected items. In the drafts I would say that the poem expanded rather than shrank, the structure stayed quite constant—an informal kind of long rhyming narrative stanza—theme and tone remained constant and practically everything in the first two stanzas as well as the last six lines came through every rewrite almost unscathed. The changes that took place were not so much in the areas you list, but were changes in substance and in direction.

My line breaks are pretty simpleminded. I end-stop fairly strongly and I lean on rhyme when it is feasible, rhyme including a lot of slant or off variations. The rhythm is largely iambic, as I think befits this sort of conversational tone of voice, or melancholy disquisition on the state of things.

As far as sound repetition goes, I don't have any principles. I try to stay away from heavy alliteration and other pyrotechnics because I think they detract from the sense of the poem and blur the imagery.

I would prefer this poem to be read aloud. Never to musical accompaniment.

On metaphor: well, metaphor is the language of poetry, it is the informing thrust of the language and practically everything is a metaphor, while at the same time pretending to be simple everyday speech. I am quite conscious of this and want all of my literal statements of detail to intensify metaphorically when I can.

As for abstract language, etc., you might say damn tootin I try at all costs to avoid. I hate them.

Nothing conscious about sentence structure.

As for reference and allusion, I am leery of literary allusions unless they are pretty readily accessible—biblical, say, or mythic—as I dislike esoterica in poetry. I would especially want to stay away from private allusive stuff directed at fellow poets, I avoid poems that are about the poetic process for the most part, even though they are very tempting to write.

As for principles of structure, I guess I almost invariably follow a sort of psychological order as in dreams or free association.

And I invariably look for a fairly conclusive ending. My pet peeve is the poem that leaves me turning the page in search of its ending—only to discover it *has* ended.

The persona is me. Why not?

I do try to stay far from cliché unless there is a way to shave it.

To appeal to the reader's eye, I like to make stanza breaks that leave a little white on the page; if a poem is all in a block, one hesitates to read it.

The tone of this poem is deliberate, reflective, brooding.

Yes, it can be paraphrased, by anybody. I don't think it's very different from my other work unless it is a little darker in tone. I don't think poets can consciously help what they write or what tone they take. I don't visualize any particular reader, I just hope the perfect audience of one is out there somewhere and I don't write for anyone in particular. In fact, I don't even write because I want to, but more because I have to.

Maxine Kumin was born in 1925, grew up in Germantown, Philadelphia, and holds an A.B. and A.M. degree from Radcliffe College. She has published *Halfway* (1961), *The Privilege* (1965), *The Nightmare Factory* (1970), *Up Country* (1972) and *House, Bridge, Fountain, Gate* (1975). She has taught at the University of Massachusetts, Amherst, Columbia University, and Brandeis University and in 1973 received the Pulitzer Prize in Poetry.

Denise Levertov

THE 90TH YEAR

High in the jacaranda shines the gilded thread
of a small bird's curlicue of song—too high
for her to see or hear.
                                        I've learned
not to say, these last years,
"O, look!—O listen, Mother!"
as I used to.
                              (It was she
who taught me to look;
to name the flowers when I was still close to the ground,
my face level with theirs;
or to watch the sublime metamorphoses
unfold and unfold
over the walled back gardens of our street . . .

It had not been given her
to know the flesh as good in itself,
as the flesh of a fruit is good. To her
the human body has been a husk,
a shell in which souls were prisoned.
Yet, from within it, with how much gazing

her life has paid tribute to the world's body!
How tears of pleasure
would choke her, when a perfect voice,
deep or high, clove to its note unfaltering!)

She has swept the crackling seedpots,
the litter of mauve blossoms, off the cement path,
tipped them into the rubbish bucket.
She's made her bed, washed up the breakfast dishes,
wiped the hotplate. I've taken the butter and milkjug
back to the fridge next door—but it's not my place,
visiting here, to usurp the tasks
that weave the day's pattern.
Now she is leaning forward in her chair,
                                        by the lamp lit in the daylight,
rereading *War and Peace*.
                                                      When I look up
from her wellworn copy of *The Divine Milieu*,
which she wants me to read, I see her hand
loose on the black stem of the magnifying glass,
she is dozing.
"I am so tired," she has written to me, "of appreciating
the gift of life."

How did the poem start?
As crystallization of long-experienced situation.

What changes did it go through from start to finish?
Not very many. The third and fourth stanzas did not at first have parentheses around them.

What principles of technique did you consciously use?
The attempt to be sonically and in every other respect as precise as possible, as described in "Some Notes on Organic Form" and in various

essays included in "The Poet in the World." However, the term *conscious use* strikes me as implying a deliberate effort not consistent with my experience of writing, in which intuition or inspiration is a more important factor than anything I could genuinely call *effort.*

Whom do you visualize as your reader?

I don't.

Can the poem be paraphrased? How?

The writer describes the old age of her mother. She tells of early memories, and of the way in which, though a person who has not valued or even approved of sensuality, yet her mother has lived intensely through her sight and hearing, which now are failing. She asserts that it was her mother who first taught her, the poet, to look at the world of nature—whether at flowers, close up, or clouds, way above the back gardens of the street where they lived. Returning to the present, the little tasks of the mother's daily life are described. The jacaranda tree places the scene in a southern or even subtropical locality. The daughter lends a hand, but she is only visiting and feels it would be inappropriate to take over too many chores. When the old lady reads it is of war and peace. . . . But she falls asleep. She has to read with a magnifying glass these days. The daughter is reading Teilhard de Chardin at her instigation. Here too the title is meaningful: the Divine Milieu could mean the afterlife but does in fact—as with all of Teilhard de Chardin—deal with life on earth (and of course "The Kingdom of God Is Within You" is a Tolstoyan concept and she is reading Tolstoy). The last sentence is too plain to be paraphrased. Is the preceding passage (here, above) a paraphrase? Not line by line, but more or less. So yes, it can be done; but is not, of course, very interesting. And since the poem is not obscure it does not seem *necessary* or *useful* to paraphrase it, except for the special purpose of a questionnaire, i.e. so that it will be possible to compare the answers of a number of poets to a set of identical questions.

How does this poem differ from earlier poems of yours in (a) quality (b) theme (c) technique?

This is an unanswerable question! How does your face differ from any other face? If the writer had only written, say, three other poems in his or her life, it might be possible to answer the question—or if the poem chosen represented a marked break with whatever the poet had written before. Not otherwise.

Checklist

1. Was this poem initiated by (1) free-association, (2) by means of an epigraph, (3) by answering the needs of an occasion, (4) by deciding on a theme and seeking to embody it, (5) by reaction to a strong emotion, (6) or by other means?

A: By the third and fifth, I suppose one could say.

Did this poem (or a part of it) first occur to you as (1) a picture, (2) a a rhythm, (3) a cluster of sounds, (4) a statement, (5) a comparison, (6) other?

A: First and third—but more than that, because as stated above it was (is) a distillation of long and complex experience.

When you were writing the poem, did you imagine any particular person or persons listening to it or arguing with it? If so, who?

A: No.

2. How many drafts did the poem go through?
What intervals of time elapsed between the drafts?
Did the poem shrink or expand?
Did the structure change? How?
The theme? How?
The tone? How?
Which lines remained unchanged? Why?
Of those lines which changed, did the changes fall more in the area of rhythm, sound, imagery, denotation, connotation, other? Why?

A: Two drafts, roughly speaking; i.e., from first pencil scrawl to legible ink, from ink to typescript, then possibly a retyping, with minor changes made in that process.

3a. On what principle or principles did you lineate the poem? Are alternative lineations possible?

A: I have written extensively on lineation and don't feel inclined to try to recapitulate here.

3b. On what principle or principles did you provide stanza or paragraph breaks? Are alternative breaks possible?

A: Same for stanza spaces. No alternatives possible once firm decision has been arrived at.

3c. What rhythmical principle did you use? Iambic, accentual, syllabic, speech cadence, the cadence of idea groups, the cadence of a particular emotion, the cadence of a bodily rhythm, other?

A: The cadence of the thinking-feeling process.

3d. On what principle or principles did you use sound repetition (end or internal): exact rhyme, assonance, alliteration, consonance, onomatopoeia, phonetic intensives, other?

A: See answer to 3(a).

3e. Would you prefer this poem to be read silently, aloud, to musical accompaniment?

A: Aloud.

3f. On what principles did you use the metaphorical process (conventional metaphor, simile, symbol, etc.; surrealism; or literal statement of details implying metaphor)? Or did you consciously avoid metaphor? Or did you unconsciously achieve metaphor by using literal details in such a way that they implied metaphor?

A: The last, if the word *semiconscious* is substituted for *unconscious.*

3g. Did you consciously avoid or seek abstract language, esoteric language, "poetic" diction, or any other specific kind or mannerism of diction? Did you consciously avoid or seek any pattern or mannerism of sentence structure, such as questions, imperatives, direct address, series, parenthetical expressions, fragments, other?

A: As an experienced artist I can't help saying, even if it sounds arrogant, that I don't *have* to "consciously avoid or seek" these types of diction—I intuitively use what seem to me the right words. If they don't seem quite right at first I continue to feel out and listen within myself for the words I want. I do not have to refer to anyone else's standards.

3h. On what principles did you use reference and allusion: conventional historical and literary reference and allusion, personal reference and allusion recognizable by only a small group of friends or fellow poets, contemporary reference and allusion recognizable by the public at large, other?

A: One's feeling about some particular material would cause one to reach for particular structures of *syntax* that would be expressive of that material (i.e., would constitute the inscape of one's relation to the raw material, of raw material plus response—that Gestalt). The question of whether such syntax—or, more broadly, of structures of *allusion,* reference, tone, etc., etc., etc., might or might not be familiar, common, esoteric, and so forth, seems to be a separate one, involving the ethics of elitism versus accessibility—and that is a matter about which every poet must search his or her conscience in relation to each new poem, rather than adopting a fixed position, I think. As far as possible I myself would like to maintain a fairly constant balance between aesthetic and humane needs or demands that occur in the life of a writer. I don't want to sacrifice one to the other but to reconcile the two—and I believe it is possible. I also believe that it is often not the fault of the artist but of the society (and its educational shortcomings) that much aesthetically sound work appears, without intrinsically being so, to be elitist.

3i. By what principles did you structure the poem? A familiar prose structure such as cause and effect, thesis-amplification, question-answer, or a psychological order as in dreams or free-association? Other?

A: A psychological order would be the closest of these terms.

3j. Did you consciously avoid or seek an open-ended conclusion, a firmly conclusive ending, a climatic or anti-climatic ending, other?

A: No.

3k. Is the persona in the poem yourself, a part of yourself, other? Why did you use this persona?

A: Myself and my mother are the people in the poem. I would find it pretentious to speak of them as personae.

3l. How did you use cliché in writing this poem? Avoid it altogether, incorporate recognizable cliché phrases with a new twist, exaggerate and so satirize clichés, other?

A: I don't know about this poem, but I sometimes like to incorporate clichés unabashedly, if they are not *too* obvious—partly to maintain a fairly idiomatic tone, partly to salvage them, for every cliché was once a viable folk-observation, after all.

3m. By what principles did you appeal to the reader's eye in arranging the poem on the page? Or did you make no conscious attempt to appeal to his eye?

A: The appearance of the poem is a purely secondary effect, as accidental as the visual effect of a musical score.

3n. How would you describe the tone of this poem? Nostalgic, satiric, reflective, ambivalent, other? What factors most conspicuously create this tone? Did you create it deliberately?

A: I suppose *reflective*. . . . The nature of the material makes this inevitable and there is no need for any deliberate effort.

5. If it cannot be paraphrased by a prose statement, why not?

If it can, give that paraphrase and explain what aspects of the poem are necessarily omitted in the paraphrase.

If a person who had had no experience with poetry written since World War II were confused by this poem, what steps would you take to help him read it?

A: An account of it can be given, as I did on an earlier page—but the poem itself has its own sounds, its own diction, its own pace, and its images; and these can only be experienced by reading (or hearing) the poem itself, not by reading or hearing something *about* it.

To help an inexperienced poetry reader to experience this (or any other) poem I would first explain that a poem *is* a sonic, sensuous, event and not a statement or a string of ideas, though it may incorporate a statement; also that he or she should try to be open to phanopoeia (having first explained what phanopoeia is). I would then try to get them to *listen* to it a number of times. If there were words or allusions they did not understand I would explain them, e.g., *jacaranda* or who wrote *The Divine Milieu* or *War and Peace* (also I might point out that these are long and/or heavy books for an old lady of ninety who doesn't see very well to be reading—and I'd make them notice it says *re*reading *War and Peace*). But at the same time I'd point out that none of these things are secrets, and that anyone could look the words and titles up in reference books at the public library.

Addenda

Diction: My usual practice is to frankly and unashamedly use my normal vocabulary, with whatever may be its peculiarities (e.g., anglicisms, archaisms, rare words) and limitations. Written *syntax* may differ from the sloppiness I share with most people in speaking—and does of course eliminate the um's and er's of speech—but the *diction* of my poems is no different from what I would use in a letter or a diary (unless I were writing with conscious limitations of vocabulary to someone semi-literate, or to a young child, or someone who did not know much English).

Metaphor: The use of figurative speech should not really be a stumbling block to a person unused to reading poetry, since the least educated people the world over tend, like poets, to naturally use figurative language themselves. Of course, some of the people one might meet who were having difficulty understanding poetry would be those who are not strictly speaking uneducated but whose education has been so abstract in its emphases that they have lost touch with common speech as well as with poetry. One of the special potentials of poetry is to reawaken the imaginative faculty which makes folk speech so vivid.

In this poem there are two figurative phrases which could puzzle a person whose imaginative power of association is undeveloped: (1) the visualization of the bird's song as a gilded thread, which comes about not only as simile but because of the glint of gold on the edge of leaves and seeds and on threads of cobweb up in the tree: these have seemed to me the visual equivalents of the bird's fine high song.* And (2), the mention of the clouds as "sublime metamorphoses" unfolding over the back yards, without the word *cloud* being actually used. As I retyped this poem to send it to

* And so, if a reader were baffled, one could of course explain; but really what would be indicated would be a longer process of re-education so that the associative, figurative imagination would be stimulated (or restimulated, since children probably have it until it is inhibited) so that not just this, but other tropes, might begin to be readily accessible to him or her.

you, I decided this allusion really was confusing and so I added the word "or," as you can see. I don't *want* to use the word *cloud*, for I want the impact of "sublime metamorphoses" to occur unmediated by the stock response of the reader to "cloud," a response which might be a memory image of a particular cloud or clouds, or a comic-book shorthand "cloud" consisting of a scalloped-edged blob, but would in any case be likely to be static, whereas I want to invoke the kinetic. Without "or," however, despite the semicolon the syntax might suggest that I am still speaking of flowers (tall ones, maybe, such as tree-blossoms or high-growing vine-flowers like clematis) so I conceded that it had to be clarified and I think the "or" does it, without significantly altering the rhythm, tonal structure, or pace.

Sense: In my account, or semiparaphrase above, I have failed to say that I feel the poem *celebrates*, and does not merely reflect elegaically. As I retyped it I re-experienced the meaning of it, which I think concerns courage and vitality as well as decline and weariness. It is a tribute more than it is a lament.

Denise Levertov was born in England; educated privately; came to the United States in 1948. Formerly married to the writer Mitchell Goodman, she has one son, Nikolai. She has taught at Vassar College, University of California at Berkeley, MIT, etc., and is currently teaching at Tufts University in Medford. The author of many books, her most recent is *The Freeing of the Dust* (1975).

Lou Lipsitz

CONJUGATION OF THE VERB, "TO HOPE"

I hoped
—the night came anyway

I hoped
—the night came anyway

Is this the way to
do it?

No. Begin again.

I hoped,
today.

I will still hope,
tomorrow.

One day,
I will risk everything.

How did the poem start?

I was working away on my usual daily routine—preparing political science classes, going through the mail, etc.—and decided to do some writing. In the back of my mind were some unresolved issues about my own past, erotic attachments, feelings of constraint I found in myself and that it seemed difficult to overcome. I started several poems that day as I had on some previous days and then "out of nowhere" this particular idea struck me: a poem on the pattern of the conjugation of a verb, as if in a foreign language. For me it contained the feelings of constraint and structure and a kind of "reaching out" that I was in fact feeling at the time.

What changes?

Very little. I played with several of the lines, experimenting with different arrangements of the words. But the basic sense of the poem, the short, two-line segments, were there from the start.

Technique?

This poem is deeply indebted to the Eastern European poets I enjoy reading, particularly Zbigniew Herbert—and then also the American poet Charles Simic. There's a conscious understatement about it and also a kind of conversation within the poem. Herbert has several poems of a similar sort, if not exactly the same. I had no conscious "poetic" principles in mind while writing. But given the idea of a verb conjugation, the form seemed fairly straightforward.

The Reader?

I don't know. Anyone, but especially a person sensitive to his own limitations, or worrying about life's possibilities. Also, other poets and friends. I read it to a high school class, and they seemed to like it better than any others; no doubt, verb conjugations strike close to home. Let me add that the roots of that conjugation idea go back to my own anxieties and doubts when I first had to learn a foreign language and had a very intimidating teacher, back in the seventh grade.

Paraphrase?

Doubt it. Of course the inner idea of hesitation or failure, to be followed by a new, more hopeful attempt, is not exactly new—say, try try again. But I somehow don't think that conveys or evokes the emotions involved. It's the notion of constraint or structure implied by school discipline and then the breaking free as with the strange turn of an irregular verb. In Spanish the verb *ir* (to go) becomes in conjugation, *voy* "I go."

Differ?

Very different from most of my poems, but like a few of them. It's much more self-contained, less imagistic, much more understated, matter-of-fact almost. I've written a few others along this line, all influenced by Herbert's poetry—which has a pleasant, although slightly resigned, sanity to it.

Lou Lipsitz, born in 1938, grew up in Brooklyn, New York. He attended the University of Chicago 1954–57, then worked for a year as a journalist and spent two years at Yale, studying political science. From 1961 to 1964 he taught at the University of Connecticut, Storrs; since then, at the University of North Carolina, Chapel Hill, where he is a professor of political science. He has published *Cold Water* (1967) and has been included in numerous anthologies. He received a National Endowment Writer's Grant in 1968. His new book of poems, *Reflections on Sampson*, will be published in 1977.

Cynthia Macdonald

THE STAINED GLASS MAN
for Donald Hirst

Dresden, October 3rd 1928

Professor Oakes Ames
Director, Botanical Museum
Harvard University
Cambridge, Mass.

Dear Professor Ames, It seems easiest in this very long letter to separate the description of the glass work from the more personal part; so I have done this, and will tell you about the making of the models later. I have been out to Hosterwitz, half an hour by auto and have passed two whole afternoons, long ones, looking at the models. Then I inspected the work room and its contents and was shown all the great improvements made by the Blaschkas in the house since his marriage.

I have found, my dear Miss Ware, a new way of coloring the glass
Since you were here in 1908. I use no surface paint at all;
See this budding rose. You could leave it on the roof a year;
The shading would not change a micrometer. I know because I have
Done exactly that. The color is in the glass. Layer after
Layer I build it up. Not one, but many, like light itself.

I think he said he no longer paints at all except with the powdered colored glass which he can anneal.

Here a sheet of cashew lake and one of violet beneath the luteous
Combine to form yellow of high intensity and brilliance,
A requirement of this liliaceous group. Their cups contain
The sun of early June, radiant, but with a touch of cooling blue.

I am covered with leaves. Leaves I have made.
They stick to me, annealed by the heat of
Loneliness. I am covered with glass
Of my own making. Leaves. The leavings.
The parting. The final leaving. The left-overs.

The green of this ligulate corolla contains a drop of milk,
A happy accident, the accident for which a long apprenticeship
Prepares one. One day I ate, or at that moment drank would be
More accurate, my lunch while searching for a way to soften color
At the junction of the blade and petiole. You ascertain
The rest without the tale. You see the milky green.

He is just as modest and honorable as he ever was, but now he has a sense of his own worth, his own unusual force of intellect and character; and there is everything to justify that.

I regret this group of fungi is not complete for I can
Only do them as and when I can obtain the specimens.
My old gatherer died at sixty-eight three months ago and then
The new one died of tasting, though I warned him. The smuts and rusts
I grow here, but the mushrooms I must leave to someone else.

Rusting. Rusting. Spores through skin.
Molds forming skin. Molds.
Molds stiffening. The marriage mold becomes
The man. The armor.
Clost to cupid's sound, but further than
The new moon shining: a cutlass,

A scimitar, a blade,
Slashing the air between us,
Cutting, parting.

The molds are wonderful, and I think you will be delighted with them all, but, of course, I know nothing of fungi.

The problem with Laver is it spoils when removed from the sea.
Its purples drain. It browns.
Fluidity becomes flaccidity. So I have had to work looking
Through the double barrier of glass and water. You would say
Both are clear, but clarity is an illusion.

Mr. Blaschka's head and bearing are very expressive and I wished I could catch a photograph of his profile as he stood for a few minutes, a plaque with a model on it held with both hands. His whole expression of absorbed, concentrated study was worth keeping, had it been possible.

Now, the land grasses. The lemma here, the lower bract—
Enclosing as it does the flowers in the spikelet of the grass—
Is smooth and tousled. I see a field of wheat within
This single stalk before me as I work.

Transplanting them to the museum is
The next-to-sharpest agony. Another
Parting. Worse by far than
The splinter of glass
Under the nail. It is the pain of sudden
Feeling come too late. O, Lilianne,
I dream you have not left.
I keep the Boecklin *Flora* over the mantel.
The keeping, the keeping. The dreaming.
The parting.

You are most kind: supper and *Der Freischütz* are indeed
A lure. But I must put the next-to-final touch on the asparagus.

These stalklets will have lost their velvet by tomorrow.
Now the flowerets curve in like cat's claws holding to
The branch. There is a desperation of the parts within the flame.

It troubles me very much that he and his wife cannot come over to see his life's work now that you have the models so beautifully arranged, and he looks so eager and pathetic when I describe the mise en scène.

This is the laver where I wash away the residues before
I trace the veins. Bronze. Because a brazen vessel clarifies
The light without refraction. Now, I will show you how
I do the leaf annealing. Cups of paraffin. I light them till
The flames drive at each other. This lever moves the apparatus.
The tips in first, then, bit by bit, the whole until it all turns
Red, as the after-image of a leaf stared at in sunlight.
And then the turning and the twisting for vein and edge.

Lilianne, I tell this all to you.
I speak to you whether I am silent
Or talk aloud. The rest
Is only the fragment of the whole. Like half
A phrase of the Schubert we heard
The night you left.
Or like that single leaf. There.
On the red crepe pillow.
Single.
The turning, the twisting.
Single. The seeing. The parting.

The strawberries were fascinating—plants, fruit and molds: also the result of frost on the developing fruit.

The strawberries, my strawberries.
Clustered like the nipples of Venus.
Of Aphrodite. To suck. To bite.
I picture babies crying at the case,

Their milk need roused by my rosy artifacts.
I picture you,
Lilianne, holding the baby.
Smiling, Rocking. Holding.

My last visit to Hosterwitz was most happy. Miss Niklason went with me and enjoyed it as much as I did. Supper was excellent, informal and pleasant, and I regaled them with all the Museum gossip I could think up. Mr. Blaschka did some leaf work again and Miss N. felt, just as I do, that it is a great experience to watch that man at work. His whole head and hands are a study, and he worked until it was about dark without turning on his electric light. She also felt that the work was enough to wear anyone's nerves to madness.

You said you would not have me.
Encased in glass. Encasing.
Now I make what I make from
The material of myself.
The leaving, the parting.
Then the loving.
Within my case I drown.
The leaving. The parting. The living.
Drawn out. Long drawn out. What works
Is work. Look at me.
It is all clear.

I know it has given him fresh courage to see me. I have been out there five times and I am sure that I accomplished what I came for. Please remember me to Louis and, with most cordial greetings to you and Mrs. Ames,

Very sincerely yours,
MARY LEE WARE

This poem's generation interests me particularly because it was my first "willed" poem. My poems usually start as a combination of feeling and idea that has sufficient intensity to transform itself into two or three phrases. This transformation precedes a conscious decision to write. But I willed *The Stained Glass Man*, determined I would write it as a companion poem to *The Stained Glass Woman*. I knew I didn't want a masculine version of a poem about a woman made out of stained glass, a stained glass mate for her. But if not that, what?

Because our family moves so often, we all have to do a lot of sorting out of accumulations, a lot of removing. My daughter, Jennifer, was going through just such a sorting process and asked me if I'd like to keep a booklet she planned to throw away. It described how the famous collection of glass fruit and flowers at a museum in Cambridge, Massachusetts, was made. The techniques of Rudolf Blaschka, the glass craftsman, were detailed in a letter written by the collection's patroness, Mary Lee Ware.

Three months later, at Yaddo, I wrote the poem. I knew I would incorporate sections of the actual letter into it as I am fascinated by shifts of diction and perception that occur over a relatively short period of time; the letter was written less than fifty years ago. The shifts interest me because of the difference in the sound of the prose and because of the illumination we get about what was taken-for-granted (Miss Ware's almost feudal sense of her own benevolence) and what was not (the mention of the Blaschka's *electric* light).

I have written a number of dramatic monologues. The form is so natural to me that Rudolf Blaschka's voice, giving the guided tour, came unbidden. It is more formal and more sentimental than the voices of characters in my other monologues, probably because Blaschka was German and was speaking in 1928. His voice was used in counterpoint to Miss Ware's. For a time, the poem looked as if it would consist of that counterpoint.

But I felt constrained by how little of himself Blaschka would reveal to her. I decided another strand was needed. My first attempt was to have Blaschka talking to his wife. That didn't work. He refused to say much to her either, no matter how I tried to force him to. No wonder: he knew about his secret, his relationship with Lilianne even though I still did not. Finally, his interior monologue developed. And with it the scenario of finding and losing a lover, which related to that of *The Stained Glass Woman*. Both the glass man and woman use almost the same words. She: "I protect myself/With the material of myself." He: "Now I make what I make/From the material of myself." I did not try to find a phrase in the first poem that could be used in the second. Nor did I speculate on why the phrase changed when he used it. Now, though, the female/male distinction seems an accurate one.

The length of Blaschka's external monologue was determined by my decision that the internal voice should not come in immediately, that there should be more of the letter and the external voice than of the internal, and that the internal required a certain amount of time to speak so that its scenario would be natural to it, not forced, yet have a somewhat obsessive quality. These decisions sound neat now. But they were not, and developed only as the work developed.

For a number of years I have been interested in writing poems that are interrupted repeatedly by insertions of prose, lists, or just a very different-sounding poem (for example, "Inventory" and "Instruction from Bly" in *Amputations*, and "The Amherst, Houston, New York Triangle" and "The Present" in *Transplants*). I like the resonances that reverberate in the spaces between the sections. Perhaps these resonances are similar to those which occur in the space which is lept over in Robert Bly's description of poetic leaping. But even if the leap is over a canyon, the ground is joined somewhere. The difficult joinings in *The Stained Glass Man* were those between the internal monologue and whatever preceded it. I worked back and forth between these sections for a number of weeks. So they were all somewhat changed by each other.

It is obvious that in the external monologue I constructed formally formulated sentences with long lines set in rectangles, and in the internal monologue, repeated words in fragmented sentences set in a wavering pattern. The different construction seemed to mirror the difference in feeling between the two.

After I'd been working on the poem for a while, I discovered that I had been using an unusual number of words with "l" sounds in them. So I decided to emphasize that sound even more, a decision which influenced some of the content of the poem. For example, the word laver is used twice near the beginning of a stanza, and the stanzas grew out of the two meanings of that words, a word which I had put on a list of possibly usable "l" words. Many of these were in my vocabulary, but I looked in the dictionary for technical words such as luteous, ligulate, petiole. I don't remember whether Lilianne got her name before or after the decision.

I've answered questions 1, 2, 3, and 6 in the previous statement. As to question 4, I visualize a few close friends as my "reader." Three are poets, one is a painter, one a political scientist, one a doctor, one a folk singer. But most of my poems are actually written to one person; they are direct communications, thought not necessarily delivered communications. That one person may or may not be one of my envisioned readers. On the level of the one person to whom they are written, the poems are messages. But I do not intend them to be private; I am certainly aware, at least during the revising stage, of the larger, though still small group, that makes up my "reader."

As to question 5, *The Stained Glass Man* can be described: it is a poem about a man who made glass flowers and fruit, who discusses how he makes them, etc. It cannot be paraphrased, I hope. A poem must be more than the sum of its describable parts. As Blaschka says about his work: "Layer after/ Layer I build it up. Not one, but many, like light itself."

Cynthia Macdonald was born in New York City, and except for four years in Southern California, spent her childhood there. She received a B.A. from Bennington College, married, had two children, and realized her ambition of becoming an opera singer. In 1961, after she had been singing for six years, she began to write poetry. She continued to write and sing while following her husband to Vancouver, B.C., and Tokyo. On her return to the New York area, she enrolled in the graduate writing program at Sarah Lawrence College and received an M.A. She has been a faculty member there for six years and is now a visiting professor at The Johns Hopkins University. She has published *Amputations* (1972) and *Transplants* (1976). In 1973, Ms. Macdonald received a grant from the National Endowment for the Arts; she has had two Yaddo residence grants and, in 1976, a CAPS grant.

Sandra McPherson

A COCONUT FOR KATERINA

Inside the coconut is Katerina's baby. The coconut's hair, like Katerina's brown hair.
Like an auctioneer Katerina holds the coconut, Katerina in her dark fur coat
covering winter's baby, feet in the snow. Katerina's baby is the milk
and will not be drinking it.

Ropes hanging down from the trees—are they well ropes? Ropes on a moss
wall. Not to ring bells but used for climbing up and down
or pulling, I mean bringing. Anchor ropes on which succulent ropy sea-plants grow.

And floating like a bucket of oak or like a light wooden dory, the coconut bobs,
creaking slowly, like a piling or a telephone pole with wet wires
downed by a thunderstorm over its face.

This baby's head, this dog's head, this dangerous acorn is the grocer
of a sky-borne grocery store where the white-aproned grocer or doctor imprints it
with three shady fingerprints, three flat abysses the ropes will not cross.

What of it? There is enough business for tightrope walkers in this jungle.
The colonizers make a clearing
for a three-cornered complex of gas-stations, lit with a milky spotlight
at night.

And here we dedicate this coconut to Katerina. We put our hand
on the round stomach of Katerina. We put our five short ropes of fingers on the lost
baby of Katerina and haul it in to the light of day and wash it with sand.

Coconut, you reverse of the eye, the brown iris in white, the white center
in brown sees so differently. The exposed fibrous iris,
the sphere on which memory or recognizing must have latitude and longitude
to be moored

or preserved in the big sky, the sea's tug of war. The tugging of water
held in and not clear. Lappings and gurglings of living hollows half filled,
half with room
for more empty and hopeful boats and their sails.

DRAFT 1

```
Women pat each others' stomachs
like the tops of childrens heads.
So, while you were talking in English
   about Greeks teaching your class
you miscarried and went on talking
```

DRAFT 2

```
Inside the coconut/is Katerina's baby/The coconut's
  hair/ like Katerina's, brown hair
Like an auctioneer / Katerina holds the coconut,   Kat.,
  in her dark fur coat
                             feet in the
covering winter's baby ~~white as~~ snow/ Kat's baby is the
  milk
  will not
I ~~won't~~ be drinking it
```

Ropes ~~hang~~ hanging down from the trees/ ~~or~~ — are they well ropes?/
  ropes, ~~in~~ — on a ~~dark~~ moss
~~place~~ wall anyhow/not ~~ringing~~ to ring bells/ but used for climbing
up & down or unclimbing
(or) pulling, I mean bringing/anchor ropes ~~from~~ on which lithe
  ropy seaplants grow

and floating like a bucket of oak or like a light wooden
  dory the coconut bobs
creaking slowly, like a piling or a telephone pole with
  wet wires
downed by a thunderstorm over its face

Within the coconut a fine suet the birds line up for
  birds in row on row
like ~~fishing~~ yachts tied to port a fan of birds like the fan
  of a palm leaf or the spray
of a huge bunch of green palm leaves [splaying / spreading / bursting] from the
  brown fist of the trunk

This then is the concoction in the coconut the goats
  milk caramelizing
in a brown angora wasp's nest the aerial uterus with
  aerial roots
this steamy tropical sponge will surely lick up like a
  rope swallower or ~~is~~ make it

~~make~~ ascend ~~and~~ haughtily like a cobra, ½ calm jewelled
  gulf ½ waterspout

~~anyway~~ This baby's head: this dog's head: this dangerous
  acorn is the grocer

of a sky-borne grocerystore which the white-aproned
  grocer or doctor has imprinted
with 3 gruesome fingerprints 3 flat abysses the ropes
  will not cross
~~but~~ what of it there is business enough for tightrope
  walkers/suspension bridge
cablers/ & barefoot log-bridge crossers in this jungle
  the colonizers make a clearing
for a 3-cornered complex of gas-stations lit with a
  milky white spotlight
at night

and here we've/I've dedicated this coconut to
  Katerina *we* I put *our* my hand
on the round stomach of Katerina *we* I put *our* my 5 short
  ropes of fingers on the lost
baby of Katerina & haul it in/(in)to the light of day
  ~~the daylight of the nut meat~~ *+ wash it with sand*
~~the hollow in the sand the sun cleans~~
~~the sun cleaned~~
~~and (illegible) off with sand & brush (illegible)~~
  ~~coconut (illegible)~~
~~sunbleach the fish grayness~~
coconut the reverse of the eye/ the brown iris in white/
  the white center
in brown sees so different ~~sees~~ such differences/ the
  exposed fibrous iris
the sphere on which [*sight* memory *illegible*] (illegible) have latitude
  & longitude to be moored

saved in the big sky the sea's tug of war the tugging of
  water held in

```
& not clear   lappings & gurglings of living hollows
  ½ filled
½ with room   for more hopeful boats & their sails.
```

How did the poem start?

Was this poem initiated by free-association, by means of a epigraph, by answering the needs of an occasion, by deciding on a theme and seeking to embody it, by reaction to a strong emotion, by other means?

A: I assigned my class a long period of close observation of a fruit or vegetable. Notes (1–2 pages) on same. I did the assignment along with them. But it unexpectedly combined with an extraordinary event. A woman poet from another country taught my class one day then immediately went off to the hospital with a miscarriage. So the poem began with a double purpose: I regarded it as an exercise in observation and as an attempt to come to grips with an extraordinary human event. I suppose I wanted to make something beautiful to compensate for her tragedy. The poem is totally associative, one metaphor reminding me of the next.

Did this poem (or a part of it) first occur to you as a picture, a rhythm, a cluster of sounds, a statement, a comparison, other?

A: I could visualize it as something which ran from the left edge of the page to the right edge, with no margins. I visualized all its images and simply recorded what I saw.

When you were writing the poem, did you imagine any particular person or persons listening to it or arguing with it? If so, who?

A: My husband would be its first audience. While writing it I felt aided by almost every poet I've ever admired.

What changes did it go through from start to finish?

How many drafts did the poem go through?

A: My husband and certain students here at Iowa liked the first draft so well that they suggested very few changes. I changed two or three words and sent the poem to the *New Yorker*, which soon rejected it, and next to the *American Review*, which also turned it down. A second set of changes on the poem were made while reading it aloud ten times in as many days on the Ohio Poetry Circuit: I could sense audience reaction to confusing or repetitive parts, I also felt some of my phrasing was stilted. *Field* asked for the poem upon hearing it read aloud. Reading it on the page, the editors pinpointed its excesses. After trying to rewrite seven lines in the center of the poem (more description and metaphor), I settled on cutting all of them. The poem appears in *Field* in that final form.

This small number of drafts is very rare for me. The poem was written in one sitting, and revision amounted not so much to rewriting as to cutting, cutting words which did not add to the poetry.

Principles of technique

What principles of technique did you consciously use?

A: Concentration; observation; losing myself.

On what principle or principles did you lineate the poem? Are alternative lineations possible?

A: I thought I was writing a prose exercise and ended up keeping the lines prose length and making the paragraphs stanzas.

On what principle or principles did you provide stanza or paragraph breaks? Are alternative breaks possible?

A: Each line a road on a map, going through many towns, offering about three events or images.

What rhythmical principle did you use? Iambic, accentual, syllabic, speech cadence, the cadence of idea groups, the cadence of a particular emotion, the cadence of a bodily rhythm, other?

A: Images as fast as they could come, things for the senses and cadences for the emotions.

On what principle or principles did you use sound repetition (end or internal): exact rhyme, assonance, alliteration, consonance, onomatopoeia, phonetic intensives, other?

A: Unconscious. I suppose I used sound association to help the poem grow.

Would you prefer this poem to be read silently, aloud, to musical accompaniment?

A: I don't care. (I've seen a couple of my poems danced to and been pleasantly surprised.)

On what principles did you use the metaphorical process (conventional metaphor, simile, symbol, etc.; surrealism; or literal statement of details implying metaphor)? Or did you consciously avoid metaphor? Or did you unconsciously achieve metaphor by using literal details in such a way that they implied metaphor?

A: I made rich use of metaphor, fearlessly switching metaphors in midline, knowing the drive of the poem would hold them together. My metaphors were the world I created out of a wordless and limited object. I trusted both the object and my helpless associations to form a poem and I don't take credit for the poem: the images wrote it.

Did you consciously avoid or seek abstract language, esoteric language, "poetic" diction, or any other specific kind of mannerism of diction?

A: I wanted mostly concrete words, accurate short words which together would have a rich texture like the world.

Did you consciously avoid or seek any pattern or mannerism of sentence structure, such as questions, imperatives, direct address, series, parenthetical expressions, fragments, other?

A: I wanted sentences that would help me get to the next sentence. So I was emphatic in a few places, fragmentary in others, declarative here and there.

On what principles did you use reference and allusion: conventional historical and literary reference and allusion, personal reference and allusion recognizable by only a small group of friends or fellow poets, contemporary reference and allusion recognizable by the public at large, other?

A: I keep my fingers crossed that close readers will understand Katerina lost her baby.

By what principles did you structure the poem? A familiar prose structure such as cause and effect, thesis-amplification, question-answer, or a psychological order as in dreams or free-association? Other?

A: I let the sensuous aspects of the coconut limit the poem. The poem sort of fans out. I wanted to do justice to Katerina and to the coconut. When justice was done, I stopped.

Did you consciously avoid or seek an open-ended conclusion, a firmly conclusive ending, a climactic or anti-climactic ending, other?

A: I wanted the ending to leave room for hope. I felt affirmative; I wanted an image to suggest this.

Is the persona in the poem yourself, a part of yourself, other? Why did you use this persona?

A: I avoided mentioning myself. The "we" is anyone who likes Katerina and cares for her.

How did you use cliché in writing this poem? Avoid it altogether, incorporate recognizable cliché phrases wth a new twist, exaggerate and so satirize clichés, other?

A: I may have used it as relief—something everyone could have thought of, something to give the wild metaphors a common, accessible ground.

By what principles did you appeal to the reader's eye in arranging the poem on the page? Or did you make no conscious attempt to appeal to his eye?

A: I wanted the poem to look big and healthy.

How would you describe the tone of this poem? Nostalgic, satiric, reflective, ambivalent, other? What factors most conspicuously create this tone? Did you create it deliberately?

A: Affirmative, energetic, authorless.

Audience

Whom do you visualize as your reader?

A: No one, as I wrote; everyone now that the poem is written.

Can the poem be paraphrased?

Can the poem be paraphrased? How? If it cannot be paraphrased by a prose statement, why not?

A: It cannot at all be paraphrased. It is all connotation. A real blizzard is better than "it snows."

If a person who had had no experience with poetry written since World War II were confused by this poem, what steps would you take to help him read it?

A: I'd forget his reading it and find out what he knew of life that I don't. If forced to help him, I'd give him a coconut.

The poem in the context of one's other poems

How does this poem differ from earlier poems of yours in (a) quality (b) theme (c) technique?

A: It has longer lines than any poem I've written before. It has more energy than any I've written in years. It has more of an unconscious rhetoric than I've used before. When I wrote it I was extremely unhappy with what I'd been writing for several months previous. This poem renewed my confidence.

Sandra McPherson was born in 1943 in San Jose, California, where she lived for twenty-one years. She was educated at San Jose State College and the University of Washington, then took a job for nine months as a technical writer for Honeywell, Inc., Seattle. After publishing *Elegies for the Hot Season* (1970) and *Radiation* (1973), she taught for two years in the University of Iowa Writers' Workshop. She has received an Ingram Merrill Foundation grant; aid from the National Endowment for the Arts; a Guggenheim Foundation fellowship; the Helen Bullis Award from *Poetry Northwest*; and two prizes, the Bess Hokin award and the Blumenthal-Leviton-Blonder prize, from *Poetry*. She lives in Portland, Oregon.

William Matthews

NURSE SHARKS

Since most sharks have no flotation bladders and must swim
to keep from sinking, they like to sleep in underwater caves,
wedged between reef-ledges, or in water so shallow
that their dorsal fins cut up from the surf.
Once I woke a nurse shark (so named because it was
thought to protect its young by taking them
into its mouth). It shied from the bubbles I gave up
but sniffed the glint the murky light made on my regulator.

My first shark at last. I clenched
every pore I could. A shark's sense of smell
is so acute and indiscriminate that a shark crossing
the path of its own wound is rapt.
Once a shark got caught, ripped open by the hook.
The fishermen threw it back after it flopped
fifteen minutes on deck, then caught it again
on a hook baited with its own guts.

Except for the rapacious great white
who often bites first, sharks usually nudge
what they might eat. They're scavengers and like

food to be dead or dying. Move to show you're alive
but not so much to cause panic, that's what the books
advise. The nurse shark nibbled at my regulator
once, a florid angelfish swam by, the shark
veered off as if it were bored. Its nubbled skin
scraped my kneecap pink, no blood
but the rasped kneecap pink for a week.

Another year I swam past a wallow of nurse sharks asleep
in three feet of water, their wedge-shaped heads lax
on each other's backs. One of them slowly thrashes
its tail as if were keeping its balance in the thicket
of sharks sleeping like pick-up-sticks. Its tail sends
a small current over me, a wet wind.
I swirl around a stand of coral and swim
fast to shore, startling the sharks to a waking frenzy:
moil, water opaque with churned-up sand,
gray flames burning out to sea. Last time I go diving
alone, I promised myself, though I lied.

How did the poem start?

Almost always my poems begin with a small scrap of language—a few words or an image. There were two scraps for *Nurse Sharks:* the word *wallow* and the image of sharks lying on each other like pick-up sticks. Divers who have spent a hundred times more hours than I have in the water say that they dive because the world they enter is strange. No matter how well you come to know it, it isn't your world: you live in air. In a strange world, things are not like themselves because the first way we know strange things is by comparing them to things we already know. The sharks being more like pigs or pick-up sticks than sharks seemed close to the strangeness of being underwater. I was already in the poem.

Another way we deal with what is strange is to accumulate facts. So in two ways, I must have sensed, the poem I had only two scraps from was going to be about curiosity, among other things.

There is curiosity about the strange, the other, that makes me want to dive. This is a curiosity about possible experience: I might go into the water and be among sharks.

Then there is curiosity for information. I might read a lot about sharks, and what I learn could help me be among sharks if I go into the water. Or it could just be part of the information I accumulate, like a pack rat, more because I love to gather such things than because I imagine very clearly how I'd ever use them.

A lot of what I've just described happens intuitively, far more quickly, and by a process far more like trial and error than it sounds when I describe it retrospectively.

The shark's restlessness, his aimless slow circulation, seems to advertise by withholding it how much force he has, how at home he is in the water that is strange to us. When I first learned that most sharks have no flotation bladders, I wondered immediately how they slept. I imagined an exhausted shark sinking deeper into sleep and into deeper, blacker water. I was curious to learn what I could about shark behavior, and I wanted to learn from people who had studied shark behavior long and exactingly enough that they didn't anthropomorphize the shark. But it was the legends about sharks I hoped my shark book would explode that had led me to read the book. And I was already using the metaphors of science to augment my own metaphors. I'd imagined an insomniac shark.

Besides, there is no such thing as "the shark." There are individual sharks, members of distinct species.

I wanted the poem to move by this kind of thinking—assertions and corrections—that resembled the tentative diver's curiosity.

What changes did it go through from start to finish?

As usual, I took out a few lines during my last revision. I wrote *Nurse Sharks* quickly, with one large revision (described in the next section) between first draft and final revision, which often, for me, is like the step described in cookbooks by "Correct for seasoning." Often in an early draft of a poem I say things that, it turns out as I go along, are apparent without my saying them. They're said by implication, or by the poem's pace or shape, and so don't need to be explicit. Such lines are notes to myself. I may have needed them to write the poem, but the poem didn't need them. Its needs and mine are always different. The better the negotiations between them, the better the poem.

What principles of technique did you consciously use?

Most of my technical decisions in writing a poem are made intuitively, the way a basketball player puts a higher arc on his shot when he senses an opponent will jump high enough that the usual arc would result in the shot's being blocked. Such decisions are neither conscious nor unconscious. I suspect they're both.

But if we take "conscious" decisions to mean those we make very deliberately, rather than so swiftly we don't know exactly how they're made, I made such a decision, important to the poem and startling to me. In its first finished draft the poem was in shorter lines. The first line read

Since most sharks have no flotation

and the lines, though they varied in length, were as much shorter throughout the poem as that first line is than the first line of the finished poem. The first version was too choppy. I had written it the way it stood in the first draft more from habit—the length of the first line in the first draft is a comfortable and supple length for me—than from a good negotiation between the poem's needs and mine. My needs—they turned out to be false needs—were to do it in a way I'd already learned, i.e., to be lazy. The poem needed longer lines to accommodate the relaxed, discursive pace I'd use in giving much shark data. The apparent antagonists in the poem are "I" and some nurse sharks. They turn out to be false antagonists, as do the fact-gathering and the experience-gathering curiosities of "I." I needed the longer line to make this second false antagonism have the right weight in the poem.

It was the first time I'd ever made such a revision throughout a poem, but I went back and lengthened the lines; then I made a few small changes required by the new lineation. The poem was better for it.

Whom do you visualize as your reader?

Nobody. I know there will be readers, but I can't know who they will be.

Or, a second possible answer, also true. I visualize as my reader a me who somehow wasn't present when I wrote the poem, and can thus read it as if it were written by somebody else. But this imaginary creature is as plausible as an insomniac shark.

Can the poem be paraphrased? How?

No. To use different language is to say something different. I called the angelfish "florid" because angelfish are brightly colored, like tropical flowers. And because "florid" is often used to describe someone's complexion, and a pink kneecap comes into the poem shortly after the angelfish. And also because "florid" suggests being short of breath, excited, flustered. I could say more about "florid" or any word in the poem. It's not only what a word does in its own place in the poem, but how it bounces and echos off other words. The poem isn't more than the sum of its parts. A sum is still. A poem is more than the *activity* of its parts. If it's alive, you not only can't paraphrase it, you can't even change a word.

How does this poem differ from earlier poems of yours in (a) quality, (b) theme, (c) technique?

Quality. It's better than most of them. Or, I like it more. In an important way, the comparison is impossible. Presuming that I write as well as I'm able at any given time in my writing life, I can turn from a poem and say it's "bad," but not because I am. I was more curious than capable. But I can write "good" poems easily by writing poems I've already learned to write. If I'm not writing as well as I'm able, that's another question altogether.

Theme. I don't think interesting poems have themes. To say to a student that some poem is "about illusion and reality" is to give the student a first and very crude way to think about the poem. That's fine, if it leads into the poem: words, silences, rhythms. But if the idea "theme" becomes a place to stop and look and go no further, like a "scenic overlook" at a park, then it's a useless idea. You have to go in.

Technique. After a poem is finished, technique is how it was done. While poems are being made, it's hard to say anything exact enough to be interesting about technique. It's a kind of responsiveness, really, an alertness to the poem's energies and possibilities. A crucial part of it, then, is one's own accumulated writing experience. A larger part of it is what a poet can learn from others—teachers, contemporaries, the great masters of the past. Indeed, anyone who has helped give the language the shape in which it comes to us. Perhaps technique is an active love of the language.

William Matthews was born in 1942 in Cincinnati. He took a B.A. at Yale and an M.A. at the University of North Carolina at Chapel Hill. With Russell Banks, he co-founded and co-edited *Lillabulero* and Lillabulero Press. He has taught at Wells College, Cornell University, Emerson College, Sarah Lawrence College, the University of Colorado, and the University of Iowa. His books are *Ruining the New Road* (1970), *Sleek for the Long Flight* (1972), *Sticks & Stones* (1975), plus a number of limited editions.

Jerome Mazzaro

AT TORREY PINES STATE PARK

For David Ignatow

The weather here is raw
after the long rain, but the pines, the pines,
spotting both sides of these thin paths
dwarf my dull morning pain
with other flora, classified and tagged
for weekend naturalists.

Divorced from the court fights,
by lore as rich as taught the Papagos
in drought to mash saguaro and
to eat its pulpy fruit,
make butter of the seed and of the juice
a wine, they stand intense.

Their gnarled and twisted limbs,
stately, enduring in this coastal air,
so resemble your own truths, I
sense you here. Though trees, you
write, have not had much to say to your work,
the happiness is pure.

LINER NOTES FOR *AT TORREY PINES STATE PARK*

On my first trip to Southern California in 1974, I was taken to Torrey Pines State Park on a day that included drives through Del Mar and La Jolla. We arrived at the park in late morning. The weather was chilly and damp for mid-March. The promontory we stopped at the base of was empty. Several other cars lay parked farther up the beach, but they in no way interfered with our view of the trees. Their tops rose greenly above the other plants and their desolate, eerie grandeur seemed a throwback to another time. I was greatly moved, as occasionally I am by a place, and my reaction pleased my host. He explained that the trees were peculiar to this and a second region of California and that they were almost destroyed by developers who wanted to extend the country club and provide terracing for the rich. Action by conservationists saved the trees and converted the area into a state park, but his bitterness at the irresponsibility of builders and the rich disrupted my musing and fused in my experience with the sounds of waves and the breezes. We then drove on to La Jolla where above one of the more scenic coves a chalkboard bearing *Frito-Lay* announced the filming of either a television commercial or a pornographic movie. A specter of kitsch or commercial exploitation seemed ever present, even in our later trips to San Diego and the wild cactus deserts of the Baja peninsula.

A year later I was again in Southern California giving a talk at Riverside, and I felt a desire to take another, solitary look at the trees. The year had been a hard one. My energies were drained by work on a lengthy study of post-modern poetry, and demands on my time seemed to have gotten out of hand. I had moved to a new department. New courses had to be worked up. Students had to be met, and issues of my journal, *Modern Poetry Studies,* had to be got out. Early in December word reached me that a very dear friend, Ann Scott, was dying of cancer. Visits to her first in the hospital and later at her home in Baltimore followed. Pain and pallor had touched but not stifled either her concern for others or her senses of humor and dignity. She was worried about her poetry, and I agreed to put her poems together in the next months and write an introduction to the volume. I thought the end of May was a safe deadline for the introduction. In March, the *Beloit Poetry Journal* asked me to contribute to a special David Ignatow issue. In November, I had accepted an assignment from *boundary 2* to review the *Notebooks, The Selected Poems,* and Ignatow's newest collection, *Facing the Tree.* Copies of all three books were in my luggage. The school year had ended but I felt the completion of anything else remote. The deadline for the *Beloit* piece was June. *Boundary 2* would be going to press in July.

It rained hard the morning of my second visit to the park, and the bluff was again nearly deserted. Two tables near the beach parking lot were occupied by families who had come to picnic. Along the beach a group of divers were suiting to enter the water, and a stray surfer emerged here and there. I pulled my rented car into a parking lot farther in and began to walk up one of the marked paths that wind through the park. The walk was risky, since it might affect my arthritis, but a few moments among the trees might also clear up some of the pressure that had been building. Again my reaction was immediate and expansive. I began to feel an affinity with the trees and their remarkable ability to survive and to connect the sense with my having got through the past year, Ann's humor, and Ignatow's survival as a poet. Her vitality, the generosity of my students, and echoes of Ignatow's resistance to pressure by his family to make a living and the neglect of him by critics were as real as the foliage that rustled beneath my shoes and the occasional snapping back of a branch that had been moved to allow passage. I was again in sacred space. Day-to-day problems dissolved into the intricate presence of the pines much as they had dissolved earlier in churches and concert halls I visited or attended. Just as in oriental gardens, life became relational, abstract, and musical, and it was the effect of a garden that the park seemed most to instill. My response was deep and consuming and I wanted deeply to share the feeling with others.

I returned to the car and jotted down some notes. The notes were meant to remind me later of the feeling I had experienced. Dates, names, a brochure, a phrase or line, or sometimes an impression worked in relaxed atmospheres to revive experiences and permit a chance for understanding and expression. Much as I had been schooled at Iowa in Rainer Maria Rilke's principle that a writer must be able to forget experience and have patience until it is part of him and returns as verse, I had also learned over the years that my memory needed aids for this return to happen. My writing in the past few months had been especially sparse. I had managed to put together one long poem entitled *Amnesties* out of notes I had taken in 1971. I also wrote a second, long, grim poem about land exploitation based in part on the first trip to Southern California. Yet my mood both times at visiting the park was neither grim nor angry, and the two poems offered no indication that the trickle of poetry that began in the late sixties would turn flood. Rather than clearing up matters, the walk along the bluff and its impulse toward poetry added to my concerns. I decided to handle the assignments as I was approached. I would work on the Ignatow review, then the Scott introduction, and finally the *Beloit* request. If the notes sprung spontaneously into a poem during the next few weeks, I would send it to *Beloit*. Otherwise I would not worry. I had given up working poems against deadlines long before.

Over the winter I had arranged out of corollary concerns to move out of my Buffalo house by June 1 and spend the first leg of a sabbatical year in Toronto. Hopefully, the new pace and locale would allow me to sort out confusions and return to creative writing on a regular basis. The neighborhood a friend chose was near the university. It was secluded, lively, and various. Shade trees spoke of a nineteenth-century calm and leisure, and in loud denial, building hammers and the sound of excavation for a subway extension insisted on a counter-recognition of the present. I quickly realized that work habits I had acquired in Buffalo would have to be improvised if I wanted a smooth and efficient transition into my new quarters. The improvisation was made difficult by the current economic scene. Costs had gone up appreciably. People generally were more sullen, and even something like marketing required a lot more time than I had been used to. I soon devised a schedule whereby I worked mornings at the library, first on the Ignatow and then on the Scott. The scholarly regimentation and rowed windows of the churchly quiet reading rooms allowed me to concentrate on my criticism. Evenings in the apartment, I relaxed and read and, eventually as the essays came to a close, browsed through my first collection of poems, *Changing the Windows* (1966). There were occasional house guests, an occasional night out dining, concerts, and less frequently movies. I was soon engaged in reading about conventions in the Victorian novel and mathematical logic and easing into a pace that was both productive and reinvigorating.

In my own work, two poems especially stood out. Both were lyrics, as opposed to the quasi-narrative poems I had been writing. Each displayed a keen awareness of space. One, *Ghosts*, had been singled out by John Bennett in a review as a work he especially liked. It was an early experiment in syllabics. The other, *In a Japanese Garden*, usually began my poetry readings. Its cadences and close echoings defied one's getting locked immediately into monotone. It, too, was syllabic. The experiment in syllabics was itself a response to editors and teachers who complained of a metrical monotony in my early poems. Encouraged by Bob Bly, I went in 1958 to syllable count and visual pattern as constants. The shift allowed me to concentrate on image and diction and approach effects I greatly admired in the writing of Marianne Moore and Elizabeth Bishop. It also, as Bly repeatedly pointed out, played up my "strength"—images that reinforced, undercut, and elaborated upon the syntactic sense in very much the way that musical chords related to melody. But there were other things in me and my writing that persisted in being too formal and classical for him. I rhymed. I likewise carried over to syllabics a principle of lineation that was conscious of, but not enslaved to voice cadence, and I insisted that each line have independent interest. Yet, as much as technique, the poems' investigations of sacred space interested me. My experience at Torrey Pines State Park would have to be translated into something comparable.

Actual composition on the poem began during a walk back to my apartment from the Robarts Library where I had been working on revisions to the Scott introduction. The weather that morning resembled the rains I encountered at the park. In contrast, my knees ached. Suddenly, as if stimulated by the end of the Scott essay and the weather, phrases recalling the California experiences began to surface. I stopped and scrawled down on my pad:

The weather is quite raw
after the morning rain
but the pines—
spotting the sides of the trail
still dwarf the pain

Then, as suddenly, the intensity diminished as I wrote along the next line, "as the other plants survived by a modicum of sense or as Pimas survived on cholla." Absolute "knowing" had become a situation whose relational characteristics would have to be worked out at leisure. The core of the statement was information I gained the week before. In reshelving the Life Nature Library volume on *The Desert*, I accidentally hit on mention of the survival of the Papagos and Pimas on saguaro. An original second stanza written at home the next morning owed entirely to a paraphrase of the passage. As I worked on the paraphrase, a second, alternate stanza came into existence, based on my own experience and notes along with a recollection of the court fight to preserve the pines.

The situation seemed to evolve nicely. A triangulation resulted from explaining my response to the trees to an intended reader not at the scene. He must understand the importance of the experience if not the experience itself. This reader persisted in being felt as Ignatow, and his little or no actual knowledge of the events meant I could begin to develop the poem's concepts much as I might for an unspecified reader. Having a specific person in mind, however, did permit liberties in both diction and what Paul Carroll calls the "impure" elements of the poem. An intimacy from the start allowed more risks. The "pain," for instance, in line 5 is especially meaningful to someone who knows me, though by the end of the poem it is worked into something less personal by its associations with "divorce," "gnarled," and "twisted," as well as with the Existential angst of the penultimate lines. Before reading the poems of Frank O'Hara, I don't think I could have woven so consciously upon a formal pattern a second design of "life interrupters," though the need for such a technique was present as early as my student days at Iowa. One lasting achievement of the New York School must be their educating writers and readers in such nonpoetic material, but this "personalism," as O'Hara recognized, is based completely on the poet's having friends as his audience-in-mind.

Two decisions needed now to be made: The first had to do with the form the poem should take, and the second with the presence of two, competing second stanzas. I looked at the shape that phrase, sense, and rhythm had unconsciously given the work. I then studied the opening stanza of *Ghosts*[1] and counted its syllables:

1. *Ghosts* first appeared in *Changing the Windows* (Athens: Ohio University Press, 1966), pp. 55–56.

As if in all this gothic machinery, 10+
weird spires, filigree, and 6
stone, you expected to 6
find a ghost, your eyes search out dark corners 10
of the campus, rattling 6
like winter winds small bits 6
of paper.

I also examined the first stanza of *In a Japanese Garden*[2]:

One follows each detail, 6
rare woods and sober-colored lacquer, scrolls, 10
each tree, stone, spreading pond ripple, 8
learning house and garden 6
designed as one are from each new view, 10
house to garden to house. 6

It was clear that, although I had begun with margins that resembled those of *Ghosts,* the balance and pace of the *Japanese Garden* stanza was more suitable to what I was writing. This was especially true as the poem drifted into the exposition on survival. It seemed appropriate, too, that the poem should gravitate to the sacred space of a garden rather than the cloistered campus of *Ghosts* since the impression of an oriental garden was part of my response to the park. The problem of the two "second stanzas" seemed to resolve concurrently. I would revise them into one. The stanza's new opening and closing lines would compress the personal "second stanza" at the same time that the middle lines used a reduced version of the Life Nature Library material.

My prior experience with revision, however, posed a new problem. I tend to expand rather than condense. *In a Japanese Garden,* for instance, was printed first as an 8-line poem in the *American Poetry Magazine* (1955). The 36-line poem appeared years later in *Triad* (1963). Other poems underwent transformations so similar that at one point I decided to over-write and pare down. The practice ended with *Beyond Ossining* (1967). In affecting length, I had there combined a deeply moving experience in a

2. *In a Japanese Garden* first appeared in *Triad* 1 (Summer 1963): 38; it was reprinted in *Changing the Windows,* pp. 41–42.

cemetery at Sparta, New York, with a wrong set of circumstances. My response to the reddish brown, seventeenth-century headstones had been genuine. I reacted intuitively to those stones whose markings time eroded and that now seemed to stand as anonymous gravestones for everyone and to one stone in particular that a cannonball during the War of 1812 marred. The same trip occasioned my first contact with a portion of the mothball fleet, laden with grain, lying at anchor in long rows along the "lordly Hudson." Both responses were, no doubt, touched off by my being a plains-locked midwesterner. Somehow, years afterward, at the birth of a son to Olivia and David Posner, the reactions merged with the fact of the Posners' English and American citizenships to produce an Existential meditation on life. The initial letters of each stanza spelled out the name of the child, Piers, but the heart of the poem had become an ultimately lifeless handling of the elements it pretended to honor.

I knew by this time that the center of my last stanza would be a paraphrase of the opening of Ignatow's *Talking to Myself*: "About my being a poet, the trees certainly haven't expressed an interest, standing at a distance." [3] I decided to see where this knowledge would lead me. The trees at Torrey Pines State Park had spoken to me at least of Ignatow's work or rather, had spoken a corollary or supportive message. Their insistent refusals to give in connected the opening stanzas to Ann's stubbornness as well as to an earlier poem, *Wickerwork* (1972), which the *Centennial Review* printed. I had grown to feel since the poem's appearance that it might be part of a larger statement, just as I discovered other, unsatisfactory poems were, in reality, parts of longer works. I began the next day to rework the opening lines into stanzas that might fit the Torrey Pines poem. I recast the opening into "Our friendship is constructed to/consume time, and, perhaps, to ward us from/our deaths as is this park." Immediately it became clear that, despite the common themes, the works did not share images. The artifacts that constituted the core of *Wickerwork* stood opposed to the natural landscape of the pines: One's sacred space was inner; the other's outer; one dealt with imagination; and the second with nature. The peculiar sense of sacred space that the Torrey Pines poem demanded could, by its very physicality, be assertive rather than descriptive or expository. This realization set me to canceling lines and returning the poem to what it had been the day before.

3. In *Facing the Tree* (Boston: Atlantic, Little, Brown, 1975), p. 37.

I finally had a three-stanza structure whose conception seemed workable. Compressing more of my notes into the beginning of the stanza followed naturally from "they stand intense." The shift into the Ignatow paraphrase was not so natural. The quote should break on the word "you," partly to cut down on its casualness but partly, too, to take advantage of the I-you juxtaposition that the previous line made possible. Christine Rabin had written of the richness that these juxtapositions achieved in an article on William Carlos Williams I had recently proofed for *Modern Poetry Studies*. Surprisingly, the break came without difficulty, and only a last line remained to be worked out. Again, I rejected several before I decided on the one I used. Once more, my decision was based on sacred space. The line had to be assertive. The one I selected insinuated Ignatow into the park and poem, turning the first "you" of line 16 indirectly into the apostrophe that the opening stanza invites and that the second stanza fails to deliver. He and the trees are, thus, confounded syntactically much as they are imagistically. I felt release. The *Beloit* Ignatow issue was already in press, but no matter. I had my poem.

Throughout the composition, I had hoped the workmanship of the poem might replace the surface pyrotechnics I relied on as a beginning poet. Then, I had consciously constructed oppositions, deliberately setting them off by dramatic adjectives or encasing them in anagrams much as a beginner will overdo cosmetics. Subsequently, Michelangelo's *Prisoners* and his final *Pietà* in Milan taught me the power in half-emergent structures. I now wanted surfaces that suggested emotions locked within just as his surfaces suggested submerged strength. I knew that such surfaces went against paraphrase in that restatement inevitably highlights the half-seen by calling one's attention to it; but paraphrase of poetry has always been difficult. The divorce of fact from response that occurs is unavoidable and unfortunate. My own early poetry added a second difficulty by interacting on several levels simultaneously. Expressing this interaction sequentially again violated texture. Adding nonpoetic elements increases the difficulty of paraphrase even more. How, for example, does a paraphrase connect the world of the poet with the exigencies of the form he has chosen? It divides them into "formal elements" and elements that "intrude" on the writer. Yet readers seem to respond to both without much difficulty. For me, the best paraphrase is an analogue and ends in being a new work of art. I agree with critics like Harold Bloom who make new poems misprisions of older works, though my view is not so inclusive as theirs.

This area of workmanship constitutes the biggest change in my work over the years, but the change should not be looked at as necessarily an advance. I believe that at every point in a writer's career he fulfills forms equal to his vision. My early poems do as much to complete their intentions as do my later ones. I still admire, for instance, the directness of a work like *Brother to Mars* (1961), the lyricism of *Morgan Street* (1960) and *White Forms* (1962), and the playfulness of *For Harold* (1957). I think it is a mistake to impose upon the tie between technique and vision the sole criterion of technique so that, as one gets on, one supposedly gets more proficient. Poets are not surgeons; their fifth operation is not easier than their first. In fact, each new poem seems to embody as many or more problems than the previous one, though it is true that certain rhythmic and sound qualities become less conscious and that peripheral vision increases. Despite the richnesses that these changes bring about, the main narrative does not seem to change much. Richnesses are for later readings. Readers should not have to master everything at one glance. Yet later readings determine the real worth of a piece. My meanings are still very much in the main narrative, and anyone who has difficulty understanding the sense of my work ought to consult a dictionary or handbook on the subject or simply read the poem aloud a few times. An awful lot of confusion gets cleared up by reading or just hearing a work.

The rhythms and pattern of the Torrey Pines poem please me most. I say this, knowing that in composition I emphasize the technical in order to give free play to the emotional and that often a reader's reaction lies with the intricacies of the work's emotional content. I enjoy the way the rhapsodic opening almost takes off at the end of line 2 with "the pines, the pines" and yet holds to bring the reader to a deflating, factual close in "weekend naturalists." The second stanza accepts the tone and builds the "tags and classifications" into a romantic view of Indian survival. Then, abruptly, this view turns brutal to further the poem's development by contrast. In the closing line this brutality becomes genial as response conveys the presence of Ignatow. Throughout these shifts various echoings occur—assonance, alliteration, consonance—helping the sound interest while the formal pattern suggests a more abstract, relational level. One makes it through the baroque syntax of the second stanza mainly because the visual pattern "interprets" the poem's "strict boundaries and well-defined shapes" with a sense of a force beyond yet within. This "force" moves the reader past the opening participial phrase into the extended prepositional construction that finally modifies "they." The fact that one gets through these obstacles makes him as ready as the poet to accept the "truths" of line 15. I final equally pleasurable that the form, which is that of *In a Japanese Garden*, achieves its own distinct tone. *At Torrey Pines State Park* echoes, but at the same time extends that earlier poem's senses of space and survival. The extension is what I hope for in every poem. It certainly was part of the emotional content that prompted the work.

Jerome Mazzaro was born in 1934 in Detroit, Michigan. He earned degrees from Wayne State University and the University of Iowa. He has been a resident of New York State since 1962, and since 1965, a member of the faculty of the State University of New York at Buffalo. He has traveled widely and has served in editorial capacities for a number of magazines, including *Salmagundi* and *Modern Poetry Studies.* His books include *Juvenal's Satires* (1965), *The Poetic Themes of Robert Lowell* (1965), *Changing the Windows: Poems* (1966), *Transformations in the Renaissance English Lyric* (1970), and *William Carlos Williams: The Later Poems* (1973). He has also edited *Modern American Poetry: Essays in Criticism* (1970) and profiles of *William Carlos Williams* (1971) and *Robert Lowell* (1971). In 1964, he was granted a Guggenheim Memorial Fellowship in poetry.

Vassar Miller

ACCEPTING

Lord, serene on your symbol,
you plant your flag
on pain's last outpost.

Your arms span its horizons,
your feet explore it,
your eyes are its seas.

You, pioneer in pain,
reclaim its wastes,
and so you prove it

no more an alien planet,
only our earth
whose soil stains your fingers.

Against your side woe's wildness
strings its red vines
and shadows your face.

Then name this bloody ground
firm underfoot
home, however homely.

1 My poem *Accepting* took its start after I had attended Ash Wednesday services at a Roman Catholic church where a friend of mine was deacon. It was a black parish, and the church was poor and plain, and I was touched to see how devout the people were, most of them having come to church after a hard day's work. Gazing up at the large, realistic crucifix above the altar, I realized suddenly that the crucifix is the symbol humanizing suffering, making it, as it were, "okay" to suffer. And for a few moments, long years of bitterness melted away.

The poem began in my head with the first line.

I'm not sure that I imagined anybody "listening" to the poem, because I guess I was really writing it to myself.

2 As well as I can recall, the poem went through about five drafts, all in one Sunday morning. At first I wrote the stanzas down any old way, and the poem was longer by several stanzas than now. I finally imposed order upon it by making it a syllabic poem, as many of my poems are. The first stanza remained virtually unchanged throughout the drafts.

3 The lines are short; the stanzas are syllabic. I've used some alliteration, "pioneer in pain," "woe's wildness," "home, however homely." I always try for concrete language. Even a phrase like "woe's wildness" has a suggestion of the concrete, reinforced by the alliteration, giving it weight and texture. I can't imagine poetry without metaphor, simile, and image.

I divided the lines more or less according to natural pauses, or at least tried to end each with a strong word. I don't like lines ending in "a" or "the" or "and." All in all, my poetry is fairly conventional.

I should hope that this poem could be read effectively either silently or aloud. I don't know about musical accompaniment, although some of my poems have been set to music.

The reference and allusion in this poem are available to any Western reader, since the poem is Christian.

4 I visualize as my reader anybody who appreciates poetry. He or she may or may not like my poem, but I don't think it obscure. Poetry is ultimately a form of communication.

5 I can say what this poem is about, but you can't paraphrase any poem, really. That would be like looking at a map and saying you have taken a trip. To paraphrase a poem seems a contradiction in terms.

6 Although this poem is Christian, it is less—what shall I say—narrowly so than my early religious poems. There is the subtle difference that I would earlier have written "cross" instead of "symbol." I hadn't thought of it, but to this extent the poem is more abstract. Also, it is more reflective, less intense, less lyrical.

Vassar Miller was born in Houston, Texas, in 1924. She grew up in Houston and received her bachelor's and master's degrees in English from the University of Houston. From fall of 1975 through spring of 1976 she was writer-in-residence at the University of St. Thomas. She has published five books of poetry: *Adam's Footprint* (1956), *Wage War on Silence* (1960), *My Bones Being Wiser* (1963), *Onions and Roses* (1968), and *If I Could Sleep Deeply Enough* (1974).

Judith Minty

THE END OF SUMMER

1\.
The old bitch labrador swims
in heavy circles. Under water
her legs run free without their limp.
She stretches brown eyes toward me,
snorting water, and the stick I throw
stirs gray memories of ten Octobers,
ducks that fly at the sun and fall.

2\.
On the Pere Marquette River, salmon
quiver upstream from the lake, return
to alpha. At the dam
they leap and throw themselves
through currents, stretch
and spend themselves
against the torrent from the falls.

3\.
All week the sky has been filled
with orange petals. Monarch butterflies
floating in cycles toward milkweed.

Freed from their chrysalis,
they have been waiting for the wind's
current to die. The beach
is covered with torn wings.

4.

The merganser carries fire
on his hood. This summer he has
nested in our channel, drifted
with our half-tame mallards. His sharp bill
stabs the water to catch bread I throw.
He belongs by the sea. I want him
to fly now before October and guns.

It was mid-September, a Sunday. We were at the beach, Lake Michigan, my husband, our three children, our dog, me. School had already started. It was one of those last nice days, Indian Summer. Our dog is lame, a congenital hip disorder common to Labradors. Breeders often destroy these puppies as soon as the disability shows up under X-ray. But Tar has been with us a long time; she labors with her pain in the field. And when she's not working, she fetches sticks for hours, shaking the water from her coat when she reaches shore, running to drop the wood at our feet so that we will throw it out into the lake again.

I was struck by her trust in us, her wish to continue this circular game until she exhausted herself. And the poem began with the first stanza which, after the initial fiddling with it, has remained pretty much intact.

I have a habit of writing down particularly strong images on 3 × 5 cards at the time they come to me. I am not a good journal keeper, probably because the journal is a big book that one writes in in a special room at a special time of day. But I always carry some blank index cards with me.

Actually I had witnessed the salmon episode the previous summer. Although I had tossed the card into my file, I didn't have to refer to it to arrive at my second stanza. The incident had affected me deeply at the time and it still, apparently, was troubling my unconscious. The progression through water from dog to fish seemed very natural to me.

Just prior to the poem's inception, I had been reading a lot of ghazals. I was particularly impressed by those written by Jim Harrison, how he incorporates the natural world of northern Michigan into his work, how he is able to achieve phenomenal metaphorical jumps between couplets while still maintaining a strong continuity of the "sense" of the poem.

Not until I had completed my second stanza did I realize I might be working with a form similar to the ghazal, in that there seemed to be a strange linking and jumping of imagery. Since this poem, I have done other ghazal-type pieces. What occurs during the writing process never ceases to startle me. I am never certain what place the poem will fly off to when I begin it.

The third stanza of *The End of Summer* was a movement still tied to the lake, but it picked up on the salmon's color, its battered body. This particular butterfly image came off another 3 × 5 card, but was only pulled out of the file during revision stages. Apparently my unconscious had arranged the stanzas out of the store of pictures it had accumulated. When it got the message I might be working in this new form, it sent me butterflies.

The fourth stanza came the following day, as I recall. By the end of the third section, I was more certain than ever that the linkings which had occurred so far should continue through the rest of the poem. But I wasn't sure where the poem was going or how long it wanted to be. So I put down my pencil and walked away from my desk—as I often do when I reach an impasse and become uncertain. I needed the poem to gel a bit more, I wanted the sense of discovery to work a little harder before it emerged. I wasn't ready yet.

The strange merganser had been troubling me all summer. I had never seen one before (they look a little like a roadrunner) and I knew how alien this bird was to my area of Michigan. When he finally came into my mind the following day, I knew he was right for the poem, particularly since his head feathers have a red-orange cast to them, and I intuitively felt that that color had to continue as one of the links in the poem.

I still didn't know how many stanzas there would be, but when the last line came, I knew that the poem was finished, that we had finally circled back to the beginning. And I remember being quite satisfied with my thematic material. I didn't want to *add* anything.

The merganser section was the hardest for me to get right. And I'm not sure it's finished yet, although I continue to remain satisfied with the last line. The other three sections went through two revisions or so before they got to the typewriter. After that, I only altered an occasional word or line break. This took less than a month, I would say. I can only estimate because I infrequently date my revisions. Probably because I fool myself into thinking that each is the last.

But the fourth section has undergone about six revisions. It originally began "The merganser has been living/at the channel all summer." And then a bunch of silly, sentimental stuff. The "I" took no action in this section until the fourth revision. At that point, after the opening lines had been altered to their present form, the center section read ". . . All summer/I threw bread to him, saw his sharp bill/stab into water. . . ." But of course, that wasn't right either. This last stanza troubled me enough to go to the encyclopedia to research the bird. He was the character I knew least about in the poem. I was still working on stanza 4 in the middle of winter, six months after the dog had begun swimming in the lake.

I have, by nature, a personality which requires organization. And I was more structured in my craft a year and a half ago, when *The End of Summer* was written, than I am today. I like symmetry. I was/am still convinced that a poem should "look right" on the page. So, when the first section came out to seven lines and the next fell into that same pattern, I was certain that each subsequent section should be a seven-line stanza. Looking at the early, handwritten drafts, I see that I didn't have to strain to achieve this form, except for part 4, which was originally six lines. But, anyway, that was before the bread was tossed.

Today structure doesn't nettle me so much, and I am able to work more freely. But it still seems to me that *this* poem, because of its very nature, should have that added control of stanzaic balance.

Everything I do in this odd business of writing poetry is based on intuition. I have no rules, only patterns that I fall into. Most of my reasons for *doing* what I do, craftwise, can be answered, "because it felt right at the time." And I try not to intellectualize too deeply for fear of moving from the unconscious to the conscious. I don't believe that any art form works well when it is consciously applied.

I am lucky in that I can *hear* a poem, any poem which I read silently, through my inner ear. I don't have to go through that annoyance of reciting aloud to myself. Naturally, my selection of line breaks depends upon how the piece sounds orally. But another, equal consideration has to do with imagery. To compound image on image within the same line produces far more energy than if the mind-pictures were to remain separated. For example

"All week the sky has been filled"

(Filled with what? Clouds, birds, A-bomb mushrooms? The reader briefly makes his own image.)

"with orange petals.

(Ah, the trees are shedding. No, the sun has exploded.)

Monarch butterflies"

(Yes, petals are butterflies, butterflies are petals which touch flowers. Now back to the sky—blue/orange.)

Another example would be in part 1:

"The old bitch labrador swims"

(Here I see an old, female/possibly cranky dog—head and shoulders on top of the water.)

"in heavy circles. Under water"

(Now my vision is directed below the surface of things.)

And the transition with the next line moves me from heavy (above water/ reality) to light (below water/fantasy/how we wish things to be). The same effect of moving the reader/self is gained in the last section with "I want him." Unfortunately, I'm not so lucky with all of my line breaks. But I think they work quite well in this poem.

Another item which I don't consciously strive for, but rather just let happen, is that old assonance/alliteration business. I would never consciously alter a piece *for* this purpose, but I'm always glad when it happens because that's what makes the poem a pleasure to read aloud. I will say that I do consciously alter lines/words that *don't* sound right/sound "off-key." I was pleased to find assonance/alliteration occurring naturally in the salmon episode, along with an emotionally rhythmic motion which blends well, I think, with the thematic material. By contrast in the butterfly section, because they are such airy things, the emotional rhythm *is* quite different.

Again, praise the Lord, few of these internal things took place willfully. I do so strongly believe that art originates out of our most sensitive areas, our unconscious, whatever; and the more we attempt to manipulate it intellectually, logically, the greater the risk of destroying the *real* poem and creating an artificial one in its place. You can't *smell* plastic flowers.

The poet is, after all, *very* human, a person who deals with the truth as he/she sees it, who writes about those special moments in life which have given him/her excruciating pain or joy. If we want mechanically perfect poems, we can turn to the computers.

I wrote *The End of Summer* because I couldn't *not* write it. Its energy moved inside of me with such a force that I had to get it out. The other alternative would have been to direct that energy in some other direction—which is why, I suppose, some people slam their fists into walls and cry out in their dreams.

On the other hand, I didn't write it *for* any particular person. Rather for the dog and the fish and the butterfly and the duck, all creatures whose life cycle is too short. And so, ultimately, for myself, because through the making-process I was discovering another possibility about *my* time and space here. When you discover something new, I guess it's just natural to want to share it with others. But "the other" becomes, for me, anyone who is curious, who wants to listen, who is willing to grope around and question his existence, who might possibly feel what I felt.

Because I have lived in/loved one place most in my life, I tend to mix that external world with the internal. Yet I don't envision my work as being written only for the people of my geographic region. I don't think it matters if the reader has never been to Lake Michigan or the Pere Marquette River. It only matters that he sees my channel through my eyes with his. Place certainly defines me, but it defines all of us. Only through specifics can we achieve any sense of group understanding.

And if *The End of Summer* speaks to "the other," what does it say? I can't believe that a creative work needs to be explained. But I will go this far: I seldom know what the poem is saying to me while it is being made. I sometimes get snatches of discovery part-way through. Yet I am never *positive* about its meaning, even by the time I reach the end. By its very nature a single poem can mean many things. I am only aware that I sensed something once and I know it better now.

I am glad that this piece ended up in four parts and that each of the creatures was of a different species. Perhaps this has something to do with seasons or quarters that make a whole. Certainly the poem speaks of life cycles, both in its thematic circles and in the form which it has taken. But if I said anymore, I would have to write another poem. And even then, it wouldn't be the same poem at all.

Judith Minty was born in Detroit, Michigan, in 1937. She received her B.S. in Speech Therapy from Ithaca College and her M.A. in English from Western Michigan University. She is presently guest lecturer in English at Grand Valley State Colleges, Allendale, Michigan. She lives on a sailboat in the summer and retreats to the north woods of Michigan as often as possible during the rest of the year. Her first book, *Lake Songs and Other Fears* (1974), was the recipient of the United States Award for 1973 of The International Poetry Forum. In 1974, she received the John Atherton Fellowship in Poetry to Bread Loaf Writer's Conference and the Eunice Tietjens Memorial Award from *Poetry* magazine. She is presently completing a chapbook and working on a longer volume of poems.

Linda Pastan

OLD WOMAN

In the evening
my griefs come to me
one by one.
They tell me what I had hoped to forget.
They perch on my shoulders
like mourning doves.
They are the color
of light fading.

In the day
they come back
wearing disguises.
I rock and rock
in the warm amnesia of sun.
When my griefs sing to me
from the bright throats of thrushes
I sing back.

1 My poem grew out of a strong mood, rather than from an idea or an image. It was certainly helped on its flight, however, by a specific mourning dove outside the window.

2 Usually my poems expand and contract endlessly during the month or so it takes to write them, and usually they go through nearly a hundred pages of revision. This one, however, almost wrote itself. It was a matter of polishing rather than true revision.

3 Though I have studied prosody and am usually aware of its various manifestations in the poems of others, I use little conscious technique myself. I do, however, seem to spend hours over line breaks.

4 Whom do you visualize as your reader?

the humanities 5 section man
who has been sharpening
his red pencil
these twenty years

my mother
who suspected me
of such thoughts
all along

the running back
who after the last touchdown
reads my poems by his locker
instead of the sports page

5 Unless I take to teaching, "paraphrasing" is something I would never knowingly commit.

6 I don't usually displace the emotions that give a poem its energy, and I only occasionally make use of a persona. Otherwise I think this poem is quite typical of my work. Quality? Others will have to judge. And I never seem able to escape my usual themes.

Linda Pastan was born in 1932. She grew up in New York, graduated from Radcliffe College, and received an M.A. at Brandeis University. Her books of poetry include *A Perfect Circle Of Sun* (1971), *On The Way To The Zoo* (1975), and *Aspects of Eve* (1975). She has had a fellowship from the NEA and from Bread Loaf.

David Ray

ORPHANS

In Ireland they were put in foundling homes,
so many sprung up after the great potato blight,
mothers left them in the fields, after they'd scratched
the earth up, or on doorsteps . . . and the beadles took them
into the foundling homes. There ninety percent died
in their first year for lack of touch.

The final insult is to be dragged into the orphanage
screaming "I'm not an orphan." Not as it should be,
with the orphans, who have nothing, on the bottom
of the heap. Quite the contrary, it is they
who proudly look down on the non-orphans, whose parents
have judged them unworthy, who still live in the city
nearby, who could save them if they cared.
You see that skyscraper, the one with the lights
that change all night, the colors of the rainbow?
That's where your mother lives and works and has her
boyfriends, Jim, Gary, Gerald, bedspring-
squeakers, huggers, tiptoers, laughing
at her question, "Did you forget the rubbers?"
Your mother, man, would spread her legs for any man

who asked, while joking in the hospital that you
needed no privacy, being too little for all that.
So they took away the only screen you had
and let you cry in public while someone else's roses
wilted in the sun.

In the orphanage the inmates fall in love, and Juliet of the sorrows
turns twelve and is taken off like a dog
to be put in still another home, the Francis Willard,
down a dusty road. They'll let you ride along
if you won't scream, and see her in the door
where she will lie quietly as if strapped down
and let her breasts grow and keep secret your vow
to meet at twenty-one, under the clock, at noon,
and love forever and hate them all.

Donald, whose gramma came on Christmas and gave him
an apple, the only thing she had, is the only kid
with pubic hair. Together
all of you take a shower in a huge stall
and Nazi ladies in fur coats
are escorted through to look at you; one girl
of twelve is lovely and she stares. It could
be love, but it's only more shame, and hate.
The rich who care and have each other
are strolling through
and smelling clorox and wondering what
they'll give this year, the girl stares
as if you're almost human. Her mother drags her on.
Donald fights. The boys cut pictures of their fathers
out of *Life* magazine. They're fighting, too, in jungles
overseas. Christ knows who a father is.

The matrons are chosen because they can wear
the white uniforms with thick starch—
polar regions, talcum, annihilation.

Their eyes are always angry, ready
to carry out the Court's will, be it
Death or Neglect.
They enjoy hurling the miserable child
down stairs, hearing him weep in the night,
enjoy making him eat turnips or whatever
makes him throw up, enjoy cutting the blonde
girl's braids, throwing them into the toilet,
reminding her that no mother wants a lock
of that hair to save. They enjoy pinching
the small buttons of the girl's nipples,
enjoy stuffing bananas up her quivering
cunt, they enjoy shouting "Nobody loves
you, nobody, not even yourselves,"
enjoy beating them, then saying "Sit down
by that fire escape and learn your
multiplication tables," enjoy kicking them
black and blue and livid and mottled red,
enjoy sending them to school like a chain
gang, all dressed in corduroy any cop
can spot should they break away and run,
up the tarmac road, begging at motorists.

And like a co-conspirator the blue-dressed
headmistress with stars on her bosom
has shaken hands with the pathetic
abandoning parent. What did she say
that last time, before stepping over barbed wire
to be gone forever? *So long. Be good. I'll write.*

The murdering matrons greeted orphans
as equals, credited them with killing
off that great detritus of family, emerging
alone with a bloody knife, saying "I have cut
my way into the womb of the orphanage.
I am alone."

I am alone! The matrons had always
been alone, always. They could understand.
Orphans were proud—survivors
from another life killed off, a dozen lives.
They were thoroughbreds—pure—
born from vanished breeds.
Why hadn't the train killed them too?
Why hadn't the fire? The bush of tumors?
They were *magic*. Such survivors
received from the buxom matrons
hate akin to the strokes of love,
hate that went in and out, hate that warmed.

But the children of living drunks
or women who ran off with truckdrivers
or locked their children out to eat mulberries
in the churchyard tree were marked as weak,
unworthy of love or hate, hardly worth
beating—they were not scarred over
like orphans, not hard as agates
though like orphans they had no surface
that could bear a kiss. They wept
more, they stared less.

Thus, while the orphans had ice cream
or were rocked to sleep
in the valleys of buxom matrons who had at last
relented, deciding to love only
the most needy cases, we stared at skyscrapers
where our mothers took their lovers down.
We wet our pillows with tears in the narrow
coffins of our bunk beds.
We vowed to kill orphans, whose gurgles
we heard down the hall as they enjoyed
their intolerable freedoms,
far past midnight, learning to laugh

like rats in alleys, learning to survive
as only the children of true spirits can,
whose mothers are stars,
whose fathers are ash,
whose cousins are the pebbles around rose
bushes which would not even tear
the nylons of false mothers as they fled us.

ENVOI
(for marilyn)

And the journalist will say you lie
you didn't wear uniforms, you didn't suffer,
you weren't torn from your senile grandmother's arms
you weren't forced to lift your hand
even to wash ten thousand dishes.
You spooned no pond until it was empty
and no one, no one, ever touched you.
He will tell it like it was,
as if being there disqualified *you*
from telling us.
He was right, no one touched you—touch,
Marilyn, as you knew, is such a gentle thing.
So gentle you touch me even now
who never came into my room or lay your
life frail as a rose petal against my face.

How did the poem start?

Orphans is an expression resulting from years of concern with an experience, namely that of having been placed, after a series of very inadequate foster homes, where my sister and I endured such indignities as being locked out of homes, starved, etc., in an institution called The Children's

Home in Tulsa. This unforgettable (unforgivable) experience, considering that my mother and other family members were perfectly capable of keeping us, seemed the capping indignity of a childhood defined by poverty and total rejection by both parents, the father by absolute desertion, and the mother by periodic acceptance alternating with abandonment. In the poem I have tried to express the anxieties and pains of the child who really has no certainty to rely upon. Ironically, the child who must accept the death of parents has more certainty in his life. The living presence of parents who alternately tease and cruelly reject the child with stimuli that include both the possibility of love and acceptance and the reality of repeated rejection is indeed very cruel. I have written of this experience in many ways, including fiction and other poems, because it has been very central to my life. This particular poem was just another welling-up, an abreaction as it were, of this very perplexing memory.

What changes did it go through from start to finish?

The changes this poem underwent include changes in point of view and in narrative concern with ideas that finally were discarded; for example, on the second page of the manuscript, these lines were deleted:

> And these orphans were clearly hated too,
> not roughly, crudely, but with the hyaline
> and dignifying clarity of clear water.
> Orphans were hated unfairly, and that
> made them proud . . .

This poem, like the stories and other poems I have written about these experiences, went through several drafts, at least four, with intervals of a few days between the drafts. The poem expanded somewhat, but not much. The structure changed only in that I provided in my last draft a more objective beginning, and I used changes in voice, perspective, deliberately, and somewhat deliberately distorted "facts" in the interest of emotional truth. For example, Norman Mailer insultingly claims that Marilyn Monroe fabricated much of the abuse she suffered at the orphanage and elsewhere: How would he know? He evidently assumes he is more of an authority because he was *not* there. The scientist is always like this. The outsider is always misinformed.

What principles of technique did you consciously use?

The conscious technique that I used was perhaps a declamatory one, almost trying to bombard the reader with the excesses of the experience and with the surrealism of the inverted logic which people experience when they suffer. Only through rhetoric did I feel the reader could accept the near-psychotic logic of the abandoned child. The poem's accuracy in relation to my feeling is more important than the usual considerations of poetic form. I felt that the poem was a catharsis and that it needed to be read aloud to be experienced. I also very much felt that literal details implied metaphor. The re-creation of cruelty to a child, comparing it to other situations, such as that of the Nazis and the Jews, Marilyn Monroe's life, etc., is in fact dominant in that it provides a life script for an individual who has gone through such an experience. Changing such a script is the work of a lifetime and it requires the help of therapy. In that sense the loving reader acts as a therapist who understands. The poem, then, is spontaneous, intuitive, historical in a real life sense with total personal reference, just as a confessional abreaction would be. The order is that of dreams and free association, and the climax is simply the sense of grief felt in the telling. The persona here is one that I cannot avoid since I am telling my own experience: it is impossible to keep a distance with such material. The tone of the poem could be characterized, perhaps, as nostalgic anger. We hold on to our sufferings. Any tone created is simply that implicit in stating the facts. The honesty is deliberate, but the author confesses a total lack of control over the disposition or the reception of the material. (Croce, of Vico: "poetry precedes intellect, but follows sense . . . primitive history was poetry, its plot was the narration of fact.") The confessional nakedness of my poetry is a reality I have long accepted. After readings some people from my audiences have sometimes asked me if it is difficult to be so candid about my own feelings and experiences. My answer is that it is the least difficult aspect of my technique. The real pain is in having suffered the things one is candid about, and in having held on to those sufferings.

Whom do you visualize as your reader?

My audience does not, as your questionnaire suggests, include the general run of the newspaper-reading public, nor my fellow poets. My fellow poets include some of the least compassionate people I know. In generosity I might say that it is perhaps their own sufferings that make them incapable of compassion for others. Enlightened readers can be found among any social group or age group, not excluding my fellow writers. It seems that my work has been treated cruelly in my adult life, a situation which I have often considered parallel to my abandonment and the cruelty I suffered as a child. Consequently my ideal reader has always been some concerned person, capable of feeling, an almost internalized parent that I have had to construct in myself. Ultimately, however, I would have to say that I wrote the poem for my own expression, not for "communication."

Can the poem be paraphrased? How?

I do not feel that the poem can be paraphrased. In fact, I cannot think of any poem with any real power that can be.

How does this poem differ from earlier poems of yours in quality, theme, and technique?

I have no objectivity in assessing the quality, theme, or technique of a poem like this because it is a direct and personal expression of my own experience, in other words a genuine abreaction, cathexis of strongly held feelings. It moved me deeply to write it, and the poem itself is simply the shell of that living experience. I cannot assess its value to another, any more than a clam that lived in a shell can assess the value of its discarded shell to a collector.

Some of the allusions, particularly in comparing the Nazis and the persecutors of the orphans, may be lost on some readers, or possibly misunderstood. I hope not. Also, there are references to Marilyn Monroe, who also had the experience of being put in an orphanage although she was not an orphan, and the scene described as being "dragged into the orphanage/ screaming 'I'm not an orphan!'" refers to Marilyn's experience as described by Norman Mailer (and no doubt others). Mailer's book on Marilyn moved me because of, not in spite of, its superficiality, and the fact that a genuine suffering human being was able to pierce through and survive the superficiality of Mailer's prose struck me as perfectly appropriate to a woman whose life was flattened out by the celluloid of movie scenes. Mailer's prose, and B movies, then, provide proper viewing lenses for such a lost person. Marilyn's tragedy was never muted by her successes, and any thoroughly successful exploitation of her for fantasy was no doubt merely a part of the inevitable rape of anyone forced to sell herself for survival. I too had that experience in the sense that I had to come up with a great deal of charm in order to survive, charm that many exploited.

David Ray, born in 1932 in Sapulpa, Oklahoma, is author and editor of several books; his most recent book of poetry is *Gathering Firewood: Poems New and Selected* (1974). Other recent poems are in *The New Yorker, Esquire, The Atlantic Monthly, Hudson Review,* and other places. He has also published stories in such magazines as *Epoch* and *The North American Review.* Currently he is at work on both new fiction and poetry. He has read his poems at the Library of Congress, the Poetry Center in New York, the B.B.C. in England, and numerous universities and colleges. He has taught at Cornell University, Reed College, The University of Iowa Writers' Workshop, and is at present professor of English at the University of Missouri, Kansas City where he also edits the literary quarterly, *New Letters.*

James Reiss

SUEÑOS

In my dreams I always speak Spanish.
The cemetery may be in Brooklyn,
and I may be kneeling on a rise
looking out at the skyline of the city,
but I will whisper, *Mira el sol.*

And it is true the late morning
sun will turn that bank of skyscrapers
the color of bleached bone in Sonora,
and all the window washers of Manhattan
will white-out like a TV screen

in Venezuela turning to snow.
But the gray face on the headstone photograph
has a nose like my father's,
and his voice had the lilt of the ghettos
of central Europe.

So I should kneel lower and say something
in Yiddish about fathers, grandfathers,

the hacked limbs of a family tree
that reaches as high as Manhattan.
I should say, *Grampa, I loved those times*

we ran through the underpasses in Central
Park, you with your cane, I with my ice
cream cones, shouting for echoes,
bursting out into sunlight—
if I only knew the language to say it in.

SUEÑOS: UNWINDING THE DREAM

How did the poem start?

If I remember right, *Sueños* began with my desire to capture the transfigured mood of one afternoon on a hotel balcony in Acapulco with my wife, Barbara. I had been trying to capture that mood in several unsuccessful poems written in the winter and spring of 1974.

Like a good many of my poems, *Sueños* actually started with what I thought was a snappy first line, the simple striking statement, "In my dreams I always speak Spanish." In fact, I often have dreams in which I or others speak Spanish—I have always felt very close to the language. Of course, it was an exaggeration to say that I *always* speak Spanish in my dreams. Nevertheless, I wrote the line down fast, imbued with at least a little of that faith and hope which are necessary at the outset of anything creative. Then I began looking for ways to develop or "unwind" the first line.

What changes did it go through from start to finish?

Sitting in my small study in Ohio on April 29, 1974, I penciled-in the untitled first draft in a burst of automatic writing. The result is a very bad poem about a man and wife on a hotel balcony overlooking not Acapulco but Fifth Avenue. In the first stanza the man points out the sun to his wife and says *Mira el sol* (which I rapidly changed to *Ah, le soleil* in a flurry of execrable French later changed back to Spanish). But in the second stanza I sketched the lines:

> True, the late sun will turn the bank
> of apartments the color of bleached
> bone; the window washers
> on the skyscrapers near Central Park
> will white-out like a television screen
> turning to snow.

Despite the geographic improbability of these lines, even at this very early stage some of the crucial images of the poem had arrived. Moreover, there was a seriousness and sonority locked in the words. It did not matter that I was unaware of what would ultimately be the poem's intent; what mattered at the moment was that I had come upon imagery and an underlying tone that seemed to me to be absolutely fresh and compelling. I plugged on for another five lines that are too wretched to repeat.

Excited, I went right to work on the second draft and typed a first stanza that is almost exactly like the final version. I had thrown out the hotel balcony for a cemetery, abandoning entirely my wish to describe that Acapulco afternoon. The second stanza, too, was almost achieved. But the rest of the poem described a "tiny form rising from the ground" who "has a face that is American/and a cry that is familiar." I was in fact describing my dead son Jeffrey risen from a dream-cemetery to confront his parents, Barbara and myself, who are so overcome with emotion that they can't cry out. Instead, "my wife becomes pale as a cloud./And I whisper, *Mira la luna*"!

At this point I typed a third draft with few changes and set the poem down, discouraged. I had, after all, already dealt with Jeffrey in several poems in my first book, *The Breathers*. I was determined not to repeat myself and blubber over old sorrows. Something about the way Jeffrey had crept into the poem seemed altogether too familiar and easy.

That summer Barbara and I went away to The MacDowell Colony in Peterborough, New Hampshire, for two terrific months of writing. During the first three weeks I immersed myself in other poems and completely forgot *Sueños*, which I had now dubbed *Canción*. By mid-August I had written myself out and sat at my studio desk staring out at a blue wall of spruce. I was restless. I was hell to live with.

One afternoon I became courageous and read Barbara some half-finished drafts, including *Canción.* Immediately she smiled in that telltale way she has when she likes something I've written. Of course, there were problems with *Canción*, but—most wonderful of all—Barbara suggested a solution. As she spoke with the detached clarity of an objective observer, I penciled her suggestion in the margin: "Have this be a poem about man who speaks in Spanish at most emotional moments. Or else have it be about poet's father."

From then on the writing seemed easy. I scrapped the second half of the poem and brought in my grandfather's ghost instead of Jeffrey's. I brought in my father all right but made the poem say something about all my "fathers." I counterpointed Yiddish with Spanish. And in a lyrical burst that was every bit as pleasurable as sex, I sketched the italicized portion of the poem based on a keen recollection of my grandfather and myself when I must have been less than five years old.

Again, Barbara helped. She suggested I get rid of the corny image of a "gray form rising from the ground" that had persisted from the start. She came up with the appropriately Jewish image of the face on the headstone photograph—in Jewish cemeteries it once was customary for photographs of the deceased to be placed on their headstones.

The day I thought I finished *Canción*—by now titled *Sueños*—I went out and lay down in the meadow behind my studio. It was August 16, 1974, the air was cool and dry, the tall meadow grass had not yet been mowed. I remember thinking I had done something significant, not knowing quite what, but knowing that *Sueños* had a certain very personal poignance, almost a Keatsian high-sorrowfulness about it—for me at least.

Yet even then the poem needed one finishing touch. Originally its last two lines went:

> But my heart hurts
> too much to speak in its mother tongue.

Perhaps I'd been thinking of Daniel Halpern's hilarious tongue poems!

At any rate, when Howard Moss took *Sueños* for the *New Yorker*, he wrote: "We like 'Sueños' but—to speak plainly—we all find the last two lines sentimental and not up to the level of what comes before. Do you think a possible last line might go something like

> if I only knew the language to say it in

which would seem to us to give the poem more point on several scores? The difficulty of expressing feeling. The connection between what once was Yiddish as a second language and now is Spanish. The tangled history of New York City immigration. And so on."

I pondered for a while but soon found myself agreeing with Moss's suggestion. I am happy to acknowledge him here. Indeed, I am happy to call *Sueños* a collaboration of several people: Barbara, Moss, and myself—not to mention all the "fathers." If the poem was a community effort, so much the better for me; we poets, like everyone else in this world, need all the help we can get. The point is that, for me, the poem develops or "unwinds" the initial line in the best way it could, given the conditions of my life and art in 1974.

What principles of technique did you consciously use?

By now the answer to this must be pretty clear. Consciously I tried to avoid technique and work artlessly, automatically. This kind of artlessness is in itself, of course, a technique. And so it is no coincidence that the poem appears in five-line stanzas—as if my mind, freed of its shackles, drifted intuitively toward patterns in a rage for order. As a matter of fact, *Sueños* was written during a period when I was trying to break away from quatrains!

Whom do you visualize as your reader?

My dead father. His father. All the wise old "fathers." And Barbara. I would have them read the poem aloud, sonorously, in a large room.

Can the poem be paraphrased? How?

Sure, it can be paraphrased, like any text—for whatever value and detriment paraphrase has. I'd rather leave that to the critics, though. Howard Moss's description of the poem being about the difficulty of expressing feeling might be a good start.

How does the poem differ from earlier poems of yours in (a) quality, (b) theme, (c) technique?

Quality. It may not be chic to say, but I like *Sueños* a lot, mainly, I guess, because of the italicized portion of the poem. To speak honestly, with intensity and authority, about such poignant things—such potentially sentimental things—is, for me, the highest accomplishment.

Theme. In its explicit Jewishness *Sueños* differed from most of my earlier work. I was surprised to find myself dealing with Jewish themes in several poems written after *Sueños.* I was certainly not elated with the ethnic turn my work had taken; Jewish themes do not necessarily spell the freshest, most exciting direction for American poetry in the 1970s. Still, *Sueños* spelled an exciting new direction for *me*, if for no one else, and I was glad to have written it.

As for the theme being about "the difficulty of expressing feeling," I think I have dealt with this idea before and after *Sueños.* It is a fairly constant theme in my work. Considering that, in some ways, I am a rather ordinary twentieth-century American male with affiliations with what might be called "the locker room school of younger American heterosexual poets," such a theme is easy to understand. A good number of male American poets in my generation might deny that it's damned hard to express feelings, especially love. Still, I have a hunch they know what I'm talking about.

Technique. Technically the poem was a breakthrough for me in terms of the way it moved—"unwound"—from beginning to end and broke in the middle with the word "But." While I had been mainly interested in narrative modes before *Sueños*—and, to an extent, still am—this poem helped me explore other modes of free association.

Postscript

It strikes me, as I write this essay nearly a year after the composition of *Sueños*, that the poem went through far fewer drafts than is customary with me. I progressed by leaps and bounds, heuristically as usual, with that marvelous sense of pulling innumerable multicolored rabbits out of ordinary hats.

I almost always listen to classical music when I write. While I was working on *Sueños* in New Hampshire, I listened to Mahler. The first movement of his Ninth Symphony. Over and over again. Loud. On a cheap stereo purchased with trading stamps. To get just an iota of the greatness of such music into poetry has always been my ambition.

See also my essay "How I Wrote 'The Breathers' or The Whole Truth and Nothing But the Truth," in *Eating the Menu: Contemporary American Poetry 1970–1974*, ed. Bruce E. Taylor (Kendall/Hunt, 1974), pp. 13–14.

Born in New York City in 1941, **James Reiss** grew up in Washington Heights and suburban New Jersey. He took two degrees and won two Academy of American Poets' prizes at the University of Chicago. He co-edited *Self-Interviews* (1970) with James Dickey along with his wife, Barbara Eve, and published *The Breathers* (1974, American Poetry Series No. 4). He has won NEA and CAPS grants and taught at the University of California at Davis, Miami University in Ohio, and Queens College, CUNY.

Dennis Schmitz

RABBITS

the urge to stroke the dead
        one back, handfeed life
to the animal
body even as its soft
        vision dilates,
your calluses pulling
fur like lint from the unmendable

flesh. shake your head
        & coming back, hose the hutch
before your wife
six months pregnant sees

the rabbit. later
        she can launder your sweaty
overalls & empty the few
        black rabbit
pellets your pockets
caught. in the closet you

change & relishing the bachelor
scents of your underwear
        drop it to your father-in-law's
bathroom floor. now your voice

weighs nothing though
        you sing.

1 Most of my poems begin in free-association, but the sounds of the words are more important to me than the picture they make. I discover the subject as the poem develops. I like the controlled meandering of music like *The Goldberg Variations*—the announcements, the repetitions, the revelation of units. The discredited idea that the pattern of electrical discharges in an individual's brain correspond rhythmically to the kind of music the person prefers I have admired for its metaphoric truth. Why not zip-zap?

The first line of this poem occurred to me as it appears in the poem. The title and general subject of the poem came soon after. The hesitation in the first line break now seems a good way to modulate the development of the vowel sounds. Asymmetrical lines, indentation, line and stanza breaks are ways for me to indicate the flow of my voice—to cancel or elaborate emphasis. I am encouraged to continue a poem only when I like my own singing in it.

Somehow my voice has to get along with a typewriter accompaniment once I begin a poem. I can't compose without typing—I need to see the line breaks as the poem comes out.

2 I used to be able to sit through a poem until it was finished. Now I'm not as patient, or things don't come out as easily. This poem took a couple of months of off-and-on tinkering after the first half was made. I didn't work steadily, but looked at what I had when I felt like it. It's like reconstructing some affection for the "Rose of Tralee" from old cylinder-recordings in your grandmother's basement.

Eventually the poem grew. I picked up the echoes and began to surprise myself again by making new sounds. You can notice that splice in the first two lines of the third stanza. In the third line of that stanza I try to switch my attention from the alliteration ("sweaty" followed by the line break helps). There is another splice in the last line of the third stanza. The alliteration here was not conscious either, but I see that it is modified by delaying the verb "change" and that emphasis is immediately modified by joining to it another verb and another notion.

Once I was able to start working at the poem again I could see some direction. The wife's assumed response, her misunderstanding in the gestures of emptying the pockets and redoing the disembodied overalls were clearer. The weakness of the wife is acknowledged to be the weakness of the husband. I still didn't know what the husband would do. But I was squeezing out words by the time I got to the end of the third stanza. It was natural that I would lose interest in the ideas.

I started by singing and wound up humming. Sometimes retyping the whole of what I have when I work on every draft, every false reentry into the poem, is a way to find my place in the poem. When I was writing this poem I recognized the false starts as such after a few words.

I was able to finish the poem because the last sentence came to me as I read over the third stanza. It sounded right after I tried a few different line breaks. That the father-in-law's bathroom be the place of revelation seemed appropriate, if a little too ironic. I thought that the conclusion had to be definite as an answer to the sequence of events in the poem.

3 I want a poem to keep moving, I want the information the poem gives, if the poem follows a story line (my poems often do), to be seen in the development of the poem. The line breaks should make the sense of the poem clearer by showing the delivery the poet intended. Yet a line or stanza may break against the sense of the poem. Or what appears to be a reading of the poem.

My lines are short enough that the reader will not be confused. I slow or speed up the lines so that the ear may help the eye. The last line in the first stanza of the poem, for instance, takes a long time to say. The husband must examine himself, compare his body with that of the rabbit before his reaction in stanza 2. His realization doesn't come at once. He doesn't know his own beauty.

The cadence of the first line seems to dominate the poem. The first stanza is best, most natural. You can put an ear to other places in the poem and hear the clank and whir of poetic devices. But I didn't use them consciously, a gear here, a spring there.

The first line is a declaration of intention. The poem starts in the middle of an action with no explanation. The second line is indented so the reader may complete the thought of the first line quickly. The comma is a half-stop to change the pace of the delivery of "the dead/one back," while the compound "handfeed" prepares for the emphasis of "life" with vowel change (băck to hănd to fēēd to līfe) and "f" sound. None of the effects was intended in the act of composition, but they seemed suitable once they were down.

I like to use my own words, rather than book words. If there are comparisons in a poem, I would like them to clarify the information I release piece by piece. Metaphor is cheap. A poem is not a note to the milkman, however. We have prose for that.

4 I didn't have particular readers in mind when I wrote this poem.

5 Rather than accept a paraphrase, I hope the reader will be more interested in investigating some relationships in the poem:

What is the significance of the title? What is the affection of the husband for the dead rabbit? For the wife and unborn child? How are the rabbit and the unborn child comparable? How are the husband and the rabbit comparable as intimated by the touch, flesh to flesh?

How does the husband protect the pregnant wife from the effects of the superstitition they share? What is the significance of the ritual cleaning of the rabbit dwelling?

Is there a parallel to the wife's handling of her husband's overalls in the husband's disposal of the rabbit? In the husband's disposal of his underclothes? Why are there dried pieces of rabbit waste in the husband's pockets? What may be the wife's attitude toward the waste?

Why does the husband relish his "bachelor" scents, his waste? What does his cleaning of himself suggest? The couple live in her father's house; is that important? The stanza break before the concluding two lines may make the reader believe the voice is to be thrown down as the underclothes are; instead the voice is what remains, unencumbered. Why is the voice left?

6 The poem seems much like other poems I've done, certainly as far as technique is concerned.

Dennis Schmitz was born in 1937 and grew up in Dubuque, Iowa, where he attended Loras College. After graduate study at the University of Chicago, he taught for several years at Illinois Institute of Technology and the University of Wisconsin-Milwaukee. At present he teaches at California State University, Sacramento. His books of poetry include *We Weep for Our Strangeness* (1969), *Double Exposures* (1971), and *Goodwill, Inc.* (1976).

Richard Shelton

CHILDREN OF NIGHT

I lay down
beside the body of the river
as if beside a beautiful woman
and all night she sobbed
that the light was gone
and would never return

at dawn a little wind
touched us gently
and when I woke she was singing
of the beauty of darkness

---

daylight arrives or departs
like royalty
with a fanfare of trumpets
and great banners in the sky

but darkness
sends no messengers before it
and arrives like water under the door
reminding us we are small and alone
and powerless to see

some of us accept it out of love
others out of fear
but none can send it away

---

when light is separated
into its parts
we see a rainbow
but darkness cannot be separated
darkness is all the same thing

when we enter darkness
we can no longer see where we are going
or where we have been
but we become more aware that we are

---

when the sun comes up
everything is waiting for it
but when the moon comes up
it is always a surprise

we malign the moon
when we say it is inconstant

the moon gathers whatever light
it can find in the darkness
and gives it all to us
keeping none for itself

---

when we enter darkness
we give up the light
but when we enter the light some of us
carry a little piece of darkness with us
and will not let it go
we are the children of night

1 This poem began with the first ten lines, and I do not know where they came from, especially the reference to the river. Where I live, the rivers are dry; but this is obviously a more conventional river. However, I was raised near a river, and have slept on the banks of rivers in several states, including one memorable night spent on the bank of a river in Mexico. I feel that the first section of the poem comes from one of those experiences from the past, and I am fairly sure that the line "the beauty of darkness" elicited the rest of the poem.

Once I had that line, I began to associate with ideas of darkness and night. I usually write poetry only at night, and I also wander in the Sonora Desert at night. Often, I am still up when the sun rises, and I watch that transition from darkness to light with great interest.

At about the time this poem was written, I had been writing a series of loosely structured poems about the moon as it appears over the desert. And I had become aware that most of my desert poems are nocturnal, but I attributed this to the fact that I usually write at night. As I was associating with the idea of darkness, I became increasingly aware that my fascination was not so much with the moon as it was with night itself, possibly even darkness. This poem is the record of my coming to that conclusion. It was not until I finished the last section that I realized where the poem was leading me and that I had made none of the usual associations between darkness and evil or death.

For me, writing the poem was the process by which I learned something about myself I had not previously known, at least not consciously. When I finished it, I realized for the first time that I am more comfortable and feel more secure at night than during the daytime. With that in mind, I gave the poem its title.

2 The first section of the poem was written one night and then abandoned as a false start. The three sections in the middle, as well as a fourth section which I eventually deleted, were written about two nights later. I then put the poem aside for several weeks and thought no more about it. Finally, one night when I was working on a quite different poem, the last stanza arrived almost exactly as it is. I felt it was the conclusion I had been working toward and began to polish each of the sections, deleting words, changing line breaks, and cutting some entire lines. Each section went through about ten to twelve drafts—each section except the last, which I changed very little.

At this point I discovered that one of the sections which had to do with shadows did not belong in the poem at all, and I removed it. I have not yet found the poem to which it belongs. It was a simple matter to arrange the sections in their present order since I knew which had to be first and which had to be last and that the order of the other three was unimportant.

3 I used only the techniques that I usually do, and these have become so ingrained that I am not sure their use could be considered "conscious," except perhaps sporadically. They include compression, attention to diction, and attention to stanza breaks and line breaks. I tried to break the lines into natural syntactical units. I tried, above all, for clarity, so that no line could possibly be misread.

4 Whom did I visualize as my reader? That's difficult to answer. Usually, I think, I write for myself. I try to work my way through an emotional complex or series of impressions and arrive at a conclusion I was not previously aware of. I think that was the case with this poem. At some point in the process, I suppose, I become aware that somebody else might read the poem, but other than my wife and son, I have no real idea of who this might be. Whoever it is, I want the poem to be as clear as I can possibly make it.

5 I do not think the poem can be paraphrased—at least I hope it can't. It is a series of statements describing my impressions of night and darkness, and hopefully these statements add up to more than the sum of their parts. And while one might summarize the conclusion in the last section with some such statement as "some people are nocturnal," I like to believe that the poem might make the reader feel the attraction of darkness and night rather than merely understand it intellectually.

6 *Quality.* I hope my work has improved over the years. It seems to me that it now has more depth, takes more risks, and engages a broader range of subjects than it did five or six years ago.

Theme. My work still deals with many of the same themes it did previously, although often from a different point of view. But it also deals with several other themes which have grown out of an increased awareness of the problems of marriage, the situation of men and women in the American prison system, and the destruction of the Sonora Desert.

Technique. The technique, in a broad sense, has changed considerably. My more recent work is less surrealistic, less imagistic, and less complex linguistically. I now seem to be using fewer images and more statements in an attempt to be more direct and clear. This has not been a conscious shift. It has just happened.

Richard Shelton was born in Boise, Idaho, in 1933 and lives in the mountains west of Tucson, Arizona, with his wife and son. He teaches in the writing program at the University of Arizona and conducts a writers' workshop at the Arizona State Prison in Florence. His books of poetry include: *The Tattooed Desert* (1971, winner of the United States Award for 1970), *Of All the Dirty Words* (1973), *You Can't Have Everything* (1975), *Journal of Return* (1969), *Calendar* (1972), and *Chosen Place* (1975). He is the recipient of Borestone Mountain Poetry Awards First Award in 1972 and Third Award in 1973, and the editor of *The Unfinished Man—The Poetry of Paul David Ashley* (1976).

Charles Simic

THE PARTIAL EXPLANATION

Seems like a long time
Since the waiter took my order.
Grimy little luncheonette,
The snow falling outside.

Seems like it's grown darker
Since I last heard the kitchen door
Behind my back
Since I last noticed
Anyone pass on the street.

A glass of ice water
Keeps me company
At this table I chose myself
Upon entering,

And a longing,
Incredible longing
To eavesdrop
On the conversation
Of cooks.

1 The poem didn't "start." The experience was with me as far back as I can remember—or more precisely the nagging image of just such an interior. Periodically, it would surface, and I would catch a glimpse of it and receive a jolt, a vague sense of dread, of premonition, which would remain just that as I would turn away to other matters. I began to write the poem when the phrase "a long time since the waiter took my order" occurred to me.

This is, indeed, the crucial event. The instant when that slumbering, almost anonymous content becomes audible, when its privacy is abolished and it translates itself into language. Having said that, I realize that I know nothing of the actual cause, and furthermore, that I had no choice. No wonder poets have always spoken of that event as of a gift. The experience chooses and then sends forth. Being a poet means having no choice but to submit.

Of course, the gift is no more than a possibility, a hint. It requires attending to. It requires a patience in order to hear what the words are really saying. Always and everywhere they are telling us which way the poem has to go. They are even telling us how the poem ends, the poem which is still unwritten. At that point, perhaps, there is no need to go back to the original experience. At that point one has to accept the possibility that the poem might go where one least expects it. The initial phrase, as it were, already has its own law and destiny.

2 The poem manipulates Time. Out of the simultaneity of the experience, the event of language is an emergence into linear time. That bit of language in the beginning contains a kind of clock—the poem is the unwinding. The phrase sets up expectations, and the poet manipulates time by postponing its fulfillment. This is a delicate, intuitive dialectic whose purpose is to use the tension that results in order to endow the words with resonance. When I say *resonance* I have more in mind than just the multiplicity of meaning. What the words are saying has to be *seen*. The purpose of that dialectic is to bring out the visual, to dramatize the situation and thus make it accessible to the reader's consciousness.

I knew the poem was going to be short. My additions and revisions had one aim: economy. I wanted to establish the context succinctly and quickly. I don't want to give the impression that I was in control, that I had it all figured out ahead. It took me a long time to stumble upon the obvious. This is what happens ordinarily and I'm prepared for it in the long run. For the rest, I had these hunches to guide me:

—A slow-moving poem with a number of pauses and hesitations. The voice, which is how the movement gets embodied, had to suggest a kind of weariness. I needed that slow pace in order to give the words weight. Actually, I had to imagine the effect on the reader of having these words in this order. Again, I was both manipulating and submitting to the inevitable.

—The next "hunch" is more difficult to describe. I wanted to include in the poem everything that I found unsayable. That is, retain the ambiguity of its origins. It seems to me that poetry aims to stand on that threshold. The poem as the vague figure in the doorway. Ambiguity as whatever still preserves the memory of the other side. Words which still retain the pressure of the unspoken. My hope here then to include the two realms.

—The ending was there all along. I mean, I had a premonition it would come as a surprise and my revisions were really a way of preparing the ground for the inevitable to happen. When it struck, it did so in the same unpremeditated manner as the first two lines. It was only then that I *understood* the poem, and so whatever further revisions remained, they were easy to make. Finally, as the poem took the shape you see here now, it took me a while to get used to it. That sense of separation, of distance, is the only way I can tell the poem is done with.

3 The only principle of technique I'm aware of is faith. Faith to the language and faith to the situation to which that language points. Nothing else. To play critic while in the process of writing would be distracting. This doesn't mean that I'm not self-conscious while writing. I am, but what I need to believe at the time is that the "situation" is completely without a precedent and that there are no outside solutions. In other words, I cannot live off anyone's intensity but mine.

Again, this demands some clarification. There are poems I write where the strategy is directly an offshoot of some traditional mode. There's also no doubt that the manner in which my psyche makes the material available to me is predicated by everything I have absorbed about the tradition of poetry. The act of writing, however, is something else. There I have to forget all that in order to undertake the impossible task of giving these words life. Since all words have a history and the act of composition is presumably ahistorical, the resulting tension can only be overcome if one has faith in the uniqueness of the undertaking.

4 No paraphrase. The poem is the only possible way in which whatever needed to be said was said. This doesn't prevent the reader from having ideas about it. The poet, however, has to place his trust in the poem's way of saying. Everything that he knows and holds true is already in the poem. This is the poet's unique vulnerability, his "madness," which he has to accept.

A poem is an organism. It is a projection of our existence, a cosmology of a particular experience. It is a sequence imposed on the simultaneity of that experience in order to recreate it. Its "poetry" is nothing more than the presence of someone existing and acknowledging his own life. This condition is more fundamental than any description of its properties. To define what a poem is would require defining human existence. It would require answering why is there *something*, rather than nothing.

Charles Simic, who teaches at the University of New Hampshire, was born in Yugoslavia in 1938. Educated at New York University, he had worked at various jobs before turning to teaching in 1970. Five collections of his poetry have been published: *What the Grass Says* (1967), *Somewhere Among Us a Stone Is Taking Notes* (1969), *Dismantling the Silence* (1971), *Return to a Place Lit by a Glass of Milk* (1974), and *White,* a long poem published in 1972. For these he has received the Edgar Allan Poe Award, a Guggenheim Fellowship, and a National Endowment for the Arts grant.

Louis Simpson

THE HOUR OF FEELING

Love, now a universal birth,
From heart to heart is stealing,
From earth to man, from man to earth:
—It is the hour of feeling.
Wordsworth, "To My Sister"

A woman speaks:
"I hear you were in San Francisco.
What did they tell you about me?"

She begins to tremble. I can hear the sound
her elbow made, rapping on wood.
It was something to see and to hear—
not like the words that pass for life,
things you read about in the papers.

People who read a deeper significance
into everything, every whisper . . .
who believe that a knife crossed with a fork
are a signal . . . by the sheer intensity
of their feeling leave an impression.

And with her, tangled in her hair,
came the atmosphere, four walls,
the avenues of the city
at twilight, the lights going on.

When I left I started to walk.
Once I stopped to look at a window
displaying ice skates and skis.
At another with Florsheim shoes . . .

Thanks to the emotion with which she spoke
I can see half of Manhattan,
the canyons and the avenues.

There are signs high in the air
above Times Square and the vicinity:
a sign for Schenley's Whiskey,
for Admiral Television,
and a sign saying Milltag, whatever that means.

I can see over to Brooklyn and Jersey,
and beyond there are meadows,
and mountains and plains.

The poem began with an experience: living in New York and working as an editor in a publishing house. One day a woman came in to pick up a manuscript that had been rejected. It was a peculiar piece of writing. She had invented a machine for choosing a mate. It looked like the electric chair. You put your prospective partner in it and the pointer swung to a number. Then you made some calculations. After that you were supposed to consult astrological charts. Finally you would consider whether you were compatible. The whole thing was ridiculous. The woman, however. did not look like the kind of eccentric you might have expected. She was about thirty, red-haired, slender—in fact, quite attractive.

I explained to her why we couldn't publish the manuscript. Then she started to tremble—her elbow rapped on the desk as it does in the poem. I saw that the situation was getting out of hand and tried to calm her down. Then she said, "I hear you were in San Francisco. What did they tell you about me?" I had just come back from a short vacation in San Francisco; she had been told I was there when she called to find out the fate of the manuscript. I saw that I had to deal with a person who was not sane. I wasn't the only one to see it. There was a woman sharing my office; she saw what was up and stayed at her desk during our interview, so as to be a witness if one were needed. At the end the woman with the mating machine took her manuscript and left. I was glad to see her go.

As I say in the poem, such people "by the sheer intensity of their feeling leave an impression." The impression was indelibly etched on my consciousness. A few years ago I began trying to write poetry about this period of my life. In these poems I set out to record images of Manhattan and the atmosphere of the city. I tried to work in this episode in my descriptions. The trouble was, I couldn't see what made this episode and one or two others hang together. It isn't enough to describe, you have to know why. Finally I saw what linked this character and the others: it was a feeling in myself, a sympathy I had for them. The insane view held by this woman was, in its way, an act of poetic imagination. She wished to make events in the real world conform to her vision of things. The doctors' name for her condition was paranoia.

The actual writing of the poem, as with most of my poems, took years. I had no idea how it would work out; I had some images and clusters of lines that I would push around. Sometimes I would think I had a poem in view, then it would disintegrate. I would be ashamed to have people see just how hard it is for me to finish what I consider a real poem. Some of my contemporaries don't have this problem: they write down whatever they feel like writing, hardly revise, if indeed they revise at all, and publish it right away. Some of them are able to publish a book every year or two. It takes me five or six years to finish a book of poems.

I saw the woman in the poem in the early 1950s. The images of New York were accumulated over a span of years. Here is a page from a notebook I kept. You will see the bearing this has on material in the poem.

13 Nov. 1962. Monday

B'way & 42nd St. looking North (at my back, Crossroads Cafe).
Distance: Canadian Club
          Admiral Television Appliances

N. E. corner: Florsheim (on corner)
              Books/Souvenirs
              Trans Continental Airlines Agency
       Globe: Exclusive New York Showing: No Morals/ Midnight Frolics—strictly adults only
—above, Times Square Bowling Lanes

To West (7th Ave)
       Rialto: First New York showing: West End Jungle, the film that London banned—adults only—with Naked Terror

          Cameras   Kodak Films
          Records   Columbia Records

These notes were a source not only of *The Hour of Feeling* but of two other poems as well, *The Rejected* and *The Springs at Gadara.* It sometimes happens that many things are conceived at once.

I don't usually make notes—only when I travel and come upon a scene the details of which strike me as important. As a rule, drafts of unfinished poems—of which I have boxes full—are my notes for future poems.

Here is another entry from the notebook, two pages further on. Again, you will see the connection with *The Hour of Feeling.*

42nd bet B'way & Ave. of the Americas

Sweetville candy U. S. A. nuts
Ice skates golf hunting ski equipment
American Irving Savings Time
  time   temperature
   12 27   46
  flashes off flashes on

These notes proved useful—notes aren't always useful, they can be a waste of time. But what was much more important in writing about New York was to relive the period imaginatively. This required "immersion." I would imagine myself there, immerse myself in the atmosphere of the time and place, try to see what was significant, concentrate on certain images and eliminate others, and arrive finally at my true feeling about the experience. This is the way I write poetry. I hope also that something will be given to me in the course of writing—something more than I can arrive at by the immersion I have tried to describe. If you recall, Wordsworth said that poetry "takes its origin from emotion recollected in tranquillity." Most people think he said that poetry is emotion recollected in tranquillity. But for Wordsworth, remembering an emotion was only the beginning. Something new would happen in the course of writing—more than could be accounted for in the original experience. Poetry was a discovery, a making, not merely a recollection. I agree with his view of the process. Though I may have done everything I can to get at the truth of an experience, I don't consider that I have a poem unless it begins to excite me by telling me something I haven't consciously known.

Here is a draft of a poem that was never published. It stands halfway between the notes I have given above and the poem *The Hour of Feeling.* You can see how I am groping in this draft. In fact, the last line says that I am groping.

SIGNS

Standing with his back to the Crossroads Café
this is what he observed:

Signs advertising Canadian Club
and Admiral Television Appliances.
On the North-East corner, Florsheim Shoes.
Books Souvenirs
Trans Continental Airlines Agency.

He observed that the Globe was playing
No Morals and Midnight Frolics Adults Only

```
Continuing to walk East
past Sweetville Candy U. S. A.,
glancing at his reflection
in a window exhibiting ice skates
golf  hunting  ski  equipment . . . .

 At the American Irving Savings Bank
hHe saw that the time was 7:27,
the temperature 46,

and he asked, What does it prove?
```

The corrections above are exactly as they are in the original draft.

Obviously something was lacking in *Signs*. What, indeed, did it prove? Years later—just this past year—I began another version of the episode of the woman with the mating machine. I made some changes—the incident took place in a restaurant instead of a publishers' office, and I cut out the business about the manuscript. The mating machine seemed ridiculous, and I didn't want to be satiric—I was after bigger game. In the new poem, after I left the woman and started to walk, I began to notice the signs. The advertisements in the sky, the objects in windows, the avenues, the whole city was charged with her emotion. Not only the city . . . "and beyond there are meadows,/and mountains and plains." It was human feeling that made these things memorable.

The epigraph, from Wordsworth's poem *To My Sister*, had been in my mind for years. The mind is the best notebook. When I had written the poem, my mind handed me the quotation and the title, *The Hour of Feeling.*

"How many drafts did the poem go through?" Maybe fifteen, though that is only a guess. "What intervals of time elapsed between the drafts?" Thirteen years from the notebook entries to the finished poem. "Did the poem shrink or expand? At times it expanded—then, rapidly, it would shrink. As for changes in the lines: sometimes these were changes of rhythm, sometimes of imagery, sometimes of sound.

I "lineate" my poems according to my patterns of thought and speech. I don't follow a literary convention—i.e., meter.

I make verse paragraphs so that a group of lines will be read together. They usually make a unit of thought. Sometimes, however, I will break a long passage into paragraphs because a pause seems indicated, as in speech, for the sake of a little silence. I sometimes make a verse paragraph so that the poem will look better on the page—a shaped form rather than a spate of words.

"What rhythmical principle did you use?" I write according to speech cadence and the cadence of idea groups, to use your terms. I try always to write "with the cadence of a particular emotion, the cadence of a bodily rhythm." Incidentally, I am interested to see you using these terms. I started using them myself some years ago. I don't think they were in general use—they would certainly not have been approved by New Critics and their followers.

I don't have any principles for the use of sound repetition, assonance, alliteration, consonance, onomatopoeia, etcetera. I play these things by ear. As for "exact rhyme," I hardly ever make rhymes. Rhymes occur in some of my recent poems but they are unobtrusive and irregular.

The poem could be read either silently or aloud. I have no preference. To read it to a musical accompaniment would be absurd.

In answer to the question about "metaphorical process"—I don't set out to make metaphors. Similes strike me as awkward. On the other hand, I do write so that my presentation of literal details will have a metaphorical, symbolic, or surrealist effect. I hope that my concentration on details, the thought that has gone into selecting them, the imagination that has gone into moving from one detail to another, will give my descriptions a meaning beyond the literal.

I avoid using abstract language, "poetic" diction, or any other kind of mannerism, unless I am being satiric—which I sometimes am.

I shall not answer all the other questions, so as not to weary myself or the reader. I shall answer those that strike me as more interesting.

I make allusions only when they seem necessary and then I try to explain the allusion within the poem itself. I don't think that anyone who reads my poems has to go to a library to look up allusions. This brings us to the question, "Whom do you visualize as your reader?" It's a touchy question. I certainly don't write for people who read Rod McKuen. Nor for people who want political poetry. In fact, as far as I can see, I have very few readers. On the other hand, my poems have been translated into some nine foreign languages and have been taught in schools in Africa, in Macedonia, and other places. I guess I am writing for readers in the

United States in the future. If I told people things they expected to hear, or if I said nice things about my contemporaries, I might have a kind of reader I can visualize. I can visualize that reader very clearly, indeed.

The ordering of the poem was psychological. I wanted one feeling and image to lead naturally to another.

I wanted the poem to open at the end, onto infinity.

The persona in the poem is a part of myself. As though I were a character in a novel. I use techniques of prose fiction in writing my poems. I write narrative poems for the most part—or poetry in which there are elements of narrative—and I set out writing a poem in the way that Conrad or Chekhov would set about writing a story in prose.

Sometimes I'll use a cliché but I'm not conscious of having done so in this poem.

The poem is shaped in verse paragraphs so as not to weary the eye with masses of words that just keep going.

"How would you describe the tone of this poem?" I'd rather not describe it. If the tone isn't obvious, then this poem has failed.

I would rather not paraphrase the poem for the same reason that I don't want to describe the tone. If a poet were sure of the exact meaning of his poem it would be a poem with a limited meaning. But I want my poetry to open on the unknown.

The Hour of Feeling is a continuation of work I have done before. It has the quality of my best writing. In its attempt to create the atmosphere of New York and its presentation of the woman's character the poem may mark an advance: at any rate, the material is presented in a new way and with greater understanding on my part. It is my understanding that gives the disparate elements their coherence. This is an important poem for me, one of the most important I have written.

Louis Simpson was born in Jamaica, West Indies, in 1923, and came to the United States at the age of seventeen. He studied at Columbia University, saw combat in World War II, traveled in Europe. He has worked as an editor, then as a teacher. At present he teaches English and Comparative Literature in the State University of New York at Stony Brook. He has published seven books of poetry, including *At the End of the Open Road* (1963), *Adventures of the Letter I* (1971), *and Searching for the Ox* (1976). In 1964 he was awarded the Pulitzer Prize.

William Stafford

ASK ME

Some time when the river is ice ask me
mistakes I have made. Ask me whether
what I have done is my life. Others
have come in their slow way into
my thought, and some have tried to help
or to hurt—ask me what difference
their strongest love or hate has made.

I will listen to what you say.
You and I can turn and look
at the silent river and wait. We know
the current is there, hidden; and there
are comings and goings from miles away
that hold the stillness exactly before us.
What the river says, that is what I say.

DRAFT 1

```
Some time when the river is ice, ask me
~~the~~ mistakes, Ask me whether what I have
done is my life.  Others have come
```

[handwritten: "I have made." above "Ask", with the "A" of "Ask" written over the lowercase "a"]

in their slow way into ~~the~~ my thoughts, ~~And~~ and
some have tried to help or to hurt.
Ask me what differences their strongest ~~efforts~~ hate
~~have~~ or love has made. I will listen to what you say.
You and I can then turn
and look at the silent river and wait.
We will know the current is there,
hidden, and there are comings and goings
miles away that hold the stillness
exactly before us. If the river says anything,
whatever it says is my answer. What the river says
is what I say.

DRAFT 2

Some time when the river is ice ask me
~~ask me~~
mistakes I have made. Ask me whether
what I have done is my life. Others
have come in their slow way into
my thoughts, and some have tried to help
or to hurt. Ask me what difference their strongest
hate or love has made.
I will listen to what you say.
You and I can turn and look
at the silent river and wait. We know
the current is there, hidden, and there
are comings and goings from miles away
that hold the stillness exactly before us.
What the river says is what I say.

DRAFT 3

ASK ME

Some time when the river is ice ask me
mistakes I have made. Ask me whether

what I have done is my life. Others
have come in their slow way into
my thoughts, and some have tried to help
or to hurt: Ask me what difference
their strongest love or hate has made.

I will listen to what you say.
You and I can turn and look
at the silent river and wait. We know
the current is there, hidden; and there
are comings and goings from miles away
that hold the stillness exactly before us.
What the river says is what I say.

1 My poem started from amid random writing I was doing in my usual morning attempts to scare up something by putting anything down that came to mind. I was at a country place; it was early morning; I was all alone, and feeling that way—in a pleasant way, with a fire in the Franklin stove, the dark outside. It was winter, and I guess the cold made me launch in the way I did, "Some time when the river is ice. . . ."

2 This poem stayed in much its original order—more so than most of mine. Writing it was like getting a lock on a feeling and just letting the feeling lead me from one part to the next. This is not to say that the elements mentioned stayed the same, but the changes were themselves (the changes of topic, I mean) were just a following of the feeling.

3 My impulse is to say that I had no principles of technique at all in mind. As I look back over the first draft, I do realize, though, that I was getting satisfaction out of syncopating along in the sentences; that is, I find some pleasure in just opening and closing sentences—starting and then holding before myself a feeling that the measure and flow of utterance will lend itself to an easy forwarding of what I am saying. I guess I am trying to own up to a pervasive *security* in language, but the feeling is not consciously based on use of a technique in any sense I have known others to define it.

4 As in almost all of my writing, I was not aiming toward any reader: my entry into the process was through inward satisfactions I felt as the language led me onward. If I quiz myself now, I am able to assume that I was *accompanied by* a sense of being able to tell someone, sometime, something like what I was putting down; that person would not necessarily be congenial—maybe someone I was going to *tell off*. But that person would also be participating in the steady unfolding of what was said.

5 I think my poem can be paraphrased—and that any poem can be paraphrased. But every pass through the material, using other words, would have to be achieved at certain costs, either in momentum, or nuance, or dangerously explicit (and therefore misleading in tone) adjustments. I'll try one such pass through the poem:

> When it's quiet and cold and we have some chance to interchange without hurry, confront me if you like with a challenge about whether I think I have made mistakes in my life—and ask me, if you want to, whether to me my life is actually the sequence of events or exploits others would see. Well, those others tag along in my living, and some of them in fact have played significant roles in the narrative run of my world; they have intended either helping or hurting (but by implication in the way I am saying this you will know that neither effort is conclusive). So—ask me how important their good or bad intentions have been (both intentions get a drastic *leveling* judgment from this cool stating of it all). You, too, will be entering that realm of maybe-help-maybe-hurt, by entering that far into my life by asking this serious question—so: I will stay still and consider. Out there will be the world confronting us both; we will both know we are surrounded by mystery, tremendous things that do not reveal themselves to us. That river, that world—and our lives—all share the depth and stillness of much more significance than our talk, or intentions. There is a steadiness and somehow a solace in knowing that what is around us so greatly surpasses our human concerns.

6 This poem shares with many of my poems a tone of accepting what comes. Human affairs get perspectived by affairs other than human. This poem is much more serious, unrelenting, than most—but not all—of my other poems. It is *one of the ways* that occur to me. It is like almost all of my other poems, though, in a deep way—it comes about through willing entry into whatever mood or whatever opportunities a time and place and the chances of language offer me.

Some Reflections That Come from Reading Down the Checklist

This poem, like almost all my poems, came from free association, that is, free allowing of my impulses to find their immediate interest. I was aware of a steady forward cadence. This poem went through only about three complete drafts, and the first writing of the poem was much more clear and *set* than most; the changes were a teasing out of opportunities perceived in the first draft. And I believe the poem was essentially complete within three days (and I was of course not on it all that time). The structure, theme, and tone just kept on being what they started out to be—working on the poem was like telling it—"go ahead, be yourself." My lines are generally just about equal; where a line breaks, though, means something to me, and some of the juggling was meant to preserve how definite the slash line is in such changeover sequences as me/mistakes, have/done, and/some, etc. I was aware of current *is there . . . there are*, things like that—willingnesses to repeat, coasting the sounds. . . .

I would like my poem to be read aloud in a serious voice without any relenting, but silent reading by a person feeling it would be all right.

I did not consider metaphor at all. I know—and I suppose at the time I knew with an immediacy and a gusto—that "river is ice" for instance can't just be present without an effect; but in writing I found my way forward to accepting the feelings and saying what occurred to me—metaphorical elements sweep into the utterance, but not by intent. In some ways, I now see, I was putting the reader into stern obligation to accept a forceful metaphor but without my revealing by any tremor that the metaphorical elements were anything other than *necessary* parts of what I was saying.

I ordinarily feel that I am not using abstract language; I am afraid to solicit the reader's or hearer's feelings—I yearn to hand him or her a situation or scene that will coerce human involvement, not request it.

One mannerism, I now see, is that this whole poem addresses another person as if present; the poem maneuvers another person into being the one who demands the account given. I believe I was sliding away from that kind of poem that proclaims—I was indulging a prevalent yen of mine—to keep away from the appearance of elbowing in.

I was using the tug of narrative, a thing I like to do. And I was avoiding anything high at the end. The persona is a part of myself—one of my ways (at least in fancy)—understanding but grabbing. I was not jumpy about cliché—I usually like to be pretty close, as if willing to say any dumb thing (with a nudge that keeps it from quite that—I hope).

The poem is a lump—the reader is in for a block of something—"shape" on the page.

I assume that any human being, with the right context, would respond to the surface of this poem. I believe some would assume that it did not make enough claims. That conviction on their part would be a measure of their smugness or craving for sweets, and even they might have a faint hint of missing something.

William Stafford was born in 1914 in Hutchinson, Kansas. He lived and worked in that state (construction, oil refinery, sugar beet fields) and completed schooling there (M.A., University of Kansas), then studied at the University of Iowa (Ph.D., 1953). Since 1948, with intervals on leave or for teaching at other schools, he has taught literature at Lewis and Clark College, in Portland, Oregon, where he still thrives—works, writes, socializes with the family (wife and four children)—and sends out poems to many periodicals. Collections of his poems are *Traveling Through the Dark* (1962), *The Rescued Year* (1966), *Allegiances* (1970), and *Someday, Maybe* (1973).

Frank Stanford

DEATH AND THE ARKANSAS RIVER

Walking from the killing place,
Walking in mud
The bootsoles leave little hexes in the kitchen.

One summer there was a place
Where everyone chewed dirt in their supper.

It was a place like an attic
With a chest of orchids pressed in books.
Men cleaned their fingernails
In the moonlight.

Death let a bid.

And while everyone was in hipboots
Looking out for Death's fork-lifts,
There was a shine on Death's loafers.
His poll tax was paid, so was his light bill.

In the winter Death runs snow tires on his truck,
He makes long hauls at night.
Death pays the best wage.
He keeps in touch on his two-way.

Death can afford whatever he wants.

If you listened to the ground, you'd hear
Thunder coming like a train on the tracks.
And Death would signal ahead
That the half-dollar you stole to flatten
You lifted from your father's eye.

Death dances a slow boogie
Even the awkward can follow
When he leads.

In my life Death has asked me
To trade dogs, take a fall for love,
While others have asked me
How he combed his hair.

Everytime Death gets a Cadillac
He wants to fight.
He wants to run the front door,
He wants cooking that will remind him of home.

If you try to forget
Death ties a string around your finger.

Regrets and warnings
To those who don't know what's cooking
When Death's bread rises
Out of its grave.

Death, for instance, was looking
To cold-cock my brother.

My brother thought he pulled a fast one.
He played the radio and drank whiskey.
He raised hell
With women already married.

Do you know of anyone who's got the best
Of Death?

Some say you can keep an eye
Out for Death,
But Death is one for fooling around.
He might turn up working odd jobs
At your favorite diner.
He might be peeling spuds.

Death likes the double entendre.

I for one am reminded of butterflies,
Snow blowing off pines:
Death is around you
Like a lock and dam.

So don't let Death catch you
Listening to the ground, even a place
That sounds like home.

It could be Death
Filing a quit-claim deed:
He holds a quiet title
To the land your loved ones walked.

Even if you couldn't hear
The sound would carry
Like a truck on a bridge, like a flower
Given at a ball, a sound in place,
The tradewind called Death, gentle
As children in their night clothes
Fighting with pillows, so quiet
Not a soul is wakened.

WITH THE APPROACH OF THE OAK THE AXEMAN QUAKES

There is a monastery in Arkansas. I was there for some years. My mother sent me there to school after my father died. There, I learned I was an orphan.

One summer I returned to the abbey with my wife. The monks asked us to come help with a summer camp for orphans. Every night the Brothers, the hundred boys, and I would swim in the Arkansas River. My wife would sit on the dock and drink wine Brother Tobias made. She would sketch until the mosquitoes came.

On these long swims to the island there was no telling what we might speak of. At the time I was envisioning a film which still isn't finished, *Deathward.* It was nearly my birthday; I would be a quarter of a century old.

I decided to begin shooting. The scenario was finished. This is the scene: I am in the water filming a monk in a boat. He is rowing from far-away toward me. In the bow there is a draped casket. For the sake of rhythm I have the selection of Bach I will be using on the soundtrack. I hear this with the earphone. With the bare ear I hear commercial fishermen beyond the point, cussing the moon, listening to country music.

While we are filming, my wife is putting the one hundred boys to sleep. Suddenly, a monk runs to the edge of the water. He has brought bad news. One of the students, the son of a local wine maker, has drowned.

We are up river about half a mile. It happened near buoy 25. We go down there. Some of the monks and fishermen are wading the sand bar. It is too dark to look for a body. But the boy is found.

Death is an old dog trader—and like one, that night I make a title for a poem I will write a year later on the eve of my twenty-sixth year.

We traveled back in the fog. It had been a while since I'd been in the main channel. I looked up and saw a huge sphere of concrete. I found out it was a nuclear reactor. Near the water level hung the remains of a large flathead catfish. *Arkansas Nuclear One* said the sign. A fisherman had written: *The Devil's Machine.*

I had a year with this poem; everyday in the woods at work I would say it. I never wrote a word down until I had it right in my mind. It became what they call a floater. That's a work song, a chant. Once I thought it sounded right, and undramatic, I wrote it down without changing a word.

Men sing when they work, or at least they used to. I'm liable to talk to myself. I try to get at the taproot of poetry, of that force drawing things upward. A paradox always—even on Saturday mornings when I might be a little low-down and hung-over, but clear as a bell. I talk to myself. There is a poem that goes:

Each dawn love is a captain
Without a ship.
The only instrumentation
The sad and imaginary
Sound of his voice, love with its own
Words for music, the low light
Of a fairly good star.

At the risk of sounding parabolic, I will let this go as technique. Mean and sing.

Really, I visualize the dead as well as the living. I visualize *you* who I will never know. We are constant strangers. I imagine *you*, I stare at *you* when I write. And to think, you will never know, will never hear of those people I can no longer call anonymous. People close to me have said: I don't understand what you are talking about, but I know what you mean.

I have found out that women seem to be able to get to the heart of my poems, while men are often lost in them. In the beginning I didn't like this, I tried to leave path stones along the way so the masculine psyche could follow. Men know what the sounds are, but they don't know how things sound. I no longer leave a trace on purpose.

Poetry sometimes is like going along in a big rig with no one else on the roads, no smoke, no stops by the wayside, going on with no cargo, the radio quiet, only the sound of your own voice trying to get in touch.

I really don't know if poetry can be paraphrased, set to music, or what have you. Maybe so. Many times the poem ends up down on the ground, surrounded by strangers. I believe that the metaphorical imagination can be authenticated by the cinema. I know that my wife, an artist, has "irrigated" some of her canvases with my poems.

Every two folks have their own way of loving. The poet and the poem know what they like. When a particular kind of loving is adapted, you are getting into a different and strange country.

Now when I was younger, I wrote all the time. I had time to kill. A man has to earn a living; writing has become more special to me. When the poet is young he tries to satisfy himself with many poems in one night. Later, the poet spends many a night trying to satisfy the one poem. My poetry is no longer on a journey, it has arrived at its place.

Then the poet realizes it is midnight, he is alone, and his love is with someone else. What he wanted to sing, what he wanted to mean—someone else has done it. While the poet worried what kind of nails to use, how to fasten down his love, another has hit them on the head and driven them deep.

I give as an example part of a poem from C. D. Wright's new book, *Alla Breve Loving*. Listen to what Ms. Wright has to say:

> I fear another lover
> I am afraid a hurricane might blow tonight,
> Some crazy sister to Camille and Celia
> May come of age tonight, and dash a shelter beam
> Across my skull, and give my heart to a barracuda.
> Or a scorpion may come and whip its jointed tail
> Through my dress. Or four drunken sailors in uniforms
> As tightly fitted as divers' suits, will come with bottles
> Of pulque on their thumbs. They'll screw me standing
> In their boots, one by one. And I fear Jacinto is in cahoots
> With them. Although he gave me a scarf for my salty hair
> And sketched a map so I could walk to the reef today.
> He crushed a centipede with his heel bared. And showed off
> For me with his kungfu moves, kicking sand into the eyes
> Of enemies.

Ten years and ten books and I still haven't said that. I read it in *Alla Breve Loving*, and I still want to say it. Poets friends the enemy.

You know there is no other poet on earth like me. I know there is no other poet on earth like you. We need to be read. This is the theme of poetry, now.

In my early days I was a student of all forms. I learned everything and nothing. I practiced the *Katas* of poetry. I listened to the blues. Having the equilibrium of a poet, I kept falling in love. Now, I believe content and form are not so much in opposition—as many would have us believe. They are one reality, in appearance as well as essence. If you do not know this, no progressive *study* of the art will provide you any insights. The poem eats when it is hungry, sleeps when it is tired.

In getting to the reasons for writing a poem, I suppose the poet can call the reader into the woods and lose him, or he can let him find his own way. I would say, though, in describing the poem we return to the place of poetry, the poet, and to the poetry itself. The following paraphrase from pages 46 and 47 of Daisetz Teitaro Suzuki's *Zen Buddhism and its Influence on Japanese Culture* is a good way of sending the poet on a wild goose chase—which he may need from time to time.

> There was a great poet and teacher of the art. One day another poet came to the city to see him. He came to learn. The master said, "As I observe, you seem to be a master of poetry yourself; pray tell me what school you belong to, before we enter into the relationship of pupil and teacher."
>
> The unknown said, "I am ashamed to confess that I have never learned the art."
>
> "Are you trying to fool me? I am a great teacher, and I know my judging eyes and ears never fail."
>
> "I am sorry to defy your honor, but I really know nothing."
>
> This resolute denial on the part of the visitor made the great poet think for a while, and he finally said, "If you say so, it must be so; but still I am sure you are a master of something, though I do not know of what."
>
> "If you insist, I will tell you. There is one thing of which I can say I am complete master. When I was still a boy and writing my poems, the thought came upon me that as a poet I ought to in no circumstances be afraid of death, and I have grappled with the problem of death now for some years, and finally the problem of death ceased to worry me. How does that sound?"
>
> "Exactly! I am glad I made no mistake in my judgement. For the ultimate secrets of poetry also lie in being released from the thought

of death. I have trained ever so many hundreds of my pupils along this line, but so far none of them really deserve the final certificate for poetry. You need no technical training, you are already a master."

I don't think it matters how a poet plants his garden; it is the quality of the yield which matters. Just like the stars, there are so many things to be said about poems and their poets. I can say I don't want my work to be obscure or vague—I also must say that sometimes I don't mind this trait in the work of others. I am not content in just *suggesting* things by the use of words, I want to *show* the origins, the metaphors of reality, the free movement of the spirit. Poetry is a body, all right, but in spirit it is the function which oftentimes creates the organ.

Jean Cocteau said mystery exists only in precise things—people in their situations, situations in people. Because I believe the visionary life has nothing to do with a necessarily transcendant existence, I *like* most of the poetry I *read*. I believe most poets know *this* is the world; and when you try to lead a special life or write a special poetry, you are dancing with an imaginary partner at a meaningless dance to which you have invited yourself and no one else.

So I think the visionary life is commonplace for the poet, the hair on his head, the pain in his rotting teeth. And I think there is a fear of all this good poetry. The spokesmen and spokeswomen of various constituencies of poetry are on their bulldozers, clearing away perimeters around a vast forest of poetry. This is a way of laying claim. You know what happens. They all meet in the center; everyone else is gone.

I don't believe in a tame poetry. When poetry hears its own name, it runs, flies, swims off for fear of its own life. You can bet your boots on that. Jean Cocteau said a poet rarely bothers about poetry. Does a gardener perfume his roses?

Truthfully, it is the lure of other fields, of other forces which draw me into a poem, not the techniques of a self-conscious poetics. A book like *The Secret Life of Plants* would have more influence on my poetry, add more in explaining and understanding the other systems of poetry, than would certain texts.

Every poet has a field of force not presently understood. Someone with no experience with poetry over the last thirty years says he is confused by *Death and the Arkansas River*. If I had the time, I would take him with me somewhere. I would give him another poem to read from one of the ten books. The truly confused are good and fair to deal with. Twisted minds are another species of folks.

A carpenter can tell you how a table is made, but can a medium joining hands with us over this table tell us what it is? Hug a tree.

We go back to the poetry, the poet. I see a figure in the field. There is genuine moonlight shining on his crowbar. He is prying stumps out of his ground. Poetry busts guts.

Frank Stanford was born in 1949, Greenville, Mississippi, and grew up there and in Memphis, Tennessee, and Arkansas. He left the Delta for the Ozarks about fifteen years ago. He makes his living as a land surveyor. He has brought out the following titles in limited editions over the last five years: *The Singing Knives, Saint Francis and the Wolf: Some Poems 1957–1964, Shade, Let Him Lay There: Some Early Poems, Ladies from Hell, Field Talk, Arkansas Bench Stone, Approacheth the Ship and Wonder, Constant Stranger*, and *You.* A long book of poetry, *The Battlefield Where the Moon Says I Love You*, and a book of fiction, *Observants*, are due out soon.

Joan Swift

THE LINE-UP

Each prisoner is so sad in the glare
I want to be his mother

tell him the white light will go down
and he will sleep soon.

No need to turn under eyes
to shuffle   poor soldiers   boys

in a play
to wear numbers   obey.

They have hands as limp as wet leaves
the long fingers of their lives

hanging. They cannot see
past the sharp edge nor hear me

breathe. O I would tell each one
he will wake small again

in some utterly new place!
Trees without bars   sun a sweet juice

a green
field full of pardon.

The walls come in. I am
captured like him

locked in this world forever   unable to say   run

be free
I love you

having to accuse
and accuse.

DRAFT 4–7–70

THE LINE-UP

~~It is hard to think of them having mothers.~~
~~They stand, tall and short,~~
~~skinny and stout,~~
~~all ,black~~
their   s
~~all loose-armed hanging at their sides,~~
~~blinking into the glare of the lights~~
~~of the police lights~~
~~I think of their mothers.~~
~~It is hard to think of them having mothers.~~
the men ~~They~~ stand on the platform
and blink into the glare of the lights
like ~~the badly rehearsed chorus line of a~~
~~high school musical.~~

They are tall and short,
thick-necked and skinny
all black
all mothered by women
who somehow had better hopes for them.
~~Felons and doers of gross misdemeanors,~~
~~sad-faced~~
~~Thieves and~~
Burglars

DRAFT 5–8–70

THE LINE-UP

Each one is so sad
I want to be his mother

tell him the ~~staring~~ glaring lights will go down
and he will sleep ~~and dream~~ soon

~~to wake small~~
~~just beginning~~

~~to wake small~~
~~in a green field~~

~~like a wet brown calf~~

~~the platform, the police~~

No need to turn under eyes
~~to wear a number~~
~~fold and unfold black fingers~~

shuffle ~~like~~ poor soldiers
~~or~~ boys in a play
to wear numbers
~~and number all days~~
obey

~~Wake small in a new house~~
~~unguarded~~
~~tell him~~
~~wake up wake up~~
~~the sun is a~~
~~tell him~~
~~wake up wake up~~

~~Though their names~~
~~are Thief and Despair,~~
~~Pickpocket, Rapist,~~

DRAFT 5–27–70

Each one is so sad, ~~so~~ *in the glare* __________________
I want to be his mother

tell him the ~~glaring light~~ *white light* will go down
and he will ~~be home~~ *sleep* soon.

No need to turn under eyes
to shuffle, poor soldiers, boys

in a play,
~~obey. No need~~ to wear numbers, obey.

~~only the voice of~~

They have hands as limp as wet leaves
and as brown, ~~all the~~ *the long* fingers of their lives
the long fingers all the dead-ends

~~hanging. Their eyes cannot see~~
~~past the~~
hanging ~~Their eyes cannot see past the edge~~

hanging. Their eyes cannot see
past the bright edge nor *their ears* hear me

~~breathing. O I would tell each one~~
~~he will wake small again~~

~~in some utterly new place!~~

~~breathing. Mine thinks "She won't, she will"~~
~~And in a moment I can't.~~

breathe.
O I would tell each one
he will wake small again

~~in some utterly new place!~~ ~~*its benevolent juice*~~
Sunlight ~~Water will spill like some juice~~

~~over their brows and the long sun~~
~~gleam on a field without stones.~~

~~over and the sun will be long.~~

~~over their______bodies beginning~~
~~over that beginning.~~

sweet
~~Trees without bars, sun a wild juice.~~
in some utterly new place!
Trees without bars, sun a sweet juice.

~~Now I must name him.~~

~~Now I must name him. He thinks~~
~~under the~~

~~Now I must name him. He thinks,~~
~~she won't under the bulbs' blank~~

~~Now I must name him.~~
~~Now I must give him~~
~~a name.~~

(emeralds)
~~Water spilling like~~ *the first* __________ ~~over their feet~~
~~To wish this is to forget.~~
~~A field without a warden!~~
~~The walls are closing in like~~
~~But the walls are coming in to me~~

~~But the police are watching me and watching them.~~
But now I must name the name.

Water spilling the first ~~emeralds~~ over their __________
~~Such a field has no warden!~~
~~Can such a field have a warden?~~
A field with no warden!

But the walls come in to [~~like police~~] tell me where I am:
~~They come in like his name.~~
Captured, like him.

Caught in my accusation
Caught in the need to accuse
Caught with my accusation

~~Caught with his face like a~~ [~~in my throat~~] ____________
~~forever like a chicken bone~~

DRAFT 6–9–70

~~Caught with his face in the back of my head~~
~~forever~~
Locked ___________ the world
~~Caught~~ with his face forever. Unable to say turn,

be free
I love you

having to accuse
and accuse.

Although my poem *The Line-Up* actually began at the Oakland, California, Police Department, it did not start to take form until almost a month later. I can't say exactly what it was I carried around in my head during that time: along with the grocery lists, or the plot of the book I was reading, certainly a vivid picture of six men on a platform blinking into a blinding light. The poem, I think, was a reaction to a strong emotion and a kind of apology, as well. As in many poems I write, I was getting the thing straight in my own mind, explaining the poem's situation to myself. But here I was also talking to the six men and the one of them I had to say was guilty. Although I didn't address them directly in the poem, they were the ones I would have wanted, if they could, to read it.

While living in Oakland, I had a habit of driving each afternoon to Joaquin Miller Park, where I would sit in the car, books and papers strewn beside me on the front seat, and write for two hours. I changed the location, sometimes parking under the eucalyptus trees above the amphitheatre (dedicated to California writers), sometimes under the big oak at the viewpoint farther along the hill. The doors were locked. I could do nothing but face the notebook. Most of this poem was written there and behind the lines I still hear the motorcycles roaring back and forth and dry leaves rattling in the wind.

According to my work sheets, I started writing the poem down on the seventh of April. Its tentative beginnings were random lines in free verse. After a few of these, with the "mother" image written and crossed out a couple of times, I abandoned the poem for a month. When I picked it up again early in May, I began with the same group of images I had used earlier, but formed them into a couplet. Then I wrote another couplet, which rhymed. I fiddled with some words, some simple rhymes like play/obey (again using an image from the free-verse lines), then once more dropped the whole thing. Tackling it again three weeks later, I am astonished to see now, the lines came easily, four rhymed couplets in a row. The next six were more difficult to pull out, but the form was set by then. However, I still wasn't able to go directly to the end of the poem and finish it. As I approached the closing lines, I put it aside for a third time—I frequently slide a poem out of sight just as I near the end. I don't want to make any mistakes, take the wrong turn. For this one, the final six lines didn't come for another two weeks. And I see now that they were written on June 9, the day I was to have taken the witness stand in court, had the trial not been canceled.

The couplets were deliberately unconventional, the rhymes all slant with the exception of two: that play/obey and the see/me of stanza 6, where, however, the rhyme words are not accented. (There is still another exception: the final couplet where the end word is simply repeated.) The lines are not written in meter but rather in the cadences of actual speech, varying in length from couplet to couplet and within the couplets themselves. (John Logan does this better than anyone I know.)

The images in the first six couplets, I find, came straight from the original free-verse lines. The remaining seven stanzas took off from there and presented more difficulties, particularly in stanza 7 where I tried to put thoughts into the head of one of the prisoners, and again in stanza 9 where an inappropriate image involving water and emeralds appears briefly, never to appear again. The closing couplets, once let alone, revealed themselves all at once. The going to sleep–waking up image, by the way, was quite undeliberate, as near as I can remember: a gift from the unconscious.

Some of the images that appeared in the poem's first tentative free-verse lines have disappeared from the later and final versions: I drop any reference to the prisoners' physical characteristics, their color, what their crimes might have been. I don't remember why I did this, but the poem was part of a four-poem sequence, and these references would have been repetitive. Besides taking its place in the sequence, I also wanted the poem to stand alone with a broader application. Other changes in the final version: the field without a warden becomes a field full of pardon; "turn" near the end becomes "run." These alterations apparently took place in the typing process since there is no indication they occured in the handwritten drafts.

A note about punctuation, or the lack of it: I purposely omitted all commas and replaced them with three spaces on the typewriter, unless the comma fell at the end of the line, where it was simply left out. I was striving for an uncluttered look and the simulation of thought patterns.

The poem says: The prisoners are helpless and pitiful in their helplessness. I would like to make each one of them happy and free. But I am a prisoner too, trapped by the same world which has trapped them, locked in my role of accuser against my will.

Does it say more than that?

Joan Swift was born in Rochester, New York, in 1926 and was raised there and in Pennsylvania. She has an A.B. degree from Duke University and an M.A. in English–Creative Writing from the University of Washington. Her poems have appeared in the *New Yorker*, the *Atlantic*, the *Nation*, the *Yale Review*, the *Iowa Review*, *Field*, *Poetry Northwest*, and others. Alan Swallow published her first book, *This Element*. She has lived both in California and Washington and is at present a resident of Edmonds, Washington, where she teaches a poetry workshop and is a member of the Edmonds Arts Commission.

James Tate

A BOX FOR TOM

These exquisite rags carry
the lice of history.
They've been there,
great cities turning in the night,
lamplit barges haunting
industrious rivers,
weepy adieus at a farm
alone on the edge of the prairie.

Here are worthy garments
to be worn as camouflage
for your lofty character,
to hide your misfit spirit;
fit for slumming in some
of the very best restaurants,
at home with snobs who snub you,
and generally causing a stir
among birds of flight and terrapins.

You can retrace an old ghost's
bad luck back to the pot of gold

in a pool hall getting a start,
then missing, falling, staining
everything to match his shoes
which were covered with doglime,
angel hair and bad news.

DRAFT 1

GOOD WILL

here are some garments, to be worn as camouflage
for your lofty character, to hide your obese spirit
fit for slumming in some of your very best restaurants
at home with snobs who snub you, and generally causing
a stir among birds of flight and terrapins.

these exquisite rags carry the lice of history!
they've been there, great cities turning in the night,
lamplit barges haunting industrious rivers,
weepy adieus at a farm alone somewhere on the prairie.

~~if you don't like them find some naked bum~~
~~who will wear them, they've still got miles to go.~~

~~they never were the fashion, but they blended in~~
~~as bad taste will. the no-count dude who accepts them~~
can retrace ~~my own~~ *someone else's* bad luck back to the pot of gold.
in a pool hall, ~~spilling barbecue, so much for white cords~~
getting a start somewhere, then falling, staining everything.

DRAFT 2

GOOD WILL

These exquisite rags carry the lice of history!
They've been there, great cities turning in the night,
lamplit barges haunting industrious rivers,
weepy adieus at a farm alone somewhere on the prairie.
Here are some garments, to be worn as camouflage
for your lofty character, to hide your obese spirit,
fit for slumming in some of ~~your~~ the very best restaurants,
at home with snobs who snub you, and generally causing
a stir among birds of flight and terrapins,
can retrace someone else's bad luck back to the pot of
  gold,
in a pool hall, getting a start somewhere, then falling,
  staining everything.

DRAFT 3

a Box for Tom
~~GOOD WILL~~

These exquisite rags carry
the lice of history.
They've been there,
great cities turning in the night,
lamplit barges haunting
industrious rivers,
weepy adieus at a farm
alone ~~somewhere on~~ on the edge of the prairie.

Here are some garments
to be worn as camouflage

for your lofty character,
to hide your ~~obese~~ misfit spirit;
fit for slumming in some
of the very best restaurants,
at home with snobs who snub you,
and generally causing a stir
among birds of flight and terrapins.

You can retrace ~~someone else's~~ an old ghost's
bad luck back to the pot of gold
in a pool hall getting a start.
then missing ~~somewhere~~, ~~then~~ falling,
                    staining everything,
to match his shoes
which were covered with dog~~shit,~~ lime
angel hair and bad news.

I had been sitting at my desk staring into a closet full of old clothes. I quite often go into trances before I write, and this meditation on some old clothes I hadn't seen for three years because of their inaccesibility in a trunk in somebody's basement was beginning to take me down lively but sad thoughts concerning the history of clothes, as if they had a life of their own—which I think they do.

It has been pointed out to me a number of times that I sometimes dress rather, shall we say, irregularly. I have always held on to clothes as long as I could possibly get by wearing them without being arrested. I wear shirts, slacks, shoes that I had fifteen years ago. If I like something it is alive for me. That's not strange: If you can let a plant depress you, why not love a sock? Well, such were my thoughts as I stared into my closet. And

I was thinking about a friend of mine with whom I have an old, standing joke: I give him clothes no one else would wear on a bet, and Tom wears them with the same instinctive love of clothes that have been around as I do.

When I started the poem I wasn't sure where it would go. I didn't care, it felt good. So I wrote very roughly, finding myself making images; the poem obviously wanted to express itself in images. I was thinking about my friend Tom, and I was thinking of him in some of the old cast-offs I unloaded on him this past summer, really alarming duds. The poem had a strong rhythm and was rather melodious. I started to go wrong in the poem after nine lines in the first draft. I started to make a serious poem cute, which was cheapening what I really wanted to say on the subject.

On the subject of subjects, I should interject here that I was conscious of having a subject. Many poems, what turn out to be poems, start for me with any kind of free association. I like to start out of the air and *then* find a subject, if at all, later. But recently I had felt the need to get back to the kind of poem that addresses some thing, some instance of dealing with a defined area.

But back to the poem. Four lines that were no good, that degraded the subject and I knew it; and finally three lines that got back to the mood of the first nine lines, though I knew there was a lot of work ahead to make anything of them. The first draft was just seeing what could come out; I did use twelve of the original sixteen lines but they had to be shaped and refined with some sharpening of the language—adjectives and various modifiers were weak. The word "some" got to be a problem; I like the word, as bland as it is; but I recognized that it was overused, not justified, and responsible for heightening the danger of a plague of melancholia indigenous to the subject.

What I wrote down as a second draft didn't add much to the first draft: I just wanted to see how it read with the trash lines excised and the existing lines rearranged. I liked the possibilities of the pool hall at the end, but the ending as it stood now was fake, hokey, and I wanted something with a strong, clear statement, with some hint of pathos to it, hopefully not overdone. The poem seemed to veer too quickly back and forth from the rather gentle levity of a line like "and generally causing/a stir among birds of flight and terrapins" to, say, the ending. I liked the "terrapins" line and was going to try to hang on to it as long as I could, though I knew it was slightly too light for the rest of the poem.

Where the poem went from there is not really all that far, but the steps were essential and paid off in lifting it into life. I wanted to go back to some free association, some doodling, to see if I could get something further, hopefully an extension, an appropriate ending. I wrote down what I at first thought were three outrageous lines; I didn't like them and didn't take them seriously: "to match his shoes/which were covered with dogshit/angel hair and bad news." The syntax sounded too poetic, maybe gimicky.

I tried a third draft. The long lines of the first two drafts didn't seem to be working, though, in a way, I was happy I had started the poem that way; I think they influenced the sounds and rhythm. I cut the lines nearly in two, and wanted to try stanzas. At this point in the poem, I might add, I still considered many doors open; I was still willing for it to change its character entirely if it had a good excuse.

Changing "somewhere on the prairie" to "on the edge of the prairie" was a move in the right direction. I knew that terms had to be more defined. So, brandishing my razor, I changed "someone else's bad luck" to "an old ghost's bad luck." Also I dropped the "somewhere" in the penultimate line of the poem; it wasn't adding anything except more drippy melancholy. Then I reconsidered the lines I had written down after the second draft: I thought, why not give it a try, see what it feels like.

I added them to the fourth draft. To my surprise I liked them. They were slightly bold and dramatic, but now I felt with the changes that had been made the poem might be able to hold them. Yes, they were growing on me; I was beginning to like them a lot. Reading the poem to myself again, looking for weak spots, I realized that the phrase "obese spirit" in the fourth line of the second stanza wasn't very clear; it could mean a number of things and I wasn't certain I wanted all of them. "Misfit" seemed appropriate; I liked the sound and sound was playing a sizable role in the choices that had to be made within this poem. It added a firmness. The sound and the rhythm were in charge of convincing everybody that what I was saying was true. I gave a great deal of thought also to the word "dogshit." In this case I liked the sound; it went well with "start" three lines above; and I also liked the harshness of the word. But that is where I worried: Was it trying to sound too "tough"? I finally thought it was. "Doglime" was different altogether, but now I realized it was best; the poem needed to be softened there, toned down.

Throughout the poem is trying to go back and forth on this matter of sentiment. It has an easy way about it that should help facilitate, accommodate, the paradoxical and contradictory things the poem has to say. Conning the watchdog. It ends on a low note but hopefully love has embued the clothes; life has not been wasted on them.

It's a poem of a rather limited ambition, but I wanted it to have somewhat of a "universal nature" to it—an openness anyway, I don't know about the universe. It did not stray too far from its archetype. To do this I think the poem must also give something to that archetype, you can't just reproduce it. But when you're writing you're not thinking about who is going to read what you're writing. You're thinking about how you're going to get out of this jam, or something corny such as how wonderful life is with all its mysteries and riddles.

Because most poems of any value do posit paradoxes, paraphrasing is a feeble pursuit. Because they are conveyed in images, you have little of importance when you strip them away: Life is sad, Life is beautiful—that's not saying anything. This poem *A Box for Tom,* though it tells what might be called fragments of a story, is not detachable from its music.

I might have written this poem ten years ago, but I didn't; the feeling would not have been the same if I had written it a day earlier. Technically it is not especially innovative. It is trying to do a small thing well and with care. Unlike most of my poems it was written in one day. That makes it something of a gift. The whole poem, if I'm lucky at all, is about two hairs away from being a terrible cliché. That was the challenge—see how far I could get with two hairs.

James Tate was born in 1943, grew up in Kansas City, Missouri, and studied at Kansas State College and the University of Iowa. In 1966 he won the Yale Series of Younger Poets Award for his first book, *The Lost Pilot* (1967). He has published a number of books since then, including *The Oblivion Ha-Ha* (1970), *Hints to Pilgrims* (1971), *Absences* (1972), *Hottentot Ossuary* (1974), and *Viper Jazz* (1976). He has taught at Berkeley, Columbia, Emerson College and the University of Massachusetts, where he is currently an associate professor. In 1974 he received a National Institute of Arts and Letters Award for Poetry, and in 1976 he was awarded a Guggenheim Fellowship.

Robert Wallace

SWIMMER IN THE RAIN

No one but him
seeing the rain
start—a fine scrim
far down the bay,
smoking, advancing
between two grays
till the salt-grass rustles
and the creek's mirror
in which he stands
to his neck, like clothing
cold, green, supple,
begins to ripple.

The drops bounce up,
little fountains
all around him,
swift, momentary—
every drop tossed back
in air atop
its tiny column—

glass balls balancing
upon glass nipples,
lace of dimples,
a stubble of silver
stars, eye-level,
incessant, wild.

White, dripping, tall,
ignoring the rain,
an egret fishes
in the creek's margin,
dips to the minnows'
sky, under which,
undisturbed, steady
as faith the tide pulls.
Mussels hang
like grapes on a piling.
Wet is wet.

The swimmer settles
to the hissing din—
a glass bombardment,
parade of diamonds,
blinks, jacks of light,
wee Brancusi's, chromes
like grease-beads sizzling,
myriad—and swims
slowly, elegantly,
climbing tide's ladder
hand over hand
toward the distant bay.

Hair and eye-brows
streaming, sleek crystal
scarving his throat—
no one but him.

1 Swimmer in the Rain started as an experience—or, really, as a whole series of experiences. Even as a boy I couldn't see why, when there wasn't lightning, rain made any difference to swimming. So, summering on a bay creek of the New Jersey shore, for years I've gone swimming in the rain. I love the sensations of it—the rain in face and eyes, the noise, the visual excitement of drops on the water-top, and not least the privacy of it. One day two summers ago, in the creek, it suddenly occurred to me that it was a poem. For a week or so the idea kept turning up and I tried to get a verbal start, but nothing happened until the phrase "no one but him" popped into my head. Somehow that was a key, and the poem—drawing no doubt on a very long sequence of physical memories and on some inexplicable, unforceable inner intensity or need or whatever—virtually wrote itself one sunny noon.

The *poem* began in the recognition that a familiar experience had a poem in it, and so came into being initially as a "luminous subject." The pressure of that experience, its shape and meaning, had obviously been gathering for years. I prefer to have poems "happen" in that way. Dilligence and skill alone can't produce the truest poems.

2 Over the next several months, *Swimmer* went through seven complete drafts, fewer than normal for me. And, unusually, the poem grew with each version, accumulating details and images, elaborating, rather than excluding, compressing, tightening. In its final form it was roughly twice as long as the original draft. The very simple narrative—seeing the rain's onset, being overtaken by it, and submitting to it—was implicit in the first draft, quite direct in the second which was written the same day.

Typically, the first draft's

> a glass bombardment,
> tossed, tumbled jacks of light
> everywhere, blinding,
> like grease drops sizzling
> in a pan

successively dropped the adverb "everywhere" and the adjectives "tossed, tumbled" and "blinding," as well as the unnecessary pan; and added "glints," then "blinks" in its place; changed "grease drops" to "grease-beads"; and added the line "wee Brancusi's, chromes," and then the line "parade of diamonds." The jacks are of course children's toys, and I suspect that the association of the metal jacks I remember led to the "Brancusi's." All in all, the process seems to have mainly involved replacing vague, generalizing epithets with additional images.

One alteration ran the other direction. From the third draft onward, I kept trying to decide what the tide pulled steady as. At first the best I could do was "wind"—with the idea that tide is in water as wind is in air, and no doubt I was connecting it with the "minnows'/sky." But steadiness isn't the wind's quality, and only in the final draft did the obvious suggest itself: "steady/as faith the tide pulls."

3 The choice of fairly short lines was apparently intuitive in the first draft—a way of emphasizing the quick-changingness, the movement, the multiplicity of the rain? By the second draft I could formalize that choice—for me, form is always something learned from the developing poem, not something merely imposed on it—into rough two-beat lines. The norm is iambic; but with lines so short, simple substitutions produce a startlingly varied, shifting rhythm without seeming uncontrolled or loose:

> The drops|bounce up,
> little|fountains
> all a|round him
> swift, mo|menta|ry—
> every drop|tossed back
> in air|atop
> its ti|ny co|lumn—

That quick, two-beat rhythmic pattern and the quick, balancing, piling up, syntactical elaborations of the multiplying images, I believe, were the necessary technical discoveries.

An early temptation to rhyme—"him-rain-scrim-bay"—disappeared as the first draft gathered momentum, though occasional and slant rhymes still occur frequently. That hint of initial formality, dissolved by the pace of events, remains and, perhaps, mirrors in its own way the accelerating and overcoming sensation of the rain—as, also perhaps, the formality of the poem's ending with the line it began with reestablishes the control, presents the speaker's resteadied ability to submit to and so command the unexpected and majestic. (As with the reappearance of the clothing image in the last lines, the poem just turned out that way—I certainly didn't write it with any such critical rationalizations in mind.)

4 I guess I don't visualize anybody as the reader of the poem. I wrote it to catch and clarify for myself a mysterious sort of experience, something that attracted and probably puzzled me—to objectify, and so to verify (though not necessarily to explain), a part of my feelings. Hence the importance of re-creating the physical setting and sensations. I am clear, too, for myself, not for any assumed reader, preferring clear to muddied water (or feelings).

5 I suppose *Swimmer* can be paraphrased; but I would be too impatient to want to do it, possibly because the poem is (or seems to me) so simple. If it succeeds, it re-creates an experience. Similarly, I suppose it has a theme, but, as of any experience, I'd hesitate to say it meant one thing rather than another. Ideally, it means all its meanings, whatever, to whomever. Faith, loneliness, natural intimacy are issues the poem raises, but doesn't settle. (A poem's meanings and resonances are like the endless circles that flow from a stone dropped into water. They must be concentric, but may be very faint and distant and even quite personal to the reader, and still be true to it.)

6 *Swimmer* does, I hope, what most of my poems have always sought to do: clarify experience or feelings. I can't think of any poem of mine it especially duplicates, although the pattern (reorganization in terms of a new experience) is recognizable in poems as early as *The Crayfish* and is surely as archetypal as you can get. Like all my poems that go on interesting me, it as much "came" as was "written." No magic, no poem. It is natural for a poet to value what he can least explain in his work; what is odd is that readers seem to be able to respond to and identify the same qualities.

Robert Wallace was born in Springfield, Missouri, in 1932. Educated at Harvard and Cambridge, he taught at Bryn Mawr, Sweet Briar, and Vassar, and is now professor of English at Case Western Reserve University. He has published three books of poems—*This Various World* (1957), *Views from a Ferris Wheel* (1955), and *Ungainly Things* (1968)—and co-edited an anthology, *Poems on Poetry* (1965).

FOLD, TAPE, AND MAIL

BUSINESS REPLY MAIL
First Class Permit No. 9260, New York, N. Y.

DAVID McKAY COMPANY, INC.
750 THIRD AVENUE
NEW YORK, N. Y. 10017

PACKING SLIP

DAVID McKAY COMPANY, INC.
750 THIRD AVENUE NEW YORK, N. Y. 10017

FREE DESK OR EXAMINATION COPIES FOR

PROFESSOR LOIS GORDON
FAIRLEIGH DICKINSON UNIV TEANECK

284679 1 111
24600 042777

QTY.	NUMBER, AUTHOR, AND TITLE		SRC
01	220374 FIFTY CONTEMPORARY POETS	$4.95	

WE HOPE YOU WILL FIND TIME TO USE THE SPACE BELOW TO GIVE US YOUR OPINION OF THESE TITLES, AND TO LET US KNOW ABOUT YOUR PLANS FOR THEIR USE IN YOUR COURSES.

COMMENTS

MAY WE QUOTE YOU? YES ☐ NO ☐

FOLD, TAPE, AND MAIL

Richard Wilbur

THE EYE

"... all this beastly seeing."—D. H. Lawrence

I.

One morning in St. Thomas, when I tried
Our host's binoculars, what was magnified?
In the green slopes about us, only green,
Brisked into fronds and paddles, could be seen,
Till by a lunging focus I was shown
Some portion of a terrace like our own.
Someone with ankles crossed, in tennis shoes,
Was turning sun-blank pages of the news,
To whom in time came espadrilles of pink
Bearing a tall and fruit-crowned tropic drink.
How long I witnessed, missing not a sip!—
Then, scanning down through photons to a ship
In the blue bay, spelt out along the bow
The queenly legend of her name; and now
Followed her shuttling lighter as it bore
Her jounced, gay charges landward to explore
Charlotte Amalie, with its duty-free
Leicas, binoculars, and jewelry.
What kept me goggling all that hour? The nice
Discernment of a lime or lemon slice?
A hope of lewd espials? An astounded
Sense of the import of a thing surrounded—

Of what a Z or almond-leaf became
Within the sudden premise of a frame?
All these, and that my eye should flutter there,
By shrewd promotion, in the outstretched air,
An unseen genius of the middle distance,
Giddy with godhead or with nonexistence.

II.

Preserve us, Lucy,
From the eye's nonsense, you by whom
Benighted Dante was beheld,
To whom he was beholden.

If the salesman's head
Rolls on the seat-back of the 'bus
In ugly sleep, his open mouth
Banjo-strung with spittle,

Forbid my vision
To take itself for a curious angel.
Remind me that I am here in body,
A passenger, and rumpled.

Charge me to see
In all bodies the beat of spirit,
Not merely in the *tout en l'air*
Or double pike with layout

But in the strong,
Shouldering gait of the legless man,
The calm walk of the blind young woman
Whose cane touches the curbstone.

Correct my view
That the far mountain is much diminished,
That the fovea is prime composer,
That the lid's closure frees me.

Let me be touched
By the alien hands of love forever,
That this eye not be folly's loophole
But giver of due regard.

DRAFT 1

That morning in St. Thomas, when I tried
Our host's binoculars, what was magnified?
In the steep slopes about us, only green,
Whisked by the wind to smalti, could be seen,
Till by a lucky focus I was shown
Some portion of a terrace like our own.

That morning in St. Thomas, when I tried
Our host's binoculars, what was magnified?
In the steep slopes about us, only green,
Brisked into fronds and paddles, could be seen,
Till by a lunging focus I was shown
Some portion of a terrace like our own.
Someone with ankles crossed, in tennis shoes,
Was turning sun-blank pages of the news,
To whom in time came espadrilles of pink
Bearing a tall and fruit-crowned tropic drink.
How long I watched then, giving blink for sip!
Then, scanning down through flashes to a ship
In the blue harbor, lip-read from the bow
The queenly legend of her name; and now
Followed her shuttling lighter as it bore

TRUTH IS A FIXED STAR

DRAFT 2

One midday in St. Thomas, when I tried
Our host's binoculars, what was magnified?
In the green slopes about us, only green,
Threshed into fronds and paddles, could be seen,
Till by a lunging focus I was shown
Some portion of a terrace like our own.
Someone with ankles crossed, in tennis shoes,
Was turning sun-blank pages of the news,
To whom in time came espadrilles of pink
Bearing a tall and fruit-crowned tropic drink.
How long I watched then, missing not a sip!
Then, scanning down through smalti to a ship
In the blue roadstead, spelt along the bow
The queenly legend of her name; and now
Followed her jouncing lighter as it bore
Clear and distinct vacationers to explore
Charlotte-Amalie, buying duty-free
Swiss clocks, binoculars, and jewelry.
What kept me goggling so? Was it the nice
Discernment of a lime or lemon slice?
~~Some prurient hope?~~
Some hope of lewd espials? An astounded
Sense of the depth of anything surrounded —
Of what a breadfruit or a Z became
When comprehended by a sudden frame?
All these,
Of what, within the premise of a frame,
A ______________? or ______________ became?
All these,

[Handwritten annotations: * chased; catchment; "All this beastly seeing" – DHL; at high noon / a high noon / a noonday; leaf-blades fan / petioles; Blown into / Stirred / Brushed / Jolted / Shapen to / Slapped into; lurching / plunging diving; corner / cantle; bleached / blanched; recording / witnessed / giving blink for; looked / stared / patchwork / blotches / tangles / tatters; photons / flashes, / blinkings / light-stabs / sprinkles; traced, tracked / lay, spelt out; letters; scudding / darting / shutting / skipping / shuttled / jouncing / bucking; consumers; with its; landing parties / and its duty-free / with; cutlery / knives; gawking / conning; for an hour? / for so long? / all that hour / time; Distinction / Discrimination; the hope of lewd espials / Some prurient hope? Vague prurience? Vile / rank curiosity / lubricious hope / salacious hope / hopes of a peep / some naughty hope / itchy / furtive / prying; An astonned sense of the depth of anything surrounded; almond (leaf); cameo / port(hole) / lens / frame; Within the sudden premise of a frame]

DRAFT 3

One midday in St. Thomas, when I tried
Our host's binoculars, what was magnified?
In the green slopes about us, only green,
Brisked into fronds and paddles, could be seen,
Till by a lunging focus I was shown
Some portion of a terrace like our own.
Someone with ankles crossed, in tennis shoes,
Was turning sun-blank pages of the news,
To whom in time came espadrilles of pink
Bearing a tall and fruit-crowned tropic drink.
How long I ~~watched, recording every sip!~~ witnessed, missing not a sip
Then, scanning down through photons to a ship
In the blue bay, spelt out along the bow
The queenly legend of her name; and now
Followed her shuttling lighter as it bore,
~~Clear and distinct, her charges to explore~~ Its jounced, gay charges landward to explore
Charlotte-Amalie, with its duty-free
Leicas, binoculars, and jewelry.
What kept me goggling all that hour? The nice
~~Distinction~~ Discernment of a lime or lemon slice?
A hope of lewd espials? An astounded
Sense of the moment of a thing surrounded —
Of what a Z or almond-leaf became
Within the premise of a sudden frame?
All these, and that my ~~gaze~~ eye should ~~hover~~ flutter there
Promoted to the main-deep of the air,
An unseen spirit of the middle distance
Giddy with godhead or with nonexistence

* * *

Save us, St. Lucy,
From the folly of the eye, remind us
By whom we are beheld,
To whom beholden

Save us, St. Lucy,
From the eye's nonsense, you by whom
Great Dante was beheld,
To whom beholden.

The salesman's head
Rolls on the seat-back of the omnibus.
He is sleeping, his open mouth
(Is) banjo-strung with spittle,

Correct my vision   Forbid my vision
Let not my   To take itself for a _____ angel
Remind me that I am a body also,
A passenger, and rumpled.

Charge me to see

Preserve us, Lucy,
From the eye's nonsense, you by whom
Benighted Dante was beheld,
To whom he was beholden.

If the salesman's head
Rolls on the seat-back of the 'bus
In ugly sleep, his open mouth
Banjo-strung with spittle,

Forbid my vision
To take itself for a curious angel.
Remind me that I am here in body,
A passenger, and rumpled.

Charge me to see
In all bodies the beat of spirit,
Not merely in the _tout en l'air_
Or double pike with layout

But in the strong,
Shouldering gait of the legless man,
The calm walk of the blind young woman
Whose can touches the curbstone.

Correct my view
That the far mountain is diminished,
That the fovea is prime composer,
That the lid's closure frees me.

Let me be touched
By the alien hand of love forever
That my eye not be folly's loophole
But a giver of due regard.

19 April 1975
Cummington, Mass 01026

Dear Alberta,

This answer to your questionnaire will be hammered out at ordinary letter-writing speed, and will be truthful if not felicitous. I'm going to respond in terms of my most recently finished poem, *The Eye,* which is to appear sometime or other in the *New Yorker*.

1 It is hard to say when the poem started, because I have been thinking about the various senses, and the justice of their perceptions, for many years. Back in the late 1940s and early '50s, when I was teaching at Harvard, I used to give my short-story writing classes exercises in description calculated to make my students aware of what the use of each sense might mean for the perceiver and for the thing or person perceived. At the same time, when lecturing on W. C. Williams, I used to make much of the immediacy or "contact" which he gained by a stress on the so-called "lower" senses, and I would generally quote D. H. Lawrence in support of Williams' aesthetic position—a position which was ultimately moral. Though not terribly fond of Lawrence's poem *New Heaven and Earth,* I recall being impressed at that time by the fact that the spiritual revolution which the poem describes is based upon a tactile experience—that the poet's escape from self, and his discovery of others, comes about through touch. I find, on scraps of paper in my study which may be as much as four years old, occasional jottings of this kind:

> One is consciousness, and others are body; one sees them with creased necks in the next row of the theatre, one sees them convulse as they belch, one sees them sleeping with their mouths open in public conveyances. . . . Even in "love" this can be, that one is the ringmaster and someone else the beast. . . .

There is a sheet of paper on which, at some time or other, I tried to begin a poem with the line "Others are bodies," but got no farther than that. About three Januaries ago, my wife and I made a week's visit to some friends in their rented mountainside villa in St. Thomas. From the poolside terrace there was an extraordinary view of other mountains, other villas, every sort of tropical tree and bird, the outskirts of Charlotte-Amalie, and its harbor, which was continually visited by the more famous cruise ships—among them, the *Elizabeth*. My hosts had binoculars, and for the first time in my life I found myself making leisured and fascinated use of such glasses. I did not do so in a spirit of voyeurism, yet I did find that for all of the simple and blameless "bird-spotter's" curiosity which motivated me, there was nevertheless something eerie and disturbing about seeing things without the usual proximity and degree of visibility. I thought dubiously of the medieval hierarchy of the senses, in which the eye was always purest, highest, most spiritual. I remembered, with sudden understanding, the story of Gyges' ring in Herodotus.

The St. Thomas experience caused all that I have spoken of in my first paragraph to commence to organize itself around a particular and elaborate instance of ocular perception. Evidently I had not wanted to write a poem—to quote your checklist—by "deciding on a theme and seeking to embody it," and therefore the essayistic jottings I had earlier made did not conduce to a poem. Approaching the theme through a single situation rich in physical details, and full of reactions and self-judgments, was apparently more appealing, since a poem came of it. Why more appealing? For one thing, I find it more satisfying to discover what ideas lurk in a place or event and its images, than to present my ideas as a flow of thought with illustrative images. Furthermore, to approach a theme through a full personal experience is to increase the chances of surprise, of discovery, of finding something out. There is also, in such an approach, a greater opportunity for the dramatic, for "tone"—in this case, the tone would derive in good part from the "self-judgments" I have mentioned above.

The poem, then, first came to be writeable when a specific and marginally disquieting personal experience made possible a sustained, concrete, and "dramatic" handling of old concerns—a handling in which ideas would appear to develop, as they should, out of raw perception and event.

2 I can't say why, but it was about a year and a half before I began to write the poem, which took a number of months to complete. The poem began, in first draft, with the lines

> That morning in St. Thomas, when I tried
> Our host's binoculars, what was magnified?

In other words, the poem found at once the couplet form in which it was to be written, and then proceeded slowly to develop as poems of mine generally do—step by step, the lines grudgingly put down and thereafter little altered. The difference between my first version of the lines quoted and the final version would have something to do with my desire to suggest Wallace Stevens' *Sea Surface* but not to seem to echo it supinely. I wanted to suggest Stevens (though I would not have said this to myself in so many words) because the poem was in part going to be a criticism of such stand-offish, self-protective, and coldly connoisseural use of the eye as one may find in Stevens' poems. Thus far, by the way, no one who has read the poem seems to have noted in it an oblique pertinence to Stevens; perhaps this is because the note of criticism on which part I concluded is directed at the speaker of the poem and not at any other persons.

Early in 1975, I showed what is now part I to John Brinnin, the poet, who had been our host in St. Thomas: it was presented to him as a complete poem called *The Eye*, without the Lawrence epigraph, which was added later. It seemed to him satisfactory, accurate, and complete—as I think it could be said to be, since the question of its opening lines is answered and the argument turns conclusively and emphatically against the speaker at the close. He took what I showed him, I think, to be witty and comparatively light. But for me the impulse of the poem had not yet exhausted itself, and there were long-pondered ideas which, it seemed to me, might *now* be expressed in a second movement, which must state positively what the last lines of part I had stated negatively. My feeling was that a new tone was called for, and a different form. After a period of trepidation and casting-about, I decided on a violent transition from the couplet to unrhymed lines in a stanza of varying line-lengths. I wished the tone of the second part to be free of the "smarty" quality of the first, to be graver, more direct, more openly emotional. At the same time I did not wish to sound falsely artless and "sincere"; part II had to seem continuous with the first part, another state of the same sensibility; and therefore I aimed (without, of course, saying as much to myself) at a plainness which should nevertheless continue some of the rhetorical play, elegance, and verbal trickiness which had preceded it. When the notion of a prayer to St. Lucy, patroness of the eye, came to me, the second part had discovered the graver yet still "dramatic" tone which I was looking for.

3 I've already said a bit about this. The forms chosen were chosen, of course, because they seemed to be part of what I had to say. The couplet has a long history of association with the elegant, the smarty, the wittily detached. The unrhymed stanzas of the second part, though no less artful in fact than the couplets of the first, seemed better suited to simplicity. I should say, of course, that neither in this "conscious" use of technique nor in any other decision did I think in such analytic terms as I am using now; the choices were not justified verbally.

In answer to some of the queries on your checklist: the stanza breaks occur between units of developing thought and feeling, and no other breaks would be possible. The rhythms are basically iambic, but are counterpointed to express feeling, motion in what is described, and the movement of thought. When people hear the poem read aloud, they generally ask to hear it a second time, and then feel that they have got it: I think of *The Eye* as a poem to be read silently or heard twice. It needs no musical accompaniment. The personae in the poem are two aspects of my own nature, and of most other people's natures. The poem is not arranged on the page to appeal to the reader's eye: I think such effects may amuse, but that they usually do not *move* the reader, and may interfere with emotional response.

4 I was conscious, in writing, of Stevens (whom I admire and with whom I differ) and of those who were present on the occasion described in part I. I thought also of a particular brave and cheerful paralytic whom I know, and of a particular blind girl. But the poem was not written to anyone. I can think of people who would not understand it; I should expect students and critics and fellow poets to understand it; and then, thank God, there are other likely readers and enjoyers whom I can't designate.

5 The poem can be paraphrased, but I don't want to say any more about it than I have already done. Someone, perhaps, could restate what I have "said" in excellent prose; but the concreteness, the various musics, and the immediacy of the conflict would be lost. If some reader complained of not understanding "photons," "Lucy," or "fovea," I would ask whether he had looked into the encyclopaedia or the dictionary, and if not why not; I'd also ask whether he had not, in fact, understood the poem pretty well without grasping those particular terms.

I hope all this has been useful to you. If there's any neglected query to which you need an answer, please re-ask it.

Yours,
Dick
[Richard Wilbur]

Richard Wilbur was born in 1921 in New York City and was brought up on a farm in New Jersey. He went to Amherst, served with the 36th (Texas) Infantry during World War II, and was then a junior fellow at Harvard. He has taught at Harvard, Wellesley, and Wesleyan. He is a poet, translator of Molière and others, critic, editor, writer and illustrator of children's books, Broadway lyricist, and recipient of various prizes. His latest books are: *Opposites* (for children and others, 1973), *The Mind-Reader* (poetry, 1976), and *Responses* (prose, 1976). He is president of the American Academy of Arts and Letters.

Nancy Willard

ANGELS IN WINTER

Mercy is whiter than laundry,
great baskets of it, packed like snowmen.
In the cellar I fold and sort and watch
through a squint in the dirty window
the plain bright snow.

Unlike the earth, snow is neuter.
Unlike the moon, it stays.
It falls, not from grace but a silence
which nourishes crystals.
My son catches them on his tongue.

Whatever I try to hold perishes.
My son and I lie down in white pastures
and flap like the last survivors
of a species that couldn't adapt to the air.
Jumping free, we look back at

angels, blurred fossils of majesty and justice
from the time when a ladder of angels

joined the house of the snow
to the houses of those whom it covered
with a dangerous blanket or a healing sleep.

As I lift my body from the angel's,
I remember the mad preacher of Indiana
who chose for the site of his kingdom
the footprint of an angel and named the place
New Harmony. Nothing of it survives.

The angels do not look backward
to see how their passing changes the earth,
the way I do, watching the snow,
and the waffles our boots print on its unleavened face,
and the nervous alphabet of the pheasant's feet,

and the five-petaled footprint of the cat;
and the shape of snowshoes, white and expensive as tennis,
and the deep ribbons tied and untied by the sleds.
I remember the millions who left the earth;
it holds no trace of them

as it holds of us, tracking through snow,
so tame and defenseless
even the air could kill us.

The poem started with an experience. After a snowstorm, I was pulling my four-year-old son to school on a sled. He looked back and saw the tracks left by the runners in the snow. The snow that morning was full of fresh tracks—the treads of boots, the footprints of squirrels and jays. All this brought to my mind an earlier snowstorm. We lay down in the snow one Sunday morning—I believe we had overslept and missed church—and we filled the yard with angels.

The important changes that the poem underwent were cutting and focusing. It was written in one evening and rewritten six or seven times. A month later I made two changes: "piled like snowmen" in line 2 became "packed like snowmen." "My son and I lie down in the simple pastures of snow" became "My son and I lie down in white pastures" to echo the twenty-third psalm.

The form is a five-line stanza, with a variation in the last stanza. What holds the poem together, I hope, is the snow as something that, in this time and place, gathered some parts of my life together. As for the angels: they are not a literary device or a metaphor. I believe in angels as presences which some people have encountered and to which they have given that name.

My reader is anyone who reads poetry but especially the woman who is too busy folding the laundry to read poetry and who reads it anyhow.

I suppose the poem could be paraphrased. I hope it won't be. I don't think *Angels in Winter* differs very much from the other poems about my son, which appeared in *Carpenter of the Sun.* All of them started from some common experience, working in the kitchen, picking up toys, bringing a bottle to a child at night.

Nancy Willard lives in Poughkeepsie, New York, with her husband and six-year-old son. Her most recent books are *Carpenter of the Sun* (poetry, 1974) and *Childhood of the Magician* (fiction, 1973). She has also written six books for children. She teaches in the English department at Vassar College.

John Woods

THE FIVE DREAMS

What are the five dreams of the elders?

Richard, for all his beard, has seen
mist on an autumn pond and hears
water, the color of cognac, rising
and falling in the reeds of the shallows.
He thrusts his fingers through his hair
and each nail glistens with oil.
He knows that water is giving and taking,
and that it will give and take though fists
slam shut, though the high curse
of his name burns on the door plate.

Wayne is backed against a wall of books,
and the fireplace, the *place* of fire,
reddens his forehead. In his nostrils,
two cables of air freeze, and on them
he hangs in the world. He spreads his arms,
one hand the wing of a leather testament;
the other, the one with a dead ring,
seizes a last book of poetry.
The fire eats all shadows but one.

These were two dreams of the elders.

Emily has brushed her hair forever.
Now it is earth, and pours to her feet.
Half moons glint at her fingertips,
and sand drifts from her mouth, her ears,
the corners of her eyes. She is content.
It was prophesied. Her children look in
at the windows, pale as moonlight.
Remember when they gnawed her breasts?
When she is empty, they will press her
in a book, the book of earth.

Mary knows there are dead places in her.
The doctors, well, the doctors are guessing.
Richard's kiss is dead, but we all
shed layers, and when we have been struck
too often, part of us turns to the wall.
She knows, too, that when the last cobs
of snow melt, green incoherence leaps
from eye to eye. And Wayne's ring?
Well, it turned green before it died.
She takes it off. It pings on the parquet.
The ring scar reddens. She feels better.

This is the last dream of the elders.

Each house has a room that's always locked.
This is the room of dreaming. Sometimes
it is a room of water where a huge eye
glares. Sometimes there is a bed
of glacial sheets, slow, slow, and in them
we can see our gill parents. And, praise God,
one night the young of us will lie down together
in a shallow of black hair. And one day
we will return, put down our cases,
pass through the room where the fist

opens, where the earth sifts, where the ring
spins to quiet. Then, we lie down in
the milky sheets, when the door closes
and is a door no longer.

ABOUT *THE FIVE DREAMS*

> Men who share the same rooms, soldiers or prisoners, develop a strange alliance as if, having cast off their armor with their clothing, they fraternized every evening . . . in the ancient community of dream and fatigue.
>
> —Camus, *The Guest*

I wrote the Camus passage in a journal several years ago, feeling that there was something about its gravity that would be a source. Every time I tried to write directly from its demands, the poem failed. Then I realized that most of the poems I had written that I cared for had already taken some resonance from the passage.

I wanted, always, to make more of my life available to my poetry. I wanted to be serious, goofy, casual, intent, and skilled enough that the craft becomes invisible. The Camus passage asked me to write about fundamental human concerns, cave-mouth poetry, the ancient communities of the womb, the seasons, the love bed, night-sweat despair, the communion of food and spirits, the grave.

I had been reading the poetry of George Mackay Brown, of the Orkney Islands. Several of his poems are ordered by counting: *The Five Voyages of Arnor; Shipwreck,* where each crew member is given a little story; and *The Abbot,* the story of seven brothers. He is a beautiful poet, up there at the top of the world. I took from him, too.

The poem began with the first line: "What are the five dreams of the elders?" What, indeed? I had no idea. I had assigned myself a poem. I'm sorry I don't have anything bardic to say. I was in love at the writing, but no matter. I sat down to write in the profession, so to speak. Even if I am not to be mystical, I still can't tell you how the lines happened, at least until the last part.

I made four little narratives or scenes, each with a different person, caught at some crucial moment in time. The cruciality, which is expressed as self-knowledge, does not come from a gradual summation, as in a realistic novel, but from revelation, as each private history is compressed, then yields its insight.

The theme is hardly original: mutability. For Richard, it is the give-and-take of water; for Wayne, fire and air; for Emily, earth. In spite of the holding actions of the ego (the nameplate, the texts, progeny, love), the old elements seek their domains.

By the fourth dream, I discovered that Mary had known Richard and Wayne; in fact, was married to Wayne. Here, I might have gone back and brought all the "characters" together. I decided against it, because it would have domesticated the poem, would have allowed the reader too much factual inquisitiveness (Professor Woods, maybe Richard was the young son of Mary, a hippie with a beard and oily hair, huh?).

The last dream wants to be the eldest dream I know. I wanted a room where all of us enter the ancient procession of mammalian life, the dream of the race.

I discover now, at this moment (*not* when I wrote the poem) how closely I have worked within the evocation of the epigram.

I suppose a poem is not finished until it finds a reader, but how do I visualize him? All poets are creative, that is, able to make sustained raids on their private history. Then from their readers, their teachers, their reviewers and critics, their exemplars, they develop a second nature. The Ideal Reader becomes internalized.

John Woods was born in 1926 and raised in southern Indiana. After Air Force service in World War II, he took two degrees at Indiana University. He has worked in a bakery, a paint factory, and as an inspector of jet engines. Since 1955, he has taught at Western Michigan University, with periods as a visiting professor at Irvine and Purdue. He has six books: *The Deaths at Paragon, Indiana* (1955); *On the Morning of Color* (1961);

The Cutting Edge (1966); *Keeping Out of Trouble* (1968); *Turning To Look Back, Poems, 1955–1970* (1972); and *Striking the Earth* (1976). Smaller collections include *Alcohol* (1971), *The Knees of Widows* (1971), *Bone Flicker* (1972), and *Voyages to the Inland Sea* (1972). He won the Theodore Roethke Award from *Poetry Northwest* and a publication prize in the *Second National Literary Anthology.*

Charles Wright

DEATH

I take you as I take the moon rising,
Darkness, black moth the light burns up in.

How did the poem start?

The poem started with the line "You take me as I take the moon rising, darkness." Then I tried the reversal of that line "I take you as I take the moon rising, darkness," and liked it that way much better: it seemed a more interesting concept: something over which I had no control; not a fixed, predestined, scheduled occurrence. Also it seemed to me empirically untrue, which I liked. And to make the untruth in the image convert to a truth, I needed another reversal to complete an imaginary equation. Thus the second phrase of the sentence, a second reversal, another impossibility "black moth the light burns up in." Two untruths, two impossibilities make a possible truth. And that's what I want in my poems, possible truths.

What changes did it go through from start to finish?

The poem went through no drafts, but was set down as you see it. The poem that is not there went through many drafts. I.e., I tried to add to it, thinking the poem as it now stands was merely one image in an imagined longer poem. After many additions and subtractions I decided, whatever its value, the two lines needed no more explanation, that they were non-adjunctable. I had always wanted to write a two-line poem, and here I finally had one and was trying to load it under with trappings and filigree. So I left it where it began. I also liked the idea of a poem, no matter how short, ending in two consecutive prepositions.

What principles of technique did you consciously use?

All I could muster. I tend, in all my poems, to work in a tight free verse off an iambic base. I count every syllable and every stress in every line I write, not to make them conform to each other, but to make sure they differ and that they get mixed up. This poem, even though short, is no different. I broke the first line after "rising" as a slight surprise factor. This also makes the last phrase "black moth the light burns up in," at least to my ear, hurry along, in contrast to the rather drawn-out sounds of "I take you as I take the moon rising,/Darkness." Also, I wanted the lines to more or less look equally long on the page, but to sound differently. Quantity and quality, the old song. I stress the lines like this:

> I táke yóu as I táke the móon rísing,
> Dárkness, bl(´)ack móth the líght b(´)urns úp in.

("Black" & "burns" get secondary voice stresses, but not as heavy as the main ones indicated. I also like the idea of "rising" being a falling rhythm.)

I use sound as it pleases my own ear. And my ear likes lots of sound. Sound and repitition. I like "music" in poems.

The poem is two halves of two different metaphors looking for a whole, a new whole. And, I hope, finding it.

I would prefer that the poem be read silently, by one reader at a time.

The "I" persona of the poem is myself.

I used cliché, obviously, in the second half-metaphor, hoping the reversal would make it effective and alive again.

The tone is reflective.

Whom do you visualize as your reader?

Fellow poets and myself are whom I usually write for, if you get right down to it. And more and more I write for myself. I think anyone can understand the point of this one, though, even if he doesn't see the process.

Can the poem be paraphrased?

No. It is a paraphrase, a distillation. CONDENSARE, the man said.

How does this poem differ from earlier poems of yours in (a) quality, (b) theme, (c) technique?

a. It is, obviously, shorter; otherwise it is typical.
b. It is an old theme for me, but one I'm not through with yet.
c. Technically, it's usual.

Charles Wright was born in 1935 in Pickwick Dam, Tennessee. He was educated at Davidson College and the University of Iowa and was a Fulbright Scholar at the University of Rome. In 1968 he was Fulbright Lecturer at the University of Padua; at present he is a professor of English at the University of California, Irvine. He has published three books: *The Grave of the Right Hand* (1970), *Hard Freight,* (1973), and *Bloodlines* (1975).

David Young

OCCUPATIONAL HAZARDS

Butcher

If I want to go to pieces
I can do that. When I try
to pull myself together
I get sausage.

Bakers

Can't be choosers. Rising
from a white bed, from dreams
of kings, bright cities, buttocks,
to see the moon by daylight.

Tailor

It's not the way the needle
drags the poor thread around.
It's sewing the monster together,
my misshapen son.

Gravediggers

To be the baker's dark opposite,
to dig the anti-cake, to stow

the sinking loaves in the unoven—
then to be dancing on the job!

Woodcutter

Deep in my hands
as far as I can go
the fallen trees
keep ringing.

1 My process of writing is to begin with free association, then decide gradually on theme and structure. Often a cluster of sounds form around a rhythm that also constitutes an image. That was the case here: I began with the Woodcutter section, especially the first two lines, then, very shortly after, the other two. When I had this section, I didn't know what I wanted to do with it; it seemed too slender to be a poem on its own. Then, suddenly, a day or so later, the phrase "Bakers can't be choosers" popped into my head and I had the main subject and structure of the poem.

2 I think there were about twenty drafts, some of them differing very minutely from one another. Time intervals were as little as fifteen minutes, as much as a month (poem begun around Christmas and finished in June, which is longer than I usually take, but I was abroad and working more desultorily). The poem both shrank and expanded. There were seven sections at one time, seven occupations, and finally there were five. The structure did not change in essence once I had conceived the subject and knew I wanted a series of speakers, of occupations. And tone changed only in the sense that I needed to find a way to link the silliness of the pun with the gravity of the Woodcutter section, so that revision was a gradual bridging between those two tonal extremes (although I never put it that way to myself until just now). Which lines remained unchanged? The original woodcutter lines, the baker pun, the first two lines of the Tailor section, the last line of the gravedigger. Why? I guess I felt they worked the way I wanted them to. The changes fell more in the area of imagery and connotation. I was trying to bring all the elements of the poem up to the quality I felt was in the best lines, a certain kind of resonance inhering mainly in the imagery but supported by sound and movement, and of course "voice." A little like thickening and seasoning a sauce. Also there was some tightening of relationships, e.g., the gravediggers thinking of themselves as opposites to the bakers, a last-minute inspiration at something like the next-to-last draft.

3 Lineation? The "inevitable" sense of measure in the initial section, the woodcutter, suggested a series of four-line sections, but I did not feel I had to keep the lines of similar length. In fact, I sought variety; if the lines had been of the same length throughout, the variety in the voices would be stifled. Rhythmical principle: each section had its own, developed its own. A two-stress line (chop, chop?) for the woodcutter, pretty regular. Two-stress for the butcher (another chopper?), but a loose three-stress in the three middle stanzas. I guess the answer, then, is accentual, plus cadence of emotion and bodily rhythm. I used no principle of sound repetition. I "trained" myself to be open to sound possibilities (I think them extremely important) long ago so that I don't have to seek consciously for strong sound relationships, but assonance and consonance show up most consistently in my work and I have a tendency to remove effects that seem too obvious, e.g., excessive alliteration. Often the sound of a single word— "sausage" would be an instance in this poem— is so attractive to me that I am eager to use it without any reference to its relation to other sounds. "Needle" is another example, and both words, I notice, are placed where they'll get prominent utterance and not be smothered or muffled by lots of similar sounds nearby. Too rich a sound texture, as in Thomas and early Lowell, makes it impossible for words to retain their lovely singularity. Hopkins, despite appearances, is quite another matter. From all this it should be clear that I'd like the poem to be read aloud.

Metaphor, etc. I think I use whatever seems to work. I never consider that I am using symbols; I never consider that metaphor is, or could be, absent when a poet is using language. So I don't think about either. There is certainly a surrealistic flavor to the images in this poem, including the one I began with, and I daresay I *was* conscious of that. And sought to do it consistently. Also, since "ringing" in the initial section was a pun, and my next idea, "Bakers can't be choosers," was another (though rather different in kind, I suppose, or in tone), I let *that* kind of figurative effect sprinkle itself through, e.g., "Rising," "dancing on the job," etc. What do I avoid? Abstract language, pretty vigorously. Esoteric language, anything I think suggests poetic "showing off" or pedantry, or that interferes with the possibility of a living voice believably speaking the words of the poem.

What principles for reference and allusion? None. I don't think the poem depends on any allusions for its success (except "Beggars can't be choosers," which is pretty safe unless you are translating into another language), but I can't deny they lurk in the poem—to the story of Frankenstein's monster, to the graveyard scene in *Hamlet*, all the Grimm's and other folktales in which woodcutters and bakers and tailors figure, also the nursery and skiprope rhymes that recite occupations and trades. For a well-read reader or listener allusions are inevitable and enriching, but the poem, as I've said, never *depends* on them to be meaningful or amusing.

Structure. The series or list, a contemporary favorite because it crosses a non-poetic structure (a series of any kind, days of the week, letters of the alphabet, etc.) with a poem and because it is not too confining: you can work on it a section at a time, its length is variable, etc. This for the overall structure; in the individual sections I followed what you call "a psychological order." As for ending, a poem must, I feel, begin and end strongly. A series poem has few other claims on it, really. I ended with my "beginning," my first stirrings, because it remained my favorite.

This poem is obviously a series of personas. In a sense, they are all me, trying to imagine myself into the inner life of five different occupations, half-humorously. Incidentally, at one time I had as one of the occupations "Poet," with something very silly like "Words, words, words," and was considering it as the final stanza. That was, it's now obvious, unnecessary and even traitorous to the poem.

Cliché phrases: yes, I guess I used them here, with a twist. The look of the poem: once one has seen and grasped the title, there is, it seems to me, a certain tidy attractiveness in the subtitles and four-line units, but my sense of that was and is rather vague.

The tone? Say rather tones. My tendency to mix tones has met with resistance from readers who are suspicious when art is playful, and those (often poets) who feel poems are validated by their unity of tone (monotony?). I am unrepentant. In this case, at any rate, the poem seems to me wry (about human limitations), gay (in its play with language), sad (only a little, especially toward the end, and only about the general facts of life or rather death).

4 Friends of mine who read poetry, who write and/or have high standards for what they read. That is, anyone who, given an interest and high standards, I might be able to please.

5 The poem can be paraphrased to a certain extent, but the puns resist that, the rhythms and images and quirks all resist it. One could say, for example, of the woodcutter, that he realizes his occupation so defines him (there's another allusion: Shakespeare's "dyer's hand") that if, for example, he could journey beyond the surface, the exterior, into his hands, he would still discover the tingling (first sense of "ringing") that comes from wielding his axe continually as well as the contrary process of growth (second sense of "ringing") that will always counteract or balance his activity, the resistance of the world to what he is. That captures a lot of the sense, but it requires sixty words (not counting the parenthetical comments) and is prose, whereas my original requires fifteen words and is, I hope, poetry.

How to help the reader unacquainted with poetry of the last thirty years? Same as with modern music or modern art, one must become familiar enough with the vocabulary and disciplines to recognize that they do not duplicate the art of the past, or try to, but have their own aims and methods. Familiarity with a new or developing tradition is the only sure means to real enjoyment and judgment.

6 Very difficult to answer. Perhaps it's less derivative (though I would want to admit that I think this poem owes something to Charles Simic's use of folkloric materials, his and other poets' of my time's determination to intertwine the daily with the nightly, the ordinary with the dreamlike and extraordinary). Perhaps it's more exact. I can't really perceive the differences well, if they exist. Collections are easier to characterize in these terms than individual poems. If I imagine a faithful reader, I can suspect that he or she might be quite willing to say that this poem is somehow further along than the poems in my first collection, *Sweating Out the Winter,* and yet at the same time he or she wouldn't be altogether surprised to run across it in that collection. I suppose I have written and will write poems that are more ambitious, more inclusive, etc. But a poet can't worry much about the individual magnitude of each poem. One must trust to the fact that a small and apparently casual piece can give pleasure too. Perhaps I've deliberately chosen a rather modest example of my work to make that modest point. I'm aware as I finish this (more fun than I thought it would be) that my discussion is unlikely to change anybody's mind or affect anyone's judgment. To those who dislike the poem, a consideration of its writing at this length can only be ludicrous and vain. But to acknowledge in more words and detail than one has ever used before the intricacy of a process that is painful, joyful, mysterious, and absorbing requires a kind of honesty and patience that may bring a measure of satisfaction both to writer and reader.

David Young was born in 1936, grew up in Omaha, Nebraska, and was educated at Carleton College and Yale. Since 1961 he has taught at Oberlin College, where he helped found *Field*, a journal of contemporary poetry and poetics, in 1969. He has published two collections of poetry, *Sweating Out the Winter* and *Boxcars*, as well as scholarly work on Shakespeare, Stevens, and Yeats, and has translated widely, most notably from the Italian poet Montale, the Chinese poets of the T'ang dynasty, and the Duino Elegies of Rainer Maria Rilke. He is married and has two children.